C000179226

YOU'LL NEVER WALK ALONE

LIVERPOOL
FOOTBALL CLUB

EST·1892 ®

THE
OFFICIAL

LIVERPOOL FC
FaMiLy TRee

THE
OFFICIAL

LIVERPOOL FC
FaMILy Tree

New era: Andy Carroll and Luis Suarez joined the Liverpool family during the 2011 January transfer window

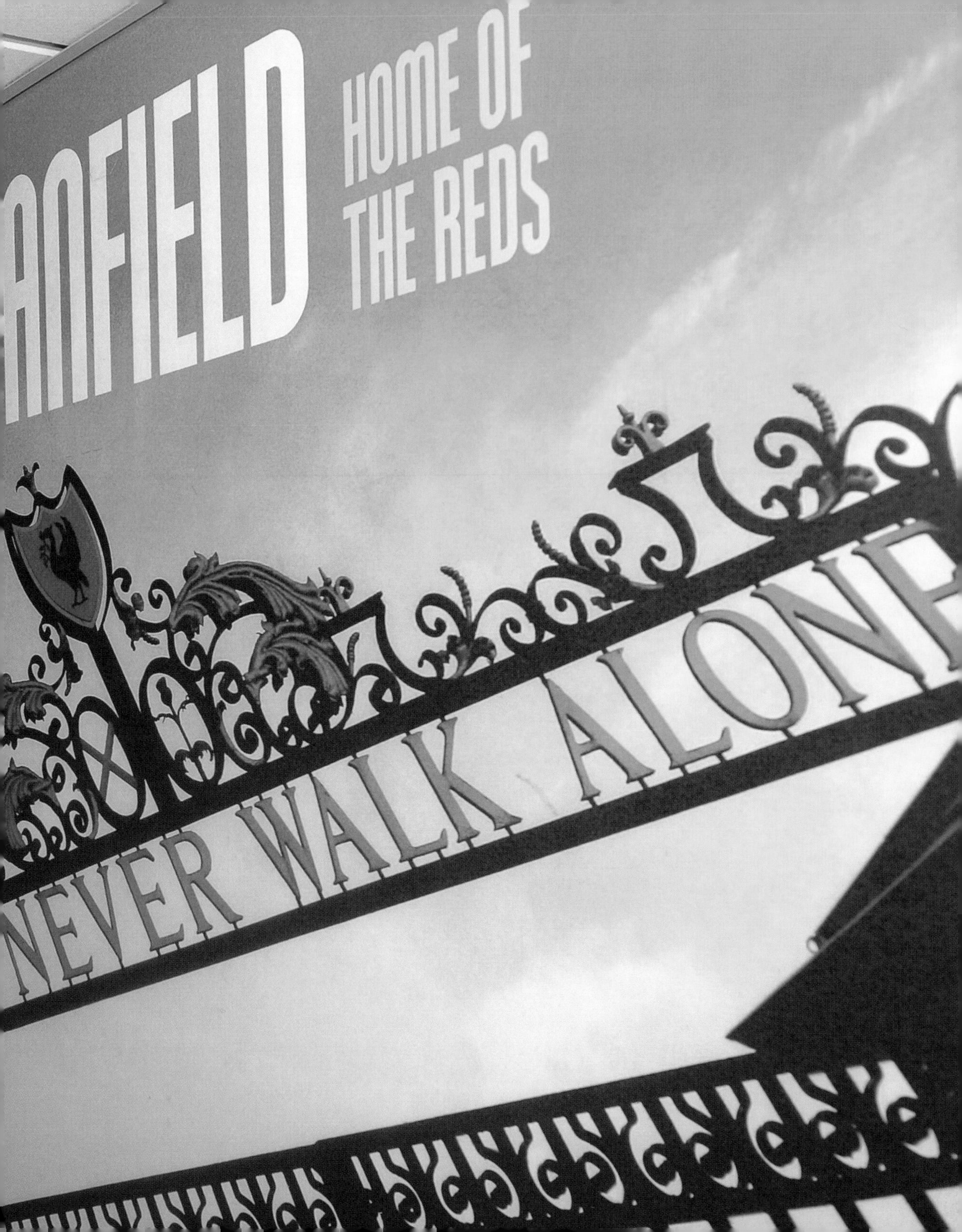
ANFIELD
HOME OF
THE REDS
NEVER WALK ALONE

Sport Media
A Trinity Mirror Business

The official LFC Family Tree has been written and produced by the team that brings you the official matchday programme and LFC Weekly Magazine.

Executive Editor: Ken Rogers
Senior Editor: Steve Hanrahan
Senior Art Editor: Rick Cooke
Editor: Paul Dove
Sub Editors & Writers: James Cleary, Alan Jewell
Liverpool FC Writers: Chris McLoughlin, William Hughes,
Simon Hughes, John Hynes
Design Team: Jamie Dunmore, Barry Parker, Colin Sumpter,
Colin Harrison, Lee Ashun, Alison Gilliland, James Kenyon
Sales and Marketing Manager: Elizabeth Morgan
Sales and Marketing Assistant: Karen Cadman
Marketing Executive: Claire Brown
Family Records: William Hughes, with thanks to Eric Doig

Published 2011

All Rights Reserved. No part of this publication may be reproduced, stored
in a retrieval system, or transmitted in any form, or by any means, electronic,
mechanical, photocopying, recording or otherwise without the prior
permission in writing of the copyright holders, nor be otherwise circulated in any form
of binding or cover other than in which it is published and
without a similar condition being imposed on the subsequent publisher.
Liverpool FC logo and name are registered trademarks of
Liverpool Football Club and Athletic Grounds Limited and are reproduced under license.

ISBN 978 1 9068 02509

Photographs: PA Photos, Trinity Mirror, Liverpool FC & Athletic Grounds Ltd

Printed and finished by Korotan

'Everybody has a part to play.
From fan to player to manager.
When we stand together
as a family we can achieve
great things'

FOREWORD
KENNY DALGLISH

LIVERPOOL Football Club is a very special sporting institution.

While I will always be extremely proud of my Glaswegian roots, this club and city has been extremely welcoming to me and my family from the moment I signed back in 1977.

Indeed, the relationship we have with the people and supporters of Liverpool means that we have always been happy in the area and was the reason why I decided to call my recent book My Liverpool Home.

Looking at the Kop choir in full voice at Anfield, sharing their passion and humour and a sea of colourful banners, is one of the most stirring sights in the game.

This book links the past and present by telling the fascinating story of the people and places who have helped make the club what it is today. There is even the odd picture of me from my early days that I admit I hadn't seen in a long time.

I hope it inspires you and fills you with pride.

Keep supporting the Reds. Everybody has a part to play. From fan to player to manager. When we stand together as a family, we can achieve great things.

LIVERPOOL FC:
FAMILY COMES FIRST

You can't choose your family, so the saying goes. You're born into it. For the Liverpool FC family, that isn't strictly true.

Many are born into it, declared Liverpudlians before birth and nurtured into the Liverpool way by loving parents who want the best for their young. Others aren't, but choose to become members having caught a glimpse of the family silver or because they've been inspired by Anfield's ethos of support, hard work, captivated by our desire and determination to achieve our dreams.

The rest are chosen by the Liverpool FC family to become members, invited into our red-clad clan to help us earn and enjoy the success that our family has become accustomed to. Those chosen ones should consider themselves lucky. To be invited to join English football's most successful family and represent us in a red shirt on the green grass of Anfield is a privilege not afforded to many. Give your all and you're a family member for life.

Our history dates back to 1892. Born from a family squabble and raised by Scottish cousins, different generations of the family, a family that lives in all four corners of the globe, have experienced glorious highs and painful lows. But over the last half-century or so, thanks to father figures such as Bill, Bob, Joe, Kenny, Roy, Gerard and Rafael, we have enjoyed unparalleled success.

We've travelled across Europe together. From Reykjavik to Rabotnicki, Poznan to Prague, Vigo to Vladikavkaz, carrying banners bearing the family name and singing songs about our loved ones.

Passion, pride, emotion and a desire to win are our calling cards. Family outings to London and Cardiff have been annual events, day-trips to Rome, Paris and Istanbul will be lovingly cherished in our family album for eternity.

But it isn't just about the football. It's about the people. Our people. The 96 brothers and sisters we lost are remembered eternally. The flame that flickers for them will never go out. The Liverpool FC family stands shoulder to shoulder.

Putting into words what this family means to us is no easy task, but a song written by two of the four Scousers behind the soundtrack to our city, the location of our family home, is as applicable as you will find.

In My Life reads like how things are in our life...

'All these places have their moments, with lovers and friends I still can recall. Some are dead and some are living, in my life I've loved them all. But of all these friends and lovers, there is no-one compares with you. And these memories lose their meaning, when I think of love as something new. Though I know I'll never lose affection, for people and things that went before. I know I'll often stop and think about them, in my life I love you more.'

Welcome to the Liverpool Football Club Family Tree, the story of a family that lives by one collective motto.

You'll Never Walk Alone

A JOURNEY OF DISCOVERY

As the popular television programme asks: 'Who do you think you are?' Liverpool Football Club has a rich heritage with supporters having a strong sense of identity and values which they hold dear.

This book looks closely at Liverpool FC's DNA and charts the genealogies of some of the key members of its family. Broken down into eight journeys, *The Official Liverpool FC Family Tree* looks at the family trees of the key managers in the club's history.

As we seek to discover more about the roots of the men who have helped shape Liverpool Football Club, we re-visit the areas where some legendary figures were raised. We return to the Scottish hamlet of Glenbuck where Bill Shankly grew up. Then there is a trip to Hetton-le-Hole to get a feel for the people and places that made an impression on the young Bob Paisley.

We take some Liverpool legends back to their roots with Phil Thompson taking us around his former haunts in Kirkby, and David Fairclough showing us around the streets where he first kicked a ball in anger. Bringing us into the more modern era, Sami Hyypia talks us through his formative years in Finland, and Jamie Carragher gives us a tour of Bootle.

Few clubs can claim to have a birth certificate. But we look at the document which effectively was just that, as far as the Reds were concerned. We also focus on the men who could be considered to be Liverpool's 'parents' as the young club took its first small steps on a road few could have foreseen leading along a path to European glory.

At the heart of every family is its home. This book revisits the Anfield story, looks at how the famous Kop received its name and examines the long links the club has enjoyed with South Africa during its near 120-year existence.

This book pays tribute to the men who showed courage and bravery by fighting for their country during the two world wars, periods when competitive football as we know it was put on hold.

The club has enjoyed strong Celtic links throughout its history and we also trace the large number of Scots selected in the early years of the club, something which led to Liverpool being known as the 'Team of Macs'.

Liverpool's first 'managers' John McKenna and William Barclay were both born in Ireland and the Reds have maintained a lasting association with players from both north and south of the country with stars such as Elisha Scott, Steve Heighway, Ronnie Whelan and John Aldridge maintaining the Anfield bond. Jim Beglin, once an Anfield left-back and now a respected media pundit, talks about the affinity for Liverpool in his home country and his own upbringing in Waterford.

In modern times, the club has cast its net far wider in the search for stars. *The Official Liverpool FC Family Tree* analyses the way in which the club has scouted for new talent down the years and assesses the impact made by foreign imports. The book also highlights the players who have gone on to appear in various World Cup finals.

Foreign managers have also played their part in the club's history and we look at the family trees of the men who gave the Reds a French flavour (Gerard Houllier) and a Spanish sizzle (Rafael Benitez).

Bringing the story up to date we look at the current set-up under Kenny Dalglish in his second spell at the club, as well as the history of the club's ownership from the original John H (Houlding) to the latest (Henry) following Fenway Sports Group's takeover in 2010.

Digging deep into the key figures who have helped make Liverpool Football Club the incredible sporting institution it is today, this book helps tell the tale of the Reds' rich fabric. It is a story which stirs the pride and passion felt whenever the team takes to the field – in the name of the city and supporters they represent.

Contents

FROM GLENBUCK TO MONTEVIDEO

CREATING HISTORY. IT'S IN OUR BLOOD

Although Bill Shankly and Luis Suarez don't appear to have much in common, they both started life in humble surroundings. Shankly came from a small Scottish mining village, whilst Suarez was born into poverty in a city on the other side of the world. Their experiences fuelled their ambition and determination to succeed

JOURNEY 1

Shankly started life in the tiny Scottish mining village of Glenbuck

While manager of Huddersfield, accepts the offer to become Liverpool manager in 1959

John Aldridge spoke about his impending move to Liverpool on January 24, 1987 – 6,700 miles away Luis Suarez is born in Salto

Suarez moves to Europe at the age of 19, impressing with Dutch clubs Groningen and Ajax

Luis Suarez becomes the latest player to wear the famous No. 7 shirt

Mr. Shankly Arrives At Anfield

Mr. Bill Shankly, new manager of Liverpool F.C., took over officially at Anfield today, although he was at ... on Saturday to watch the reserves play. Left to right in the ... afternoon are: Bob Paisley, first team trainer, Mr. Shankly, Mr. ...ams, ...han, and Reuben Bennett, the chief coach.

FOLLOWING A DREAM TO ESCAPE THE MINE

A small Scottish mining village seems the most unlikely of breeding grounds for a football managerial genius. But it was in Glenbuck that Bill Shankly shaped many of the skills that would help him lead Liverpool to glory at home and abroad.

While many escaped the misery of the mines through drink, Bill Shankly turned to football. Whether it was cards or a quick game of five-a-side on the pit surface, he was always a bad loser – or maybe just a born winner.

There was something truly magical about the tiny mining village, a proud community which once stood on the main road between the coastal town of Ayr and Muirkirk, its nearby neighbour. So magical in fact that it was torn down.

Now all that remains is a monument bearing this inscription:

"Seldom in the history of sport can a village the size of Glenbuck have produced so many who reached the pinnacle of achievement in their chosen sport. This monument is dedicated to their memory and to the memory of one man in particular, Bill Shankly."

Indeed, it produced as many as 50 Scottish sporting stars, many of whom were actually members of the clan Shankly. Sociologists, football journalists, historians and even Glenbuck's repatriated sons and daughters, have tried to fathom the reason for the success of its inhabitants. None have managed a satisfactory answer. Glenbuck itself might have been the reason. Shankly had never seen a toilet until he left the village. Money was tight, working hours were long, the conditions would be considered inhumane by today's standards and football offered an escape from poverty and deprivation for young men.

For some of them, escapism was only a dream. Shankly was one of the lucky ones. Bill, or Willie as he was more commonly known, was born to John and Barbara Shankly on September 2, 1913.

He was the ninth of ten children, and the youngest of five boys. The family home was Auchenstilloch cottages, known locally as 'Miners Row'. The Shanklys had two houses next to each other, knocked into one to accommodate their large family. They later moved to newer, custom-built council houses that were constructed in the area. That at least improved their lot a little.

John Shankly moved to Glenbuck from the nearby village of Douglas to seek work in his chosen profession of tailoring. He met and married a young woman, Barbara Blyth, who came from one of Glenbuck's most celebrated families.

Below: Shots of a young Bill Shankly, in his formative years growing up in Glenbuck

THE BILL SHANKLY PLAYERS' TREE
– December 1, 1959 to July 26, 1974

Shankly

Goalkeepers

Tommy Lawrence 1957-1971,
Dailly, Scotland
Bert Slater 1959-1962,
Musselburgh, Scotland
Jim Furnell 1962-1963,
Clitheroe, England
William Molyneux 1963-1965,
Liverpool, England
John Ogston 1965-1967,
Aberdeen, Scotland
Ray Clemence 1967-1981,
Skegness, England
Frank Lane 1971-1972,
Wallasey, England

Defenders

Ronnie Moran 1952-1965,
Crosby, England
Gerry Byrne 1953-1969,
Liverpool, England
Dick White 1955-1962,
Scunthorpe, England
John Molyneux 1955-1962,
Warrington, England
Alan Jones 1957-1963,
Flint, Wales
Philip Ferns 1958-1965,
Liverpool, England
Chris Lawler 1960-1975,
Liverpool, England
Ron Yeats 1961-1971,
Aberdeen, Scotland
Bobby Thomson 1962-1964,
Menstrie, Scotland
Tommy Smith 1962-1978,
Liverpool, England
Alan Hignett 1963-1965,
Liverpool, England
Thomas Lowry 1963-1965,
Liverpool, England
Roy Evans 1965-1973,
Liverpool, England
Peter Wall 1966-1970,
Westbury, England
Emlyn Hughes 1967-1979,
Barrow-in-Furness, England
Larry Lloyd 1969-1974,
Bristol, England
Alec Lindsay 1969-1977,
Bury, England
Chris Fagan 1970-1971,
Manchester, England
Dave Rylands 1970-1974,
Liverpool, England
Phil Thompson 1971-1983,
Kirkby, England
Max Thompson 1974-75,
Liverpool, England

Midfielders

Alan A'Court 1952-1964,
Rainhill, England
Jimmy Melia 1954-1964,
Liverpool, England
Bobby Campbell 1954-1960,
Liverpool, England
Johnny Wheeler 1956-1961,
Crosby, England
Fred Morris 1958-1959,
Pant, England
James Harrower 1958-1961,
Alva, Scotland
Tommy Leishman 1959-1962,
Stenhousemuir, Scotland
Ian Callaghan 1960-1978,
Liverpool, England
Willie Stevenson 1962-1967,
Edinburgh, Scotland
Peter Thompson 1963-1972,
Carlisle, England
Phil Chisnall 1964-1966,
Manchester, England
Doug Livermore 1965-1970,
Liverpool, England
David Wilson 1967-1968,
Nelson, England
Brian Hall 1968-1976,
Glasgow, Scotland
Phil Boersma 1968-1975,
Kirkby, England
John McLaughlin 1969-1974,
Liverpool, England
Steve Heighway 1970-1981,
Dublin, Ireland
Peter Cormack 1972-1975,
Edinburgh, Scotland
Trevor Storton 1972-1974,
Keighley, England

Forwards

Billy Liddell 1939-1960,
Townhill, Scotland
Alan Arnell 1953-1961,
Chichester, England
Roger Hunt 1958-1969,
Golborne, England
Alan Banks 1958-1961,
Liverpool, England
Dave Hickson 1959-1961,
Salford, England
Alf Arrowsmith 1960-1968,
Manchester, England
Ian St John 1961-1971,
Motherwell, Scotland
Gordon Wallace 1961-1965,
Lanark, Scotland
Bobby Graham 1961-1972,
Motherwell, Scotland
John Sealey 1962-1965,
Wallasey, England
Geoff Strong 1964-1970,
Kirkheaton, England
Ian Ross 1965-1972,
Glasgow, Scotland
Steve Peplow 1966-1969,
Liverpool, England
Tony Hateley 1967-1968,
Derby, England
Alun Evans 1968-1972,
Bewdley, England
John Toshack 1970-1977,
Cardiff, Wales
Jack Whitham 1970-1972,
Burnley, England
Steve Arnold 1970-1971,
Wembley, England
Kevin Keegan 1971-1977,
Armthorpe, England
Derek Brownbill 1972-1973,
Liverpool, England
Alan Waddle 1973-1977,
Wallsend, England

Players used: 68. **By position:** Goalkeepers: 7, Defenders: 21, Midfielders: 19, Forwards: 21. **By nationality:** England: 50, Scotland: 15, Wales: 2, Republic of Ireland: 1. **Key:** On the player information, the first date is the year the player signed for LFC and the second the date of his last senior appearance.

What's in a name?

Bill Shankly

There is no known derivation for the name but it may have been made up of a combination of a couple of others.

Shank or Shanks was a nickname for a person with long or ungainly legs. Shank was a surname scattered throughout Britain, while Shanks was mainly found in North East England and, appropriately, Scotland.

The surname Shankly was an anglicised version of the Gaelic first name Seanlaoch, meaning 'old hero'.

Football was in their blood and it passed through the genes. Bill's uncle Bob played football for Rangers, Preston and Dundee before becoming player-manager and finally chairman at Portsmouth. A second brother, Billy, played for Portsmouth, Preston and Carlisle before joining Bob as an administrator and director, and then chairman of Carlisle. Life was hard for the Shanklys during Bill's formative years and indeed for the other families of Glenbuck. However, that determined and belligerent streak that people remember so fondly in Shankly was forged in Glenbuck.

Those harsh years spent down the mine shafts as a teenager undoubtedly convinced him he would be better served elsewhere. Shankly was a man who needed fresh air. Talking to former players about Emlyn Hughes after his passing they opined that the reason he and Shanks got on so well was because both shared a love of fresh air. Rain, hail or shine Shankly loved the great outdoors. You would too if you endured what he, and thousands of others, had to go through to make their living.

The elder Shankly boys managed to avoid a life in the pit, or at least delay the agonies, thanks to their ability on the football field. Bill's eldest brother, Alec, played inside-forward for Ayr United prior to World War I, when he joined the Royal Scots Fusiliers and then the Royal Flying Corps. Following the end of the war and with his football career over, he had no option but to commit to the pit.

The next brother, Jimmy, was a centre-half and then centre-forward, playing at Portsmouth, Halifax, Sheffield United, Southend and Barrow – his final club before his retirement in 1933. The middle Shankly brother, John, was an outside-right for Portsmouth and Greenock Morton, among others. John suffered from ill health and was forced to retire from football, returning to Glenbuck and the certainty of life as a miner. Time would tell us that the only certainty of life down the mines was ill-health in later life – if you were fortunate. John died in tragic circumstances; not in the pit, but in a football stadium – Hampden Park – during the Real Madrid versus Eintracht Frankfurt European Cup final of 1960. John suffered a massive heart attack at the game, and died later that night in hospital.

The fourth brother, Bob, was to have a successful managerial career with five clubs, winning the Scottish championship with Dundee and subsequently guiding them to the latter stages of the European Cup. He is to Dundee what Bill is to Liverpool.

Bill's life was almost a reversal of his two eldest brothers. Their footballing talent shone like a beacon from a very early age and they were always destined for a career in the game. It was as obvious in the playground as

In the town where I was born

Glenbuck, Scotland

In 1786, major deposits of iron, coal and limestone were discovered in the Scottish village, resulting in the Glenbuck Iron Company gaining a licence to exploit them.

Several mines, blast furnaces and five rows of houses for workers and officials to live in were built, but by 1813 the company had run into financial problems and production ceased.

The huge coal reserve in the area and development of steam locomotives ensured the village recovered, but by 1933 a lack of orders meant that all the pits were closed for good.

Top: A picture of Glenbuck.
Left: Shankly (far right) pictured with his mother, father and a brother

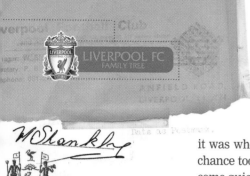

it was when they played for professional clubs. With Bill, his footballing chance took a little longer to materialise than his siblings – and it did not come quickly enough to save him from an initial career in the dank, dark, damp local colliery.

It was an experience that would stay with him until his dying day. It was 1927 and the options facing Shankly as he left school were twofold. Unemployment or the coal mines beckoned, and being a good Calvinist he decided that work was the answer.

The young Bill Shankly left school and found work in the mines earning 2s 6d – that's 12½p – per day. After six months of emptying coal trucks Shankly found himself at the pit bottom. The further down the shaft you went the greater the dangers became. Workers were forced to do 10 days out of every 14, and those who failed to meet this quota for any reason were fined 6d. Conditions varied from district to district, but the dangers were omni-present. The shafts were dark and wet. The moisture led to respiratory problems in later life for the miners while working in near darkness all day, every day was hardly good for the eyesight. When a miner lost his job there was also every chance he'd lose his home, since many properties were owned by industry. That was usually enough to turn the miners to drink, and local history is littered with tales of drunken miners, their miseries and the sadness that was served upon their families.

Not Shankly. Acutely aware of the dangers that alcohol created from his own observations of Glenbuck's drinkers, he was unflinchingly teetotal. However, he did allow himself one indulgence and that was playing cards

Not quite my cup of tea: A Manager of the Year prize for the teetotal Shankly – a giant bottle of whisky. Below right, his parents' wedding certificate

EXTRACT OF AN ENTRY IN A REGISTER OF MARRIAGES, of 17° & 18° VICTORIÆ, kept in the undermentioned P... Cap. 80, §§ 56 & 58.

No.	When, Where, and How Married.	Names (in full) of Parties, with Signatures. Rank or Profession, and whether Bachelor, Spinster, Widower, Widow, or Divorced.	Age.	Usual Residence.	Name, Surname, and Rank or Profession of Father. Name, and Maiden Surname of Mother	
128	1944 On the Twenty-ninth day of June at Wellpark Church, Glasgow. After Banns: According to the Forms of the Church of Scotland.	William Shankly W. Shankly Professional Footballer, (Leading Aircraftman, Royal Air Force).(Bachelor) Agnes Wren Stewart Fisher A. Fisher Slater's Clerkess,(Aircraft-woman:Women's Auxiliary Air Force). (Spinster)	30 23	6, New Houses, Glenbuck, (Now engaged in War Service) 128, Dunchattan Street, Glasgow. (Now engaged in War Service).	John Shankly Tailor (Deceased) Barbara Shankly M.S. Blyth James Fisher Garage Proprietor Annie Fisher M.S. Michael	

EXTRACTED from the REGISTER BOOK OF MARRIAGES for the DISTRICT of TOWNHEAD in the BURGH of GLASGOW , this 3rd day of July 1944 . In terms of the 58th Section of the Act 17 & 18 Vict. c. 80, every Extract ... ...and Marriages (Scotland) Acts, duly authenticated ...

In the town where I was born

Glenbuck, Scotland (cont.)

The village's local football team, Glenbuck Cherrypickers, produced 50 professional footballers despite only existing from 1870 to 1931 – and the village having a population of around 1,000.

Amongst them were all four of Bill Shankly's brothers including Bob, who was capped by Scotland and went on to manage Falkirk, Third Lanark, Dundee, Hibernian and Stirling Albion. Bill never played for the Cherrypickers' first XI – the club folded in 1930/31 before he was old enough – or good enough – to play for them.

in a card school that took place in the hills outside the village.

He also shared his father's love of the cinema and revelled in the gangster movies that abounded on the screens in the late '20s and early '30s. Often father and son would go together. However, by 1930 Bill didn't have the spare change required for the cinema because the final Glenbuck pit had closed and he found himself unemployed, a victim of the depression.

Fortunately, he had his football as a distraction and around the time he was made redundant his displays with Cronberry Eglinton were making people sit up and take notice. A Scottish town without a football team was like Hogmanay without *Auld Lang Syne*. Glenbuck was certainly no exception to this rule, for they had the famous Glenbuck Cherrypickers.

The club had its beginnings in the late 1870s and was founded by Edward Bone and William Brown, among a myriad of others. It was originally called Glenbuck Athletic and the club colours were white shirts and black shorts.

Sunday best: In relaxed mood with the family (top)

Family Secrets

Bernard Battles

Like Shankly, Bernard Battles was a larger-than-life character. Unfortunately, 'Barney' was a man who was lost tragically early.

A heavyweight half-back, he had two spells with Liverpool after initially joining on loan from Celtic in 1896 – just after helping the Bhoys to the Scottish title.

His enthusiasm made him a fans' favourite but after returning to Scotland, he contracted pneumonia and died at his home in Glasgow's Gallowgate, aged just 30.

The big man's funeral at Dalbeth cemetery saw 40,000 people line the route to pay tribute to a much-loved personality.

King of the Kop: At Anfield in familiar pose (top). Right: A kickaround at Melwood and wearing the national colours as a player

Over the years the Cherrypickers won numerous local cups including the Ayrshire Junior Challenge Cup, the Cumnock Cup and the Mauchline Cup. Despite all their honours the real place of Glenbuck in Scottish footballing folklore is as a conveyor belt of talent for the professional ranks. Of the 50-or-so players who plied their trade in senior football, at least half-a-dozen also played for Scotland – not bad for a village whose population never exceeded 1,200 and was believed to have averaged out at around 800 settlers. Despite the track record and Shankly's regular links with the Cherrypickers, Bill was never destined to join the illustrious band of Cherrypicker alumni.

The first year he would have been able to play for them, 1930/31, he was not considered good enough. This was no disgrace as they once again captured the Ayrshire Junior Challenge Cup. Strange, though, that Shankly was soon deemed good enough for Carlisle United – but not for the village XI. However, this victory in the Ayrshire Junior Cup was to be their final moment in the sun. The final pit had closed, and the final nail was hammered into the coffin of the village of Glenbuck. The Cherrypickers were disbanded as the men were forced to seek work in other areas. When the next season began, Shankly had no club to play for and was forced to begin his career playing right-half for Cronberry Eglinton. They were undoubtedly a decent local side but this was merely a stepping-stone for the 18-year-old Bill Shankly, for whom greater things waited around the corner.

A FATEFUL TRAIN TRIP AND THE ROAD TO ANFIELD

From Cronberry, Shankly graduated to the Carlisle first team before a dramatic change of mind resulted in a switch to Preston. Despite initially refusing the move, Shankly, encouraged by his brother Alec, rushed back to the station where he had just met Bill Scott, Preston's trainer, and joined him on his train home. He signed on in the train carriage and travelled back to Carlisle.

Shankly made a success of his move to Preston, reaching an FA Cup final and captaining the club, as well as representing his country.

His early management career took him to Carlisle, Grimsby, Workington and Huddersfield before fate came calling one day in 1959 when Liverpool chairman Tom (TV) Williams and Harry Latham, an Anfield director, visited the Terriers' then ground, Leeds Road.

Immediately Shankly was attracted to the idea of managing a club like Liverpool. He said: "I knew the Liverpool people…it was a city like the Scottish cities and the people were similar to the Scottish people."

In the town where I was born

Glenbuck, Scotland (cont.)

Glenbuck was the birthplace of Tom Bone, one of the finest British quoits players of all time.

He was born in the village in 1868, became Scottish quoits champion in 1889 and, in 1908, beat Liverpool's James Hood to become champion of Great Britain.

LIVERPOOL FC
FAMILY TREE

The story of what happened next is well chronicled. Promotion to the First Division in 1962, a league title arriving two years later before a first, historic FA Cup triumph. Another two titles, a UEFA Cup and a further FA Cup followed before Shankly handed over the reins to Bob Paisley.

Building on the foundations laid by his trusted friend, Paisley would take the club to even greater heights, conquering Europe in 1977, 1978 and 1981. But there was a sad end to the year that had witnessed the Reds' third European Cup victory. Anfield mourned, as the shock news emerged that Shankly had passed away on September 29.

On October 1, 1981, Liverpool faced Oulu Palloseura in a European Cup first-round, second-leg tie and the city's *Daily Post* newspaper summed up the mood:

'For most of the second half, the Kop simply sang the word "Shankly" to the tune of Amazing Grace. A banner in the middle of the crowd summed up the feelings of thousands: "King Shankly Lives".'

The Kop banner got it spot on. Shankly was gone but never forgotten. His legacy lives on, as new recruits quickly discover. One of the latest Liverpool signings comes from the other side of the world, but has also overcome adversity to forge a career in the sport he loves.

Above: The Kop flag at half mast as news of Shankly's death breaks. Below: A death notice in the Liverpool Echo

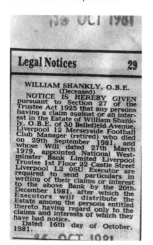

Legal Notices   29

WILLIAM SHANKLY, O.B.E.
(Deceased)
NOTICE IS HEREBY GIVEN pursuant to Section 27 of the Trustee Act 1925 that any persons having a claim against or an interest in the Estate of William Shankly, O.B.E. of 30 Bellefield Avenue, Liverpool 12 Merseyside Football Club Manager (retired) who died on 29th September 1981, and whose Will dated 27th March 1979, appointed National Westminster Bank Limited Liverpool Trustee 1st Floor 22 Castle Street Liverpool L2 0SU Executor are required to send particulars in writing of their claims or interest to the above Bank by the 20th December 1981, after which the Executors will distribute the Estate among the persons entitled thereto having regard only to the claims and interests of which they have had notice.
Dated 16th day of October, 1981.

Liverpool
Lu

LUIS SUAREZ

HAVE BOOTS, WILL TRAVEL

The legend of the Liverpool number 7 shirt was created by the achievements of Kevin Keegan and Kenny Dalglish during their playing careers at Anfield through the 1970s and 1980s. Keegan arrived from Scunthorpe in north Lincolnshire, while Dalglish came down from Glasgow in Scotland.

The latest man to wear the famous jersey has travelled a lot further to get to Merseyside. Luis Suarez was born in Salto, the second largest city in Uruguay, close to the Argentinean border and 6,700 miles from Liverpool 4. He has already packed a lot into his 24 years.

The fourth of seven children (brother Paolo was latterly a midfielder for Isidro Metapan in El Salvador), Luis was brought up by a single mother – who worked as a housekeeper. Suarez did not have a privileged upbringing and his determination to succeed in professional football was forged at an early age. Despite his talent, he did not attend a Uruguay youth training camp because his family couldn't afford to buy him a pair of boots.

Suarez explained: "I had a really hard time growing up. As you can imagine coming from a large family, we did not have many resources at home, which meant we had to carry on with a very normal life, full of sacrifices."

He and his four brothers idolised Gabriel Batistuta, the Argentinean centre-forward. "He was a complete number 9," says Suarez. "Brave, skilful – powerful. What I liked most was that he could score goals from anywhere. When I was a child and he scored for Fiorentina, I would play on the street and try to repeat what I had seen. Importantly, he was a hard worker who never had it easy. That inspired him and in turn has inspired me."

Salto is situated approximately 260 miles north-west of the Uruguayan capital, Montevideo. It is linked to the Argentinean city of Concordia by the Salto Grande Bridge, which was built on top of the Salto Grande Dam. It's a city of contrasts with slum areas and prosperity living side by side. It is known for its thermal pools, which attract tourists.

Suarez's ability was apparent from an early age. When he was just four years old, people began to notice that he ran faster with a ball at his feet. At the age of seven, he moved to Montevideo to join the junior academy of Nacional, Uruguay's most successful club. While in the capital, he lived with his grandparents. "That was where my football career began," he explained. "That was the first big change in my life, and since then I have faced many other big changes."

Below: In action on his Liverpool debut against Stoke City. The bottom picture shows Gabriel Batistuta – Suarez's first footballing hero

Montevideo, which was under British rule for several months in 1807, is a port on the southern tip of the country. The city's stunning architecture is admired and has an eclectic style, with the high numbers of European immigrants that crossed the Atlantic in the 20th century influencing the look of the built environment. It has plenty of football pedigree and Montevideo staged all the matches in the first FIFA World Cup, held in 1930 and won by the hosts.

Suarez made his first-team debut in May 2005, aged 18, in a Copa Libertadores match against Junior de Barranquilla. In his only full season for Nacional, he scored 12 goals as they were crowned champions of the Uruguayan Primera Division.

He was in his early teenage years when he met the love of his life, Sofia Balbi. It was a love so strong that he followed her to Europe when her family relocated to Barcelona. Desperate not to lose Sofia, Suarez, then 19 years old, followed her to Europe in 2006 by pushing for a transfer to Dutch club Groningen when Brazilian side Flamengo were also interested in signing him. He is now married to Sofia and they have a baby daughter, Delfina, born in August 2010.

Speaking of his move to Europe, Suarez has said: "My happiness (after winning the title with Nacional) was not complete. Sofia and I had to continue a long-distance relationship for a year. Despite this complication I could not give up on our relationship and when I got a call to play in Europe I didn't think twice. The only thing I thought about was being by her side again. That's how my European adventure started.

In the town where I was born

Salto, Uruguay

The second largest city in the country by population (just under 100,000 according to a 2004 census), and the sixth largest by land and total population.

Salto is on the east coast of the Uruguay River. Although containing many slum districts, it is considered one of the higher class areas in the country due to its standard of amenities.

Famous Salto sons include authors Horacio Quiroga (born 1879) and Enrique Amorim (born 1900), and footballers Pedro Virgilio Rocha (a Penarol and Uruguay legend, born 1942) and Edinson Cavani, who was at Napoli in early 2011.

What's in a name?

Luis Alberto Suarez Diaz

'Suarez' (translating from the Latin 'suerius' as the occupation 'swineherd') is of Iberian descent, recorded in the spellings of Soeiro, Suero, Soares and Juares. It has German origins, from the fifth century when the Vizigoths tribes from northern Germany destroyed the Roman Empire – of which Spain was a part. They occupied for several centuries, leaving behind a legacy which also includes surnames Gonzales and Ramirez.

His full name is Luis Alberto Suarez Diaz. In Spanish custom, Suarez is taken from the father's surname and Diaz from the mother's side.

"I had the girl of my dreams back but in career terms, I always had it clear in my mind that this was the big chance of my life. At the beginning it was not easy, I could not speak Dutch or English and communication was incredibly hard but I knew I could not give up.

"I kept on fighting and working hard. It was incredible to believe that I was playing for a top division team in the Netherlands at such a young age. When I look at my past I think about all my friends growing up, all the dirt fields and streets of Montevideo that I played on. I can't help but feel very proud of what I have achieved."

Suarez scored 14 goals in 35 games for Groningen, which earned him a big-money switch to Ajax in 2007. During his time in Amsterdam he scored over 100 goals in all competitions, was appointed club captain and by 2010 he was the Dutch player of the year.

Rik van den Boog, the managing director at Ajax, believes Suarez will be a big success for the Reds. "Luis is going to bring Liverpool alive because he is a street fighter," he said. "Luis was not a big player when he arrived here but he soon stood up in the dressing room and became a leader."

Marco van Basten, who managed Ajax in 2008/09, said of Suarez: "He is unpredictable…but that makes him special too." Under Ajax's next coach, Martin Jol, Suarez's goalscoring ratio was phenomenal: 49 strikes in 48 appearances in 2009/10, among them six hat-tricks (which included three four-goal hauls and one six-goal haul).

It was in the summer of 2010 that Suarez acquired a degree of notoriety after his handball on the line denied Ghana a winning goal in their World Cup quarter-final with Uruguay. If nothing else, his action demonstrated his desperation to win and his performances for the national team have been exceptional, accumulating 38 caps and 16 goals.

In February 2011, he made an instant impression at Anfield, scoring on his debut against Stoke City. Liverpool has also had a positive effect on him, especially Kenny Dalglish. In one of his first interviews after joining the Reds, Suarez remarked: "He [Dalglish] is a person who you respect after only a few minutes' conversation. He tried to speak to me in Spanish – 'hola, bienvenido' (hello and welcome) – and that impressed me. Obviously, he is a legend at this club, in this city, but I think it's very important to judge people as you see them rather than just what you hear. He has lived up to that legend in my eyes.

Below: Representing his country, Uruguay, wearing the home and away jerseys

"I could see quickly that Dalglish is a manager and a person who I can relate to and he is very determined to make the team play with a certain image – the kind of attractive football that I want to be a part of. He was very keen to bring me here and if there is one person that was influential in my signing it was him. He is very ambitious about the club and is confident he can lead the club back to the top. Now I am here, I do not want to disappoint him in any way."

Suarez recognises the significance of the Liverpool number 7 shirt, given the names that have worn it before, but insists that it places no extra pressure on him to achieve success.

"Everybody has told me about the symbolic importance of the number 7 here. First there was Keegan, then Dalglish – both fantastic players. But personally, as soon as I step out on the field, I am not bothered by the number on my back. Sentimentality has never really been very important to me – every club I've been at, I've worn a different number. My focus has always been how I can help the team win the game.

"I'm very excited about the future here at Liverpool. The club has a long and glorious history and is respected by football supporters, not just in Europe but across the whole world. Okay, the last 18 months hasn't gone as the club or the fans would have wished but I have spoken at length with the people here and I can see that they have the passion and determination to take Liverpool back to where it should be."

For all that he has already experienced, there is plenty in the future for Luis Suarez and Liverpool fans to be excited about in the future as another new member is welcomed into the family.

993

LIVERPOOL
A.F.C.

ANFIELD

Shelter

LIVERPOOL FOOTBALL CLUB

Liverpool Football Ground

1878: The Reverend Ben Swift Chambers forms the St Domingo Football Club

1891: Businessman and brewer John Houlding has a dispute with his fellow Everton committee members

1892: The birth of a new team at Anfield, named Liverpool Football Club by William Barclay

William Barclay and John McKenna team up to manage the side

1977: Born in the shadow of Anfield, a young Scouser keeps the Reds on course to be champions of Europe for the first time

FROM SHEPLEY TO ROME

OUR ANCESTORS AND THE FAMILY HOME

The origins of Liverpool Football Club can be traced all the way back to a little-known village in West Yorkshire. A church minister set the ball rolling before our founding father set us on the long and winding Anfield road that would one day lead to the Eternal City

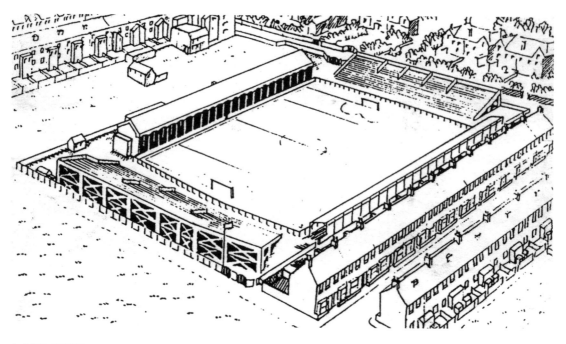

Anfield in 1894/95
with the first main
stand and uncovered
terracing at both
ends. The Kop, as
it would become
known in 1906, is
behind the goal at
the bottom of this
artist's impression

THE ANFIELD STORY

The centre of any family is its home.

For Liverpool, living at Anfield was akin to seeing your older brother move out into a new home down the road while you set about settling in and making improvements to his old pad. Everton had been resident in a couple of homes before spending eight years at Anfield. It was also their home when they were crowned champions of England for the first time in 1891. The Blues had arrived there after William Cruitt, landlord of their Priory Road base, became dismayed by the volume of noise that intruded into his home on matchdays.

It reached such a point that he asked Everton to move on. Businessman John Houlding approached fellow brewer Joseph Orrell for help. Orrell owned land in Walton Breck Road that was lying idle, and Houlding asked if Everton could rent it. Orrell agreed terms and Everton moved into Anfield for the start of the 1884/85 season, with the first match being played there on September 27, 1884 when the Blues defeated Earlestown 5-0.

It is often believed that a row over rent was the catalyst for Everton's spat with Houlding – but there was more to it than that. Personality clashes were also involved, with the strong temperance movement of the time

LIVERPOOL
FOOTBALL CLUB.

(UNDER ASSOCIATION RULES)

SEASON 1892-93.

President.

MR. JOHN HOULDING, C.C.

Vice-Presidents.

MR. B. BAILEY, | DR J. B. EDIS,
MR. E. WALKER, C.C.

Chairman:

MR. E. BERRY.

Committee:

MR. W. F. EVANS, | MR. T. C. HOWARTH,
MR. F. C. EVERITT, | MR. C. LINDSAY,
MR. W. GUNNING, | MR. J. McKENNA,
MR. W. HOULDING, | MR. A. NISBET.

Hon. Treasurer:

MR. R. H. WEBSTER.

Hon. Secretary:

MR. W. E. BARCLAY,
33, Everton Terrace, Liverpool.

VIII.—In the event of a Player requiring a new outfit, or any part of it, he must report it to the trainer, who will note it in his weekly statement to the Committee.

IX.—The Trainer shall be in attendance on Tuesdays and Thursdays, (mid-day and evening), and at any other time when required by the Committee for training purposes, and every Player will be required to turn out on these days, placing his name in the training book, as a record to be submitted to the Secretary weekly for the information of the Committee.

X.—Players shall keep themselves in fit and proper condition, and must turn up to play at the place notified, and if unable to do so must produce Medical Certificate or otherwise giving cause of absence to the Secretary.

XI.—Players and Members of Committee only, are allowed in the dressing room.

XII.—Any infringement of the foregoing bye-laws will be dealt with by the Committee, fining the offending person at their discretion, and continued breaches of discipline will be met by suspension and forfeiture of all wages for a period according to the gravity of the case.

N.B.—The Committee will not be responsible for payment for Medical attendance except that given by the Medical Officer of the Club.

The above Bye-laws having been passed at a meeting of the Committee, held on 1892, are binding upon the Members until further notice.

JOHN HOULDING, PRESIDENT.

EDWIN BERRY, CHAIRMAN.

Liverpool Football Club.
(ASSOCIATION.)

RULES.

I.—That the Club be called the LIVERPOOL FOOTBALL CLUB, and shall play under the Rules of the Football Association.

II.—That the Executive Committee shall be elected by the Members, and shall consist of a President, Vice-Presidents, Chairman, Honorary Secretary, Honorary Treasurer, and eight other Members.

III.—That the Executive Committee shall have sole control of the ground and finances, power to engage players, arrange fixtures, and have full control of all matters, including the election of Members during its year of office.

IV.—That the Annual Subscription for Members be 7s. 6d., admitting to ground and covered stands during the season except to English Cup Ties, Charity or Benefit Matches.

V.—New Members shall be elected only at Executive Committee meetings, and shall be duly proposed and seconded by two Members of the Executive. Voting to be by ballot.

VI.—Subscribers' Tickets shall be issued as follows, available during the season, except for all Cup Ties, Charity and Benefit matches, viz.:—Admitting to Ground and Uncovered Stands, 7s. 6d.; to Covered Stand, 15s., and to Reserve Stand, 21s.

VII.—Subscriptions shall be due on the 31st August in each year, and Membership ceases unless the subscription be paid on or before that date.

VIII.—The Executive shall have power to make Bye Laws and decide any point not provided for in these Rules.

IX.—The Annual General Meeting shall be held within one month after the close of the Club's playing season.

X.—Every Member shall be provided with a copy of these Rules.

BYE-LAWS.

I.—Every player, whether amateur or professional, shall appear in proper football costume, both when practising and engaged in a match on behalf of the Club, and no member will be permitted to practise or play on the ground unless wearing the authorised costume of the Club.

II.—No practice will be permitted under any circumstances on days when matches are played, either before or after the match.

III.—All reasonable commands of the Captain in the field must be promptly obeyed. He shall have power to alter the positions of the players if during the progress of a match he thinks it advisable to do so.

IV.—The team shall be complete before leaving the dressing room, and must come on the field in a body, led by the Captain, at least 5 minutes before advertised time of kick-off, unless otherwise instructed by the Secretary.

V.—All articles for the use of members, provided for by the Committee, are the property of the Club.

VI.—The Captain shall return the ball to the Storekeeper immediately on the conclusion of the match.

VII.—Players will be provided with an outfit, and they will be held responsible for any loss or damage sustained to it through neglect on their part. Every Player shall look after his football costume, and shall keep it clean and in good repair at his own expense.

02 LFC 2004

seeing a brewer such as Houlding fall foul of the beliefs held by many committee members. The use of Houlding's hotel, The Sandon, was also viewed by many as a means for him to increase his own revenues – but this was challenged by others. Tom Evans, a person of known integrity, was a member of the early Everton committee and responsible for Houlding's involvement in the club in the first place. He refuted such allegations. Things came to a head at a committee meeting on September 15, 1891 when Houlding's letter, containing the following extract, was read out:

'I am compelled to give you notice which I hereby do that you must give up possession of the piece of land situated between Anfield Road and Walton Breck Road used as a football ground with the approaches thereto after the close of the present season viz April 30th 1892.'

The Sandon today.
Opposite page:
Extracts from the
club's first official
rule book

Houlding sent the letter because Orrell, owner of the field on which the stadium stood, wanted the land for other purposes. Houlding himself had bought land next to Orrell's and saw this as the ideal opportunity to present the club with a prospectus and proposed that Everton should become a limited company and buy his land and Orrell's for a combined sum of £8,737.10s. His motives were questioned.

While sympathisers saw him as merely wanting to help take the club forward by acquiring land to increase the ground's capacity and improve facilities, others felt he was simply trying to make money as his share of the sale would net him a profit. In his prospectus, Houlding claimed:

'The site is well known to residents and football visitors to Liverpool, and is admitted to be a most valuable position for a football club to occupy. The enormous number of spectators who witness the various matches on the ground testify to this.'

At a special general meeting in Shaw Street in 1892, all but 18 of Everton's members refused his proposal to form the club into a limited liability. One last attempt at compromise was made with Everton proposing a £180 per year rent on a 10-year lease. The offer was said to stand for a week. Houlding made no reply and anticipating this, George Mahon, a prominent member of Everton's committee, had identified land off Goodison Road as a possible new home. The departure of Everton from Anfield was confirmed in the club minutes of February 8, 1892:

'As we have not received Mr Houlding's acceptance of the club's offer of £180 per annum for the ground and, as Mr Houlding had given the club notice to quit the present ground, the club's solicitors be instructed to arrange for a lease of the Goodison Road ground.'

And out of that decision, a world famous football club would be born.

No. 35668 C.

N.L. 34731.

Certificate of Change of Name

OF THE

Everton Football Club and Athletic Grounds Company, Limited.

I hereby Certify, That the

Everton Football Club and Athletic Grounds Company, Limited,

having, with the sanction of a **Special Resolution** of the said Company, and with the approval of the BOARD OF TRADE, changed its name, is now called the

Liverpool Football Club and Athletic Grounds Company, Limited,

and I have entered such new name on the Register accordingly.

Given under my hand at London this *Third* day of *June,* One Thousand Eight Hundred and Ninety *Two.*

J. S. Purcell

Registrar of Joint Stock Companies.

Printed by McCorquodale & Co. Limited, "The Armoury," Southwark.

LIVERPOOL FOOTBALL CLUB'S BIRTH CERTIFICATE

Very few football clubs can claim to hold a birth certificate, but Liverpool are able to do just that.

For at the height of Everton's dispute with John Houlding, the brewer drew up a prospectus to form the club into a limited liability. When these proposals were rejected on January 25, 1892, it effectively paved the way for the birth of a new team at Anfield. In effect, the publication of that prospectus was also the moment Liverpool Football Club was conceived.

William Barclay, a former Everton secretary-manager, had worked closely with Houlding before the acrimonious split. It was Barclay who decided that the new team should be called Liverpool. At first Houlding would not accept the idea, hoping that he would be able to keep the Everton name. But when the Football Association rejected his request, Houlding accepted Barclay's suggestion and asked him to run the team alongside businessman John McKenna.

In early 1892, Houlding's proposal – that Everton form themselves into a limited liability, in order to purchase additional land adjacent to their Anfield pitch from landlord Joseph Orrell – had caused feelings to run high.

At a special general meeting of the Everton committee at College Hall, Shaw Street on Monday, January 25, 1892 the plan as put forward in a prospectus by Houlding was formally rejected. At the same meeting, Everton's members selected Goodison Road as an alternative site should matters come to a head.

At a committee meeting held on Monday, March 7, 500 copies of a prospectus for the formation of Everton Football Club and Athletic Grounds Company Limited were distributed to members and so the seeds were sewn for Everton to go their separate way. Houlding therefore has always been considered as Liverpool's founding father, while the club's first managers, McKenna and Barclay, helped them take their first steps.

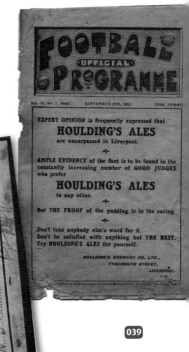

LIVERPOOL FC
FAMILY TREE

John Houlding

What's in a name?

McKenna

Both Scots Gaelic and Irish, this name is derived from the son of Cionaodh and hails from a pagan god of fire.

Houlding

This surname is thought to be a variant of Holding which means 'son of Hold', and translates as gracious and faithful.

Houlding's house

The Parents

JOHN HOULDING

Houlding was a fascinating character who possessed a variety of interests.

Born in 1833 at 15 Tenterden Street, just off Scotland Road in the city, he was a driven individual who combined his love of sport with a shrewd head for business and a keen interest in politics. As a councillor he earned the nickname 'King John of Everton' for his influence in local politics before becoming a Justice of the Peace and Lord Mayor of Liverpool.

He established a successful brewery business and owned five public houses. And, of course, he was the architect of both Everton and Liverpool and their subsequent rise to the heights of English football. He died in 1902 at the age of 69.

JOHN McKENNA

Born in Northern Ireland, McKenna was considered the senior partner in his link-up with William Barclay at Anfield.

A successful local businessman, he was appointed to be part of the club's first committee and was very much involved in the administration side of the club's early years – so much so that the first Barclay knew about Liverpool's application to join the Football League came when he received a call asking him to travel to London to discuss fixture arrangements.

Considered something of a visionary, McKenna had the foresight to recruit Tom Watson from Sunderland to replace Barclay as "secretary-manager". This was no reflection on Barclay's ability but Watson was an experienced team manager who had already led Sunderland to the Football League championship on three occasions in the 1890s. McKenna believed that experience to be vital to Liverpool's future plans.

John McKenna

McKenna, known as 'Honest John' to complement Houlding's 'King John' nickname, was elected to the Football League's management committee in 1902. He became a vice-president in 1908 and president two years later, a position he held for over two decades until his death. He also served as Liverpool chairman between 1909 to 1914 and 1917 to 1919 as well as being a club director for several years. Widely admired and respected, he was a major influence on the formative years of the club.

He died at Walton Hospital in March 1936.

What's in a name?

Barclay

This popular surname has a host of origins, from place names in Gloucestershire and Scotland, to the old English name meaning 'birch wood'. It is now chiefly a Scottish surname.

The Premier League is sponsored by Barclays Bank. The bank's name comes from James Barclay who, in 1736, became a partner in a banking house established in Lombard Street, London.

Rev. B. S. Chambers.
1877 – 1882.
Also 1890 – 1894.

WILLIAM BARCLAY

Born in Dublin in June 1857, Barclay played a key role in Liverpool's early days alongside McKenna.

His organisational skills had been well utilised as headmaster of what were then known as the industrial schools in Everton Crescent.

A firm ally of John Houlding, he had been with him at Everton and was the Blues' secretary for their first season in the Football League. He remained loyal to Houlding following the split and was deployed in a similar role at Anfield until the appointment of Tom Watson.

Known as a great enthusiast in football management and a sound judge of a player, he was well regarded and had a wealth of contacts in the game. He also served on the Lancashire FA.

Barclay took his own life in 1917, two years after his wife's suicide.

BEN SWIFT CHAMBERS

The Reverend Ben Swift Chambers is widely considered to be the man who was the driving force behind the creation of Everton Football Club. If there hadn't been an Everton, there may never have been a Liverpool.

In 1877, Chambers was appointed circuit superintendent and minister of St Domingo Chapel in the Everton district of the city. After forming St Domingo Cricket Club for members of his congregation, Chambers established a football team to keep the cricket side fit during the winter months of 1878. The St Domingo Football Club soon attracted players from churches outside the parish and so in November 1879, it was felt appropriate that the football section of the cricket club be re-named Everton.

When Chambers' grave was found in a dilapidated state by author Peter Lupson while researching his book on the church's early influence on the game 'Thank God For Football,' Liverpool and Everton joined forces to

PRE-BILL SHANKLY MANAGERS' TREE
March 1892 to December 1959

Phil TAYLOR
1956-1959
Manchester, England

Don WELSH
1951-1956
Manchester, England

George KAY
1936-1951
Manchester, England

George PATTERSON
1928-1936
Birthplace unknown

Matt McQUEEN
1923-1928
Harthill, England

David ASHWORTH
1919-1922
Waterford, Republic of Ireland

Tom WATSON
1896-1915
County Monaghan, N. Ireland

John McKENNA
1892-1896
County Monaghan, N. Ireland

William BARCLAY
1892-1896
Dublin, Ireland

What's in a name?

Watson

This means son of Wat, a pet form of Walter. The Watson surname can be mainly found in northern England or Scotland.

Ashworth

Derived from the old English name for 'enclosure in the ash trees', this is also a place name in Lancashire and Yorkshire.

McQueen

A Scottish Gaelic surname which is also popular in Skye. It is derived from Mac Shuibhne which translates as 'son of Suibhne' (pleasant).

Patterson

One of the most popular Scottish surnames, there are 10 different coats of arms for the Patterson clans. It derives from the shortened form of Patrick, Pat or Pate and means 'noble son of'.

(Above) One of the first known squad line-ups, taken outside the bowls pavilion at the rear of the Sandon Hotel, summer 1892 (John Houlding is seated front, centre). (Below) Representatives from Liverpool and Everton pay their respects at the grave of Ben Swift Chambers, without whom there may never have been a Liverpool FC

rededicate his grave. The service in Shepley, Yorkshire was held on July 2, 2008 – exactly 131 years to the day that the Reverend Chambers held his first service at St Domingo.

Both clubs contributed to the cost of restoring the grave. The stonework and engraved words on the headstone have been cleaned up and undergrowth cleared around the plot. It is now inscribed: 'In Memory of the Rev Ben Swift Chambers. Born: Aug 30 1845. Died: Nov 24 1901. Also his beloved wife Elizabeth who died 9th June 1925 aged 80 years.'

The Latin words 'In Te Domine Speravi' were also engraved alongside one side of the grave which translates as: 'In thee, O Lord, I have hoped.'

A tablet was also added at the bottom of the grave which reads: 'In memory of the Reverend Ben Swift Chambers who set the ball rolling that led to the birth of Everton and Liverpool Football Clubs.'

What's in a name?

Welsh

An ancient surname, it has been recorded in a number of spellings including Welch, Welsh and Walsh and has two distinct sources. The first is medieval English, and the second Irish. The English form of the name derives from the Anglo-Saxon word 'wealisc' meaning a stranger or foreigner, and this was originally given as an ethnic name to the 'natives' of the lands that were being conquered. Early English examples of the surname from this source include Simon Welsche of Bedfordshire, in 1279 and Roger Welch of Colchester, Essex, in 1334.

Kay

George Kay served as Liverpool manager for almost 15 years between 1936 and 1951. The surname has several possible meanings, ranging from a maker of keys to a hedge, an enclosure or a place of security. In German the word Kai means a quay or a wharf.

Taylor

A name of trade. An English surname, it has French origins. It derives from the word 'tailleur' meaning 'a cutter-out of cloth', the surname being adopted from the medieval job description after the 12th century. The first recorded spelling of the family name is shown to be that of Walter Taylur. This was dated 1180, in the records of Canterbury Cathedral, during the reign of King Henry II, 1154-1189.

BORN IN THE SHADOW OF ANFIELD

You can't get any more local than David Fairclough. The Anfield favourite was brought up in the shadow of the floodlight pylons which then towered over the area, close enough to follow the course of a game through his ears alone.

"We lived right by Anfield and you could hear the crowd," he recalled. "I remember when they played Inter Milan in the European Cup in '65. That night we stood in the street and listened to the crowd singing. We heard the roars when Liverpool scored, you knew it was a Liverpool goal. As the crow flies it's only a couple of hundred yards. I never thought that one day I'd play for Liverpool because it was just a dream and those type of things don't happen."

Liverpool FC was his life and more often than not he accompanied his father to the game, willing the team and his hero, Roger Hunt, to success.

If Fairclough wasn't watching football, he was playing it – morning, noon and night – although for him it was more the 'Streets of Anfield Road' than fields. He lived on Carmel Street, which no longer exists because the area off St Domingo Road has been extensively redeveloped. Take a trip back, though, and he can pinpoint instantly where things were – his house, gran's home ("probably where this lamp-post is, it's very weird to stand here"), the area where he and his mates kicked the ball around for hours on end.

Liverpool was in the blood. Alan Banks, who played for the club under Bill Shankly, was a cousin of Fairclough's mother. His mother and father's families were all devoted Reds. "Football was our life," admits Fairclough. "My dad was the type who would go the away games; he would think nothing of going to watch Liverpool against Leyton Orient in a midweek game. We went to reserve games. He had a season ticket in the Kemlyn Stand when it was originally built. Life was all football-based when I was young."

Going back to where it all began stirs many emotions, some of them contrasting. It's all changed in some respects, not in others. His primary school down the road is still there, although the name is different. Some roads remain, others are gone. It's sad that landmarks have disappeared but nice that it's not as 'grotty' as the last time he was here. Fairclough makes a good tour guide as he takes a walk back in time, although he confesses it feels 'eerie' returning to his childhood haunts.

"This is Robson Street," he begins, stepping out of his motor. "I used to mind cars here when I was a young lad. This was all my patch; Robson Street, Mere Lane and going down to St Domingo Road. You played football

Hero: Roger Hunt

What's in a name?

Fairclough

A Lancastrian name said to derive from a family group which held land in Ormskirk as early as the 14th century.

Some also believe it hails from Fairclough Farm near Clitheroe, which was named in Middle English as fair clough meaning 'beautiful ravine'.

inside St Thomas White Gardens. There were all these tenement buildings but inside there were squares and they were all set out as football pitches. They were the perfect size, a big one and a scaled down one.

"This is Penrose Street now. We played football all around here. It's changed markedly. Carmel Street, Afghan Street and Penrose Street was a block. We used to have races around the block; it was seen as a stadium, like a 400 metre track. Life revolved around football and running and playing outdoor games. There was nothing else to do. You were living in little back-to-back houses so you didn't spend much time in the home."

David went to school at Major Lester (now Hope Valley) on Walton Breck Road, the shortest of sprints down the hill from his home.

"I don't think my mum ever had any trouble getting me out of bed because we would be in the schoolyard at quarter past eight and would play football before nine o'clock. Bell rang, in for school, out for break, football. Back home for lunch, quick bite to eat and it was back to school for more football. Every little gap in your life was taken up with football. I was very happy and I have very vivid memories of growing up."

The schoolyard is steeply sloped and it would be grossly unfair if the boys who play there did not swap ends at half-time. Little David lost his two front teeth on it, playing football one lunchtime. "I butted the floor. I had to go home and my mum was devastated. She said: 'Oh, you had lovely teeth'. That started years of treatment."

A smashed-up mouth was never going to deter Fairclough from the game. "We played football until we were called in, literally. I know that's all comic book stuff but that's how it was. I never strayed too far; they always knew where we were going to be. We would play football and break windows, not deliberately. It was just that we were playing in a confined space and accidents happen. We were never wicked – breaking the window, running away and that was the end of it. We stumped up the money and paid for the damage, which was 1/9 or 2/11 in old money. There was always a whip round to pay for broken windows."

School holidays were taken up with more football or collecting autographs at Anfield, Roger Hunt's particularly.

"I moved house a few years ago and found all the pictures I'd cut out and put into scrapbooks. It was signed by all the lads, Tommy Smith, Ron Yeats and Bill Shankly. I was an avid collector of programmes and those kinds of things." Gazing out over the city landscape, breathing in the fresh winter air, Fairclough is full of the particular pride which infuses all Liverpudlians when they're 'home' again.

"We were playing on the streets and by the time I was eight years old I was two-footed"

"From the streets you could look out to the sea, you felt very much part of the Liverpool community. It was a very busy, active place to live. Lots of little shops. It was a great place to be brought up. I'm very proud of my roots here."

The skills and stamina he unconsciously developed amid the tight tenements and steep hills of Anfield helped to make him a better player.

"St Domingo Road is steep in a car but walking and running up and down was good training for footballers. When we were kids we walked up from Walton Road, across the valley and then up St Domingo Road, that was quite a steep climb. It goes to one of the highest points in Liverpool at St George's Library. We were playing on the streets and by the time I was eight years old I was two-footed. Those little games got rid of your fears of kicking with your bad foot. You learnt to bend a ball around gas pipes. You went to the shops with a ball at your feet. You would dribble down the street, on the way down passing it against the wall with your right foot and using your left foot on the way up. You weren't thinking what you were doing – but it all helped."

Stanley Park was another area where he spent much of his childhood. "Our school played there or down at Clubmoor Rec. I had my first experience of organised five-a-side football at Stanley Park on a little court. It was a real thing of beauty. There were beautiful bowling greens; kids wouldn't walk on it. You might walk on the edges and that was daredevil stuff."

Aged nine, Fairclough won tickets to all the 1966 World Cup games at Goodison Park and Old Trafford plus the final, in a *Liverpool Echo* competition. "There was a picture of me juggling the ball in the air, I've still got it in my scrapbook."

After one match at Goodison he was walking home through Stanley Park and excitedly spotted Helenio Herrera, Inter Milan's legendary trainer. Whispering, he told his dad who was walking towards them and plucked up the courage to ask for an autograph. "I've probably still got it. That's a big memory for me."

Family Secrets

Jimmy Case

Up until the 1980s it was not unusual for top-flight footballers to have another trade. In the case of midfield hard-man Jimmy Case, that trade was an electrician.

Brought up in Allerton less than 10 miles from David Fairclough, Case continued to serve his apprenticeship after signing for the Reds from South Liverpool in 1973.

Small in stature as a young player, he developed his strength by joining a Liverpool dockers team and went on to go toe-to-toe with some of the toughest midfield men in the country as he played his part in the Reds' success story.

CATCHING THE EYE OF THE SCOUTS

Fairclough was now playing most of his organised football at the park, demonstrating his ability and versatility. The lad with the unruly ginger hair always stood out from the crowd but his talent was more than enough to attract attention in schoolboy matches.

"When I was under 11, I played for Liverpool Primary Boys and played right-wing, left-wing or centre-forward. It wasn't a problem for me and I think that all came from growing up in an environment like this. I played for the Under-11s at my school when I was seven. The dad of a lad I used to hang around with, Phil Redfearn, said from when I was eight or nine that I had something. Everyone would liken me to Alan Ball because of the red hair. People always said I was going to play for Liverpool one day.

"When I look back I never remember worrying about getting into Liverpool Boys' U11s, U14s or U16s. Things just seemed to fall into place. I was a winger (and the record goalscorer for Liverpool Boys U11s) and I began to play Sunday League when I was 12 as a centre-forward (for Fazakerley Colts in the Bootle and Litherland League).

"My pace was a huge asset but at that stage [playing for Liverpool] was just a dream. I never consciously thought I'd play for the first team until the day I was chosen for the squad."

Within a week of moving to Cantril Farm, aged 13, Fairclough signed for Liverpool as a schoolboy.

"My first knowledge that Liverpool had noticed me was when we played in a district competition on Stanley Park where the car park is now. A guy came up to me afterwards and asked what my name was and told me: 'I'm from Liverpool Football Club'. One or two other things were happening, unbeknown to me. People were mentioning my name in Bootle. I think Liverpool were getting this information together.

"Tom Saunders [youth development officer] had taken over at Liverpool and he stressed that I should play schoolboy football. I played largely for Liverpool Schools and Liverpool FC just kept an eye on me."

David had always been a bright boy, attending a grammar school in Rice Lane. He could have left at 15 but stayed on to do his 'O' Levels, despite his mate Max Thompson signing as an apprentice for Liverpool at the same time. Fairclough got reasonable 'O' Level results but admits he was distracted by football and underachieved. But things were progressing on the soccer front.

"My school was disappointed with me. All my end-of-year reports said I should go on to higher education and train to do other things. The football

Above: Fulfilling a dream – donning the famous red shirt.
Opposite page: A trip along memory lane as Fairclough drives down St Domingo Road. He is pictured by a lamp-post just off Penrose Street, where he and his mates kicked a ball around for hours on end

Above: Fairclough returns to his old school, Major Lester, now known as Hope Valley

thing got in the way and was a huge distraction. I didn't think of the down-side: that it might all go wrong. We were very naive.

"In that year I had got into the youth team and the 'A' and 'B' teams, so the signs were all good. At 16-and-a-half I signed apprentice and on my 17th birthday I signed pro. A year later I made my debut. It all just happened. I never thought it would be so soon."

The seamless progression continued from when he made his first-team debut on November 1, 1975 at Middlesbrough. Fairclough had been in great form for the reserves, Steve Heighway had a problem and David was informed on the Friday morning after training that he would be travelling to Teesside and, in all probability, playing. It was a pleasant surprise.

"I travelled home to Cantril Farm on the bus to pick my kit up and then went back to Anfield. I rung my dad when I got home and my mum and dad made plans to go to Middlesbrough the next day with my auntie and uncle. I played, and it was great. There was not much time to worry.

"I came back on the evening after the game. The following morning I went and watched the kids playing on Cantril Farm in the Sunday League. There was a bit of celebrity status as I was walking across the field. Different people were coming up and saying, 'Well done'. I became the local celebrity. On the Tuesday night, we played in San Sebastian in the UEFA Cup. Bob Paisley put me on at half-time and I scored."

'SUPERSUB' FRUSTRATIONS

The 'Supersub' tag that follows him around to this day was established in March and April of 1976.

He came off the bench to score all of Liverpool's goals in successive wins over Norwich, Burnley and – best of all – Everton ("You can imagine how it lifted off then"). Without them, the league championship would almost certainly have gone elsewhere. Of all his goals, the winner against the Blues remains his favourite, ahead of the winner against St Etienne in '77.

One senses his frustration at being viewed as the eternal number 12.

"I had run-ins with Bob Paisley over the Supersub thing because at times I think he over-used it. I went in on numerous occasions and said, 'I don't want to be sub. I want to go and play with my mates in the reserves.' In those days they played at the same time as the first team. It was a very frustrating time. I think the fact that I was a young, local boy made it very easy for the boss to leave me out. Ron Greenwood told me that if Steve Coppell wasn't fit or playing very well then I was his stand-in for England. But I had to be playing for Liverpool's first team for that. I knew I was good enough to do it.

Fairclough fondly remembers kicking a ball in the playground at every opportunity, although he did lose two teeth one day when he fell and hit his head on the yard

Below: It wasn't long before he was kicking a ball around the corner at Anfield as a schoolboy, and later for his beloved Reds

Fairclough's iconic St Etienne celebration in 1977 and (below), souvenirs from his Reds' career

"With the start I had it should have been more successful"

I just needed more games really. That is a huge disappointment for me."

After bursting onto the scene in a blaze of goals, the frustration of not being a regular starter would stay with Fairclough for the rest of his Liverpool career. Not being selected for the FA or European Cup finals in '77 was a particular low point. He sought advice from his father, who suggested: 'You're always going to get the rough end of the stick'.

However, before serious thoughts of leaving Liverpool could form, Fairclough's father died suddenly of a heart complaint.

"Perhaps had he lived it would have been different and I would have tried to impose myself a little bit more with Bob Paisley. As it was, my mum was relatively young and I had a sister who was only 11 living in Cantril Farm in a council house. It wasn't an easy situation to run away from."

THE LOVING AND LEAVING OF LIVERPOOL

Fairclough had a good 1977/78, playing in the European Cup final win over Bruges at Wembley, but his Liverpool career petered out somewhat after he suffered a serious knee ligament injury in 1980, at a time when he was in the team and scoring goals. "That scuppered everything."

By the time he was fit again, Ian Rush and Kenny Dalglish were an established partnership. He left for North American Soccer League side Toronto Blizzard in 1983, then moving on to Swiss club Lucerne the following year. He went on to play for Norwich City, Oldham Athletic, Beveren (of Belgium), Tranmere Rovers and Wigan Athletic. Fairclough admits frankly: "With the start I had it should have been more successful."

Now resident in Formby, he is still involved in football, through various business ventures and media work. He is a regular on LFC TV, providing match commentary and studio punditry. Despite harbouring regrets, his spiritual home remains Anfield and to be brought up within 200 yards of the ground and play for the Reds made him hugely proud.

"I think you do feel a little bit more passionate if you grew up here and go on to play for the football team. I'm very pro-Liverpool and am very grateful that I played for the team I supported as a boy."

Fairclough flicks through one of his football scrapbooks

A PART OF THE COMMUNITY

David Fairclough was not the only Liverpool player to live in the vicinity of the stadium he would later illuminate.

Matt McQueen, one of the great characters in the club's early history, was resident close to the ground. As well as winning two championships with the Reds – one as a goalkeeper and the other as an outfield player – he went on to manage the club, despite losing a leg in a car accident. Inside-left Joe Hewitt, who joined the club in the 1903/04 season, later lived at Skipton Road in Anfield. Several stars of Bill Shankly's side also lived in close proximity to Anfield. Jimmy Melia was born in Penrhyn Street on Scotland Road and, as his passion for the game developed, grew up kicking a ball around cobbled streets which had been bombed during the war.

Tommy Smith is the epitome of a dyed-in-the-wool Liverpudlian. He had worked as a groundsman at Anfield before going on to serve the club as a player, captain and coach. Born within spitting distance of the stadium, he was taken to Anfield as a 15-year-old by his mother, who requested that Shankly take good care of her son.

Another local lad, Gerry Byrne, came through the ranks at the club and demonstrated a similar courage and devotion as Smith to the Reds' cause. His uncompromising style and bravery were famously showcased during the 1965 FA Cup final. He was injured early in the showpiece Wembley occasion against Leeds United. Bob Paisley, then Liverpool's trainer, suspected that Byrne had broken his collarbone after a tough tackle and was in danger of puncturing his lung if involved in a similar challenge. This was in the days before substitutes and Byrne concealed his pain throughout the 90 minutes and subsequent period of extra-time, helping the Reds to win the FA Cup for the first time.

While several stars became part of the Anfield community in more ways than one, Bill Shankly became known for living a brisk walk away from the club's Melwood training ground. When Shankly was appointed Liverpool manager in 1959, he and his wife Nessie first looked at accommodation in the Southport area. But they opted to live a little closer to the training headquarters by moving into Bellefield Avenue, a West Derby cul-de-sac that was actually closer to Everton's training base than Liverpool's. When Shankly arrived, Melwood was in a dilapidated state, overgrown and with only one mains water tap. He set about revamping the facilities as well as revolutionising the training methods. Following his shock decision to stand down as manager in 1974, he continued to visit Melwood. The Shanklys felt very much at home in Liverpool and never thought about leaving the area.

Top left: Local lad Tommy Smith is full of pride and passion as he leads the Reds out as captain at Anfield in 1972

Top right: Jimmy Melia tries to keep the swelling down on an ankle injury, dipping his foot in a bucket of icy water in his living room

Left: Gerry Byrne sets out to strengthen his thigh muscle following an operation in 1967 by cycling to training

FROM HETTON TO AFRICA
NORTH-EAST HERO, KOP PIONEER

Bob Paisley won more than most thanks to a winning mentality chiselled by a tough upbringing in the North East of England. Paisley also served his country, collecting war medals that would one day be outnumbered by his many football honours. The famous Spion Kop will never forget him or the other heroes who came from a far foreign land to represent our club with pride and distinction

JOURNEY 3

Bob Paisley's dad, a miner, suffers an accident and vows that his son will not follow him down the pit

Paisley turns down Sunderland to join Liverpool. He later succeeds Shankly and becomes Britain's most successful boss

Paisley's playing career at Liverpool was interrupted by the outbreak of war. Other Reds were called up

Spioenkop Hill, the scene of a Boer War battle, provides the inspiration to rename one end of the Anfield terracing

The Reds recruit their first South African stars after the Spion Kop is named

LIVERPOOL FC
FAMILY TREE

BROUGHT UP WITH THE NEED TO BETTER YOURSELF

Much has been made about the coincidence of Bill Shankly, Sir Matt Busby, Jock Stein and, latterly, Sir Alex Ferguson being raised in mining communities within about 30 miles of each other in the west of Scotland. All four overcame the harshest of upbringings to rank amongst the most successful and influential managers in British football history.

Bob Paisley was born and brought up not far over the English border in Hetton-le-Hole, itself then a pit village. He won nearly as many European Cups as the four mentioned above combined, which puts into stark perspective the scale of his achievement. He can look down on some of the giants of the game.

Paisley lived in the County Durham town until he signed for Liverpool in 1939. Situated seven miles from Sunderland, it was a place, according to the man himself, where "coal was king and football was a religion". Little Bob was "kicking a ball from the time he was born, practically", according to the testimony of his widow, Jessie. His father, Samuel, first bought him a pair of boots when he was four, costing six shillings.

Later in life, Bob would reflect on how growing up in Hetton shaped his character and helped him develop into a manager of unparalleled achievement. "Where I come from in the North East, we were all brought up with the need to better yourself. That, and the belief in football as a religion, produces a certain kind of driving force for this job. It gives you that little spark of ruthlessness – a need to win."

Paisley could reflect on his childhood and admit: "Although we never went short of life's essentials, there was never much money left over by the end of the week". This understates the difficulties the family faced. Samuel and mother Emily had to scrimp and save to buy him kit. Paying for a ball was certainly a problem, forcing Bob and his mates to improvise when they fancied a kickabout. Uncle Alan worked in a butcher's and would provide his nephew with a pig's bladder on a Monday morning. The bladder could be blown up and used as a ball. When that was worn out, the resourceful boys of Hetton improvised with rolled up newspaper or bits of cloth tied in a rough sphere.

He first showed a talent for football at Barrington primary school. A plaque commemorates Paisley's achievements on the site of the school, which became a Somerfield supermarket. In a talented team Paisley stood out and he was called up for Durham county schoolboys' team, playing

Young Paisley
as a schoolboy
footballer

THE BOB PAISLEY PLAYERS' TREE

July 26, 1974 to July 1, 1983

Paisley

Goalkeepers

Ray Clemence 1967-1981,
Skegness, England
Steve Ogrizovic 1977-1980,
Mansfield, England
*Bruce Grobbelaar 1981-1994,
Durban, South Africa

Defenders

Chris Lawler 1960-1975,
Liverpool, England
Tommy Smith 1962-1978,
Liverpool, England
Emlyn Hughes 1967-1979,
Barrow-in-Furness, England
Alec Lindsay 1969-1977,
Bury, England
Phil Thompson 1971-1983,
Kirkby, England
Brian Kettle 1973-1977,
Prescot, England
Phil Neal 1974-1985,
Irchester, England
Max Thompson 1974-75,
Liverpool, England
Colin Irwin 1974-1981,
Liverpool, England
Joey Jones 1975-1978,
Llandudno, Wales
Alan Hansen 1977-1990,
Sauchuie, Scotland
Alan Kennedy 1978-1985,
Sunderland, England
*Avi Cohen 1979-1981,
Cairo, Egypt
Richard Money 1980-1981,
Lowestoft, England
*Mark Lawrenson 1981-1988,
Preston, England
Steve Nicol 1981-1994,
Ayrshire, Scotland

Midfielders

Ian Callaghan 1960-1978,
Toxteth, England
Brian Hall 1968-1976,
Glasgow, Scotland
John McLaughlin 1969-1974,
Liverpool, England
Steve Heighway 1970-1981,
Dublin, Republic of Ireland
Peter Cormack 1972-1975,
Edinburgh, Scotland
Jimmy Case 1973-1981,
Liverpool, England
Ray Kennedy 1974-1981,
Seaton Delaval, England
Terry McDermott 1974-1982,
Kirkby, England
Sammy Lee 1976-1986,
Liverpool, England
Howard Gayle 1977-1981,
Toxteth, England
Graeme Souness 1978-1984,
Edinburgh, Scotland
*Kevin Sheedy 1978-1982,
Builth Wells, Wales
Ronnie Whelan 1979-1994,
Dublin, Republic of Ireland
*Craig Johnston 1981-1988,
Johannesburg, South Africa

Forwards

Phil Boersma 1968-1975,
Kirkby, England
John Toshack 19701977,
Cardiff, Wales
Kevin Keegan 1971-1977,
Armthorpe, England
Kevin Kewley 1972-1978,
Liverpool, England
Alan Waddle 1973-1977,
Wallsend, England
David Fairclough 1974-1983,
Liverpool, England
David Johnson 1976-1982,
Liverpool, England
Kenny Dalglish 1977-1990,
Glasgow, Scotland
Colin Russell 1978-1981,
Liverpool, England
Ian Rush 1980-1987;
1988-1996,
St Asaph, Wales

• Although born in different countries, players marked with an asterisk either went on to play international football for another nation or were considered to be of a different nationality.

Players used: ?? **By position:** Goalkeeper: 3, Defenders: 16, Midfielders: 14, Forwards: 10.
By nationality: England: 27, Scotland: 6, Wales: 3, Ireland: 4, Zimbabwe: 1, Australia: 1, Israel: 1.
Key: On the player information, the first date is the year the player signed for LFC and the second the date of his last senior appearance.

In the town where I was born

Hetton-le-Hole

Situated south-west of Sunderland, charters going back to 1187 suggest the village was originally called 'Heppedune' – a combination of two Anglo-Saxon words spelt together. An ancient manor there was owned by the 'le Hepdons' family and divided into two parts – Hetton-on-the-Hill and Hetton-in-the-Hole, the latter being where the present town arose from.

In 1984, when the village was hit by the miners' strikes, local bands The Pigeon Fanciers and Hasewell Crisis recorded a single to raise money for the families and to raise awareness of how miners have served their community. 'Knocking on Hetton's Floor' – an adapted version of Bob Dylan's 'Knocking on Heaven's Door' – sold over 1,000 copies, but failed to chart.

Bob's parents

regularly for them from then on. Bob was soon signed as an amateur by Wolves at the age of 13, where Major Frank Buckley reigned supreme. They tried to build up the physically frail Paisley but eventually rejected him because of his size, or lack of it. "I was heartbroken and thought my chance was gone," he later said.

At the age of 14, he left school and began playing for Hetton Juniors (HJ), which was a nursery side for Bishop Auckland, the great amateur team of the time. After two years' success at HJ, he was signed by The Bishops, where he got into the side as a left-half.

BOB THE BRICKIE AND BARNEY'S MUM'S CHIPPY

Once Bob left school he followed the inevitable path that led to the pit, although he didn't follow it all the way below ground level – Paisley had a surface job.

He hadn't been there long when he experienced the trauma of seeing his father carried out on a stretcher after suffering a serious arm injury. The injury was so severe amputation of the limb was almost necessary and he didn't work again for over five years. Samuel decided in the immediate aftermath that Bob would work at the pit no longer which, given the dangerous conditions, could have put his dreams of a professional football career in jeopardy. He was out of work until he landed employment as an apprentice bricklayer.

Bob's brother Hughie explained: "It was at Blackhall, 12 mile away. We got an old bike off Uncle Dave, my father's brother, and Bob used to pedal from the Downs Lane to Blackhall, 12 miles there and 12 miles back. Twenty-four miles a day – a boy on an old bike." When he got back to Downs Lane, Bob ate his dinner before going out to meet his mates outside the ice cream shop on Front Street. They'd then walk two miles to the cinema in Houghton. After the show was over, they'd walk back to Hetton and end the evening with a chip supper from Worlock's fish shop. The woman who served him, Sarah-Anne Donnelly, would later give birth to a boy called Alan Kennedy. Sadly, she died in April 1978, four months before Bob signed her son for Liverpool.

Hughie also started work as a bricklayer in Hartlepool in 1936 but he was only earning six shillings and fivepence a week. The Paisley family were living from day-to-day until football brought them a cash bonanza that same year. It was nothing to do with any playing achievement, though. The Littlewoods Tote playing pool had only been in existence seven years

An early shot of
Paisley, at Anfield

What's in a name?

Paisley

A habitational name from the Scottish town, the name has also been derived from the Latin word 'basilica' meaning church and cemetery, or the English 'pasture slope'.

It was first recorded in 1157 as Passeleth, then in 1158 as Paisleth and in 1163 as Passelet, Passelay.

Moran

An Anglicised form of the Gaelic name 'O (descendent of) Morain', meaning 'great' or 'large'.

It is also a Spanish surname deriving from place-names found in Asturies, Galicia and Aragon.

Spot the ball: Paisley and friends jostle for possession

but it was becoming increasingly popular, acting as a potential passport out of poverty for the football-loving working-classes – if only they could get lucky. The Paisleys did. "That was our saviour," Hughie recalled with a mischievous delight. "I think I got 14 out of 15 teams right. I had York City to beat Port Vale in an away match and Port Vale beat them 2-1, otherwise we would have had £9,000. "But we were quite happy with the £315, nine shillings and a penny. We were millionaires! We were real posh. The first thing my father said was 'I'm having a new coat'. I can't think what our Bob wanted." It's almost certain that he requested something football-related.

MY WORD IS MY BOND

The pain of rejection he felt at Wolves was nothing compared to the crushing disappointment of being deemed not good enough by the club he supported, Sunderland. Aged 15, he had a trial for the Roker Park team but was considered too small to progress further. He idolised them as a boy and to be told he wasn't going to make it by them hurt deeply. He was, however, amused that the men who turned him down were no more than 5ft 4ins tall.

Bob was aware that his lack of height was seen as a handicap so when he joined Bishop Auckland, he would stay behind after training and spend hours leaping at a swinging ball to improve his performance in the air.

What's in a name?

Kennedy

An Irish name from 'O (descendant of) Cinneidigh' (helmeted/ugly head). Cinneide was the nephew of Brian Boru, High King of Ireland (1002-1014), and the surname O Cinneide came into being in Ireland in the 11th century.

As well as being linked with two fine players of the Bob Paisley era, Kennedy is also the family name of the Marquesses of Ailsa.

Keegan

Another name with Irish roots, Keegan is the reduced anglicised form of the Gaelic 'Mac Aodhagain', meaning son of fire or of 'Mac Thadhgain', son of poet.

In the town where I was born

Seaton Delaval
(Ray Kennedy)

Seaton Delaval is a village in Northumberland and is the largest of five villages in the Seaton Valley. Situated close to Newcastle-upon-Tyne, it is one of the few places in Northumberland to have the Tyneside area telephone code of 0191.

The village's most famous landmark, Seaton Delaval Hall, occupies an agricultural and industrial estate which has been owned by the Delaval-Hastings family since the time of the Norman conquest of the north of England, around 1080. The house was designed by Sir John Vanbrugh in 1718 for Admiral George Delaval although neither man was alive when it was completed in 1728. Seaton Delaval Hall is now a Grade I listed building, owned by the National Trust, and has been open to the public since May 2010.

The Valley Players are an amateur dramatics group who have been performing to audiences in Seaton Delaval since 1965. Formed by Jim Leslie, they have members from all over the north-east.

Bob's brother Hughie, back where it all began in Hetton

Sunderland came back in for Paisley when they heard Liverpool were making a move to sign him but Bob had given his word to the Reds and he wasn't going to break that, not even for his local club.

Opting to move to Liverpool and not Sunderland was a turning point not just in Bob's life, but indeed in the fortunes of our club. He had begun a lifelong relationship with the Reds. On reluctantly agreeing to follow in Shankly's footsteps in 1974, a record three European Cups and six league titles found their way into the Anfield trophy cabinet during his spell in charge, along with other silverware.

However, the road to becoming Liverpool's most successful manager wasn't without obstacles. Paisley was aged 20 when he became a Liverpool player on May 8, 1939, after catching the Newcastle Express to Liverpool Lime Street. He signed for the club on the same day as Billy Liddell.

His Liverpool career was put on hold before it had properly began as war broke out in September of that year. He had managed just a couple of reserve appearances in the Central League before competitive football was suspended. Seven years passed before it resumed.

Left: Bob meeting old
friends on a visit to his
hometown of Hetton, and
(below) on the Anfield turf
after another title triumph

What's in a name?

Heighway

This surname has
two distinct possible
origins. It is most likely
sourced from the English
place name Highway
in Wiltshire, which is
recorded as Hiwei in the
Domesday Book of 1086.
 The name may also be
of topographical origin
from 'residence by or on
the high road.' The name
first appeared in records
in the late 13th century.

Family Secrets

Harry Beadles

Harry Beadles played 18 Liverpool games in the '20s, his bravery one of his key attributes. That should have come as no surprise, as he had been awarded a medal for gallantry in World War I.

Forced to leave school at 12 to help earn money for his family, he worked at Pryce Jones Welsh Warehouse in Newtown as a furrier and hosier.

He enlisted soon after war broke in 1914. While serving as a Rifleman in Gallipoli, he was awarded the Serbian Gold Medal. A Serbian observer officer had been wounded in no man's land and despite heavy fire, Beadles saved him.

Later in life he ran the Hillside Hotel in Huyton before taking over as licensee of The Canon pub near Anfield. He also attended home matches, paying to stand on the Kop.

Bob in uniform during the war years

FOR QUEEN AND COUNTRY – THE WAR YEARS

Many families lost loved ones as they went about the duty of serving their country in the two world wars. Liverpool Football Club were no exception.

Yet throughout the conflicts, football continued. When the First World War broke out in September 1914, the Rugby Football Union was quick to suspend all matches. The football authorities decided to continue, attracting criticism from both those in favour and those against.

On the one hand, the game's rulers and clubs were accused of cowardice; on the other, questions were asked of those attending the matches. A letter in the *Daily Post* in March 1917 expressed concern at the large crowd watching the Everton v Liverpool derby at Goodison Park:

'A crowd of 25,000 people watched a game of football between the Everton and Liverpool clubs. A very considerable percentage of that assembly must have been of fighting age.'

On the flip side, the matches provided supporters with good entertainment and a momentary escape from the harsh realities of war. An earlier letter published in the local press in November 1915 said:

'Our two clubs are being well patronised by the football-loving public of this city and the surrounding districts, which simply goes to prove that the authorities acted wisely when they determined to continue the game during the war time.

'Deprived of their wages at one fell swoop, our footballers have engaged themselves in munition works and other Government employment, and have also come forward and provided thousands of persons with a delightful entertainment each week either at Anfield or Goodison Park.'

Fans particularly enjoyed seeing Thomas Bennett in action. He was a prolific war-time marksman, scoring 77 times in 70 games. The letter to the press also made the point that many servicemen were among those present on matchdays. It stated:

'It is a matter of common knowledge to those who have visited our grounds at Anfield and Goodison Park this season that the number of men in khaki has been pronounced. Special entrances have been allotted to these gallant fellows; they have been admitted free, and extra privileges have been granted to these wounded heroes who having done their duty at the front, have returned maimed and handicapped, and who need some little enjoyment and recreation to make them forget the horrors of war.'

Liverpool lost Wilf Bartrop, who played three times in the 1914/15 season,

Family Secrets

George Latham

Like Harry Beadles, Latham's bravery in service was later recognised. In World War I, he was a captain in the 7th Royal Welsh Fusiliers.

Latham was given the Military Cross for gallantry on the Turkish front in 1917, and the Bar in 1918.

He had played only occasionally for Liverpool in a three-year spell with the club, but later went on to be a part of the unit that won the British Forces (Egypt) Football League Cup in 1919.

Some of Bob's service medals

What's in a name?

Balmer

Principally a County Durham/Lancashire surname, it came from the occupational term for 'a seller of spices or ointments'.

Palk

Records suggest that only six people in every million Brits have this surname. The origin of the name is not known.

towards the end of the First World War as he was killed in action in 1918. Other players who died in the war were Joe Dines, Donald Shone, David Murray and reserve player Wilfred Watson – with Tom Gracie also dying in service, but of infections.

By the time the Second World War came around, Liverpool Football Club were well prepared. A number of players had signed up for the Territorial Army during the 1938/39 season but Liverpool were the first to join the Territorials as a club. Their 20-player entry was also supplemented by manager George Kay and assistant-secretary Jack Rouse.

Germany invaded Poland on Saturday, September 2, 1939 but a Home Office bulletin stated that the situation did not warrant the cancellation of matches. Liverpool were due to play Chelsea in what turned out to be their last Football League game until 1946. The Reds had a number of players due for sentry duty at the time the game was due to kick-off but thanks to the generosity of some Territorial friends who volunteered to take their places, Dirk Kemp, Bernard Ramsden, Matt Busby, Tom Bush, Jimmy McInnes, Willie Fagan, Jack Balmer and Cyril Done were all able to start the match. Done marked his debut by scoring the only goal of the game and would go on to have a prolific scoring streak during the war years.

Stationed somewhere 'in the north', the players had slept on a railway station floor before starting four hours' sentry duty at 5am. It didn't seem to have any adverse effect and the Reds held on to their 1-0 advantage, despite having Jim Harley sent off.

However, the political landscape was changing on a daily basis, as the impact of the war effort was constantly re-examined. Later that week, a ban on the assembly of crowds followed after a Government order to close places of entertainment. The football authorities were keen to change the situation and on September 14 permission was granted to stage friendlies, subject to police approval. Two days later, Liverpool won 5-0 at Chester.

Members of the Liverpool family were keen to play their part in active service and several players were promoted within days of war breaking out. Of those who volunteered for the 9th King's Liverpool Batallion of Territorials, Arthur Riley and Dirk Kemp were made sergeants, while Tom Cooper, Willie Fagan, Bernard Ramsden and Tommy Bush were promoted to lance corporals. Players developed key skills: Fagan became a trench mortar expert, while Jackie Balmer and future manager Phil Taylor learned to drive tanks. Berry Nieuwenhuys worked as a driller on Merseyside, drawing on the trade he developed from his days in South Africa.

There were some incredible acts of bravery. Utility player Bill Jones was honoured with a military medal for rescuing wounded comrades under fire. Full-back Ted Spicer, a lieutenant in the Marines, captured a German non-commissioned officer, who turned out to be a football international. A Commando, Spicer had been commissioned in May 1942 and was later promoted to the rank of captain.

Yet the grim realities of the conflict became all too real when Tom Cooper lost his life in a motorcycle accident near Aldeburgh. Serving as a sergeant in the military police, the England international full-back's motorcycle was involved in a head-on crash with a lorry. A subsequent inquiry into the accident led to an order that despatch drivers were not allowed to ride their motorcycles without wearing crash helmets. Ron Jones, who played a handful of games in 1938 and 1939, was also killed in action.

While Anfield was fortunate enough to come through the war relatively unscathed, the proximity of L4 to the docks saw some damage at Goodison Park. Football's popularity continued to see great numbers pouring through the turnstiles and the derby matches were a major draw. In January 1944, 43,000 witnessed Liverpool's win at Goodison Park while in 1945/46 a crowd of 60,926 saw a 2-2 draw at the same ground.

By the 1940/41 season, regional league football was in place in the north and during the course of the war years, the club and its family twice found themselves in hot water. When Northern Ireland star Peter Doherty went to watch a Liverpool match at Blackpool he was asked to play for the Reds. He did so, but the club were later censured when it came to light that George Ainsley had been due to play before Doherty's surprise appearance. The RAF, who had granted Ainsley special leave to play, were furious and threatened never to grant leave to any of their footballers again. Liverpool Football Club apologised to the RAF and the League. On the second

Jack Balmer: Served his country during WW2

"There were some incredible acts of bravery...Bill Jones was honoured with a military medal for rescuing wounded comrades under fire"

occasion, Reds captain Berry Nieuwenhuys was banned for life. The South African's crime was to ask for more than the regulation fee of £2 per game. He was soon reinstated.

Some notable figures played in the matches held during this period. The legendary Tom Finney made his Preston debut at Anfield against a Reds team that included Don Welsh of Charlton and Wolves' Stan Cullis. Inside-forward Wille Fagan was a regular guest in the Northampton team that won the 1941/42 League Cup qualifying competition.

As for themselves, Liverpool enjoyed a strong 1942/43 season. After finishing second in the table, four points behind Blackpool in the 18-game North One League – which ran until Christmas Day 1942 – the Reds topped the North Two League, which was held over 20 matches between Boxing Day and May.

Two key men of the future made an early impact. Bob Paisley had impressed in the 1939/40 trial matches, but spent most of the war overseas in the Army. Meanwhile, Billy Liddell, a teenage winger, was described by manager George Kay as "the best thing that has come out of Scotland in the past 10 years".

A FORGOTTEN HERO – CYRIL DONE

When the abortive league programme began, Cyril Done scored Liverpool's last pre-war goal. His debut winner against Chelsea was merely the start of things to come. He became LFC's leading scorer in the regional matches played during the hostilities, netting 40 goals in a season on two separate occasions.

Having rejoined the club nine games into the 1946/47 season, his goals – 10 in 17 games including two hat-tricks – went a long way in helping the Reds to win the league championship.

In all Done netted 148 goals during the war years and it would doubtless have been more, but for the fact that he was unavailable for 18 months after breaking his leg against Manchester City in September 1944.

When this total is added to his eventual tally of 38 other goals for Liverpool, it is worth remembering that had his war-time goals counted officially, Done would have been fifth in Liverpool's all-time list of goalscorers with 186, three more than Robbie Fowler.

What's in a name?

Done

This surname is believed to have originated from Cheshire. Although not very common, most of the Dones have traditionally lived in Cheshire, Lancashire or Staffordshire.

Harley

Derived from place names in Shropshire and Yorkshire, meaning rocks or a fenced enclosure or farm.
Famous examples are William Harley, who joined forces with Arthur Davidson to produce the first Harley-Davidson motorcycle in 1903. Harley Street in London was built in the mid-1700s on land the Duke of Portland had inherited from his wife, Lady Harley.

Final goal: Unsung hero Cyril Done (right), promoting a boxing event at Anfield

The great Billy Liddell, in action at Anfield in 1957

PETER PRICE REPORTS   The Stage of Sport

Players chair Billy Liddell on his final exit from Anfield

WHILE Everton and Arsenal players lined up to applaud refe...
Anfield the players were even more demonstrative. Ronnie Mo...
Nicholson hoisted Billy Liddell on their shoulders an...
fet, what may be his last exit from Anfield...

Although it was only a reserve team game, a large...
crowd attended to give Liddell a fitting send off, and...
it he thought that when he reached the quietude of the...
dressing rooms that was the end of the farewell scene...
how wrong he was.

A crowd awaited his return to his car and after a session of...
signing autographs, his admirers took up the chant: "For...
he's a jolly good fellow." It will be a long time before...
Liddell is forgotten on Merseyside, and the youngsters will...
always recall him as the player who never refused them...
an autograph.

His saddest experience you might think was in defeat by...
Arsenal at Wembley but you would be wrong, for Billy...
worst moment was when as a sixteen-year-old he had...
stand down from the "A" team to make room for...
trialist. When the trialist did not appear Billy jum...
at the instruction to "get changed," and then in w...
his rival and there was n...
game for Billy.

His happiest moment? That is...
a difficult question, for...
there were so many, but...
Billy picks out the Anfield...
game with Barnsley on...
Good Friday a couple of...
years ago, when after...
their out of the first team...
he came back with two...
great goals to a roar that...
has rarely been equalled on...
the ground.

Liddell was invited to join the...
club party on their trip to...
echoslovakia, but he finds...
f unable to accept.

073

The Kop's last stand,
season 1993/94 and
(above) a street view of the
Spion Kop, circa 1900

ORIGINS OF A FOOTBALL INSTITUTION

While the war impacted on every family in Merseyside and beyond, another conflict had already become a part of Liverpool Football Club folklore.

In January 1900, scores of Scousers were part of the Lancashire Fusiliers that went into battle in the Boer War. A fierce battle took place on a hill near Ladysmith, South Africa, known locally as Spioenkop Hill. The battle ended in defeat, with more than 300 of the Fusiliers losing their lives.

Six years later, a huge terrace was built at Anfield as a reward for Liverpool supporters after the club had lifted its second league championship. The ground already had a small terraced area at the Walton Breck Road end, but chairman John Houlding and club secretary John McKenna decided there was room for improvement. A steep, cinder bank with wooden steps and no roof was designed by respected architect Archibald Leitch and constructed that summer. All that was needed was a name.

The 1900 Battle of Spioenkop Hill: Inspired the name of Liverpool FC's new stand

The season kicked off and the new stand, which held around 20,000 spectators and gave some splendid views across Stanley Park, remained nameless. One story goes that it was Ernest Edwards, the then sports editor of the *Liverpool Echo*, who had a flash of inspiration. He suggested that Liverpool's new terracing reminded him of the hill where the battle of Ladysmith had taken place, so why not call the stand the Spion Kop? The name stuck, probably because local men had lost their lives on Spioenkop Hill.

A 1-0 victory over Stoke City on September 1 (Joe Hewitt the goalscorer), played in blazing heat, was watched by 30,000 fans. Many of those in attendance became the first to see a game from the Kop – home to what would become Liverpool's legendary 12th man in years to come.

Arthur Riley:
Liverpool's first
overseas player

FROM OUT OF (SOUTH) AFRICA
The make-up of the Liverpool family was to be changed significantly in the mid-1920s as a result of a touring party.

South Africa had already influenced the naming of the club's famous Spion Kop terrace in 1906 and a couple of decades later, the Reds were to have their first South African players.

In 1924, a group of two dozen white South Africans embarked on a three-month trip that saw them play 26 matches in the UK, Ireland and Holland. Significantly, one of those games was played against Liverpool at Anfield on October 1, 1924. Liverpool lost 5-2 and were so impressed by two of their opponents that they made concerted attempts to sign them. The pair would go on to became two of the greatest players in the club's early history.

Gordon Hodgson became one of the most prolific strikers Anfield has seen while goalkeeper Arthur Riley was a loyal servant who made 338 appearances, after accepting the unenviable task of succeeding the legendary Elisha Scott in goal. It was Riley who became the first player born outside Britain and Ireland to represent the club when he made his debut at Tottenham Hotspur in October 1925. Hodgson made his bow later that same season. He scored 15 times on the South Africans' tour and his striking prowess was enough to tempt Liverpool to sign him in December 1925.

The club's first-choice striker for 11 seasons, Hodgson set a then Liverpool record of 233 league goals in 358 games, a tally which featured 17 hat-tricks. He played in three internationals for his adopted country of England, and was also capped by South Africa. To illustrate the impact he had, only Roger Hunt and Ian Rush have scored more league goals for Liverpool.

The success of Hodgson and Riley meant Liverpool were happy to recruit other South Africans in the years that followed. In 1928, Jimmy Gray made a solitary appearance in the 2-1 home defeat by Sheffield United. Gray was actually born in Scotland, but was a South African international who had previously played for Transvaal. A longer-lasting impact was made by winger Berry Nieuwenhuys, a natural entertainer who played 260 games for the club after signing in 1933. A member of the incredible 1946/47 title-winning team, 'Nivvy' left the club when he received the blessing of the directors to follow through a desire to become a professional golfer. Liverpool's South African contingent often possessed talents in numerous sports. Riley and Hodgson were both useful cricketers, with the latter going on to play county cricket for Lancashire – taking 148 first-class wickets during a five-year spell with the Red Rose county.

Gordon Hodgson:
Overseas pioneer

What's in a name?

Priday

A rare name in the UK, it is thought it may have been born from Priddy, a surname which came from a place name in Somerset.

What's in a name?

Grobbelaar

Translated from the original Dutch, there is an irony in the meaning of this surname as 'clumsy'.

A very popular name in South Africa, Bruce Grobbelaar joked in his 1986 autobiography that he had so many cousins he gave up on tracing his family tree – once he had reached 75 of them!

In the same year that Nieuwenhuys arrived at Anfield, the Reds signed anther versatile sportsman in Johannesburg-born Lance Carr. Carr was an accomplished cricketer and boxer but struggled to make his name as an attacker with Liverpool, after being bought from Boksburg. He made only occasional appearances until enjoying a regular run on the left-wing during the 1935/36 season. By the conclusion of his Liverpool career, he had scored eight goals in 33 appearances.

In December 1936, the Reds signed their first player named Dirk. Goalkeeper Dirk Kemp made 33 appearances for the club but, ironically, his opportunities were limited by the fine form of his compatriot Riley. The following year winger Harman Van Den Berg also signed for the club. The Cape Town-born player made 22 appearances in the two seasons before the outbreak of the Second World War. Nonetheless, his spell at Liverpool made quite an impact on Van Den Berg. He wed a Merseyside woman and the pair were married for more than 60 years.

The post-war South African influence on Liverpool began in December 1945 with the capture of winger Bob Priday. He was signed on board a liner as it arrived in Southampton after sailing from his Cape Town home. Priday was part of George Kay's 1946/47 championship-winning squad but didn't qualify for a medal, as his nine appearances didn't meet the necessary criteria. Even so, he made an invaluable contribution to Liverpool's championship success. A second-half goal earned a point at Brentford in a mid-May fixture, and he then scored a crucial winner against Arsenal at Anfield in the Reds' penultimate match.

Half-back Hugh Gerhardi played six league matches during the latter stages of the 1952/53 season. He made his debut at Middlesbrough in February 1953 and played in the following four matches, but was only called upon once more before the season ended with the last of his six appearances coming in a 4-0 defeat at Cardiff City in April 1953.

The Reds' next two South Africans continued the tradition of goalkeepers started by Riley and Kemp. Like Riley, Doug Rudham was on tour with the South African national team when he attracted Liverpool's interest. He signed for the Reds in 1954 at a time when the club couldn't settle on a regular number one: Dave Underwood and Charlie Ashcroft shared the duties during the 1954/55 season, while Rudham somehow retained his place after conceding nine goals in one game at Birmingham City! In total, he made 66 appearances for Liverpool, playing his final match for the club in November 1959.

Bruce Grobbelaar: Always
expect the unexpected

Family Secrets

Billy McOwen

There are many who would give their eye teeth to play for Liverpool, but McOwen left the Reds to pursue a career in dentistry.

He had helped the team win promotion from the Second Division in 1893/94, but opted to practice as a dentist as he would be able to command far more money.

As a goalkeeper, he was known for his cunning on the pitch. It was reported in December 1893 that: 'McOwen...jumps up and pulls the crossbar down when the ball appears likely to hit it. It makes the crowd laugh, but it doesn't look fair.'

Having said that, he was also a good shot-stopper in his own right. During his playing career, he faced 13 penalty kicks – and saved 12 of them!

Family Secrets

Craig Johnston

Part of the 1986 Double-winning team, Johnston was a colourful character whose creativity stretched beyond the pitch.

A South African-born Aussie who played representative football for England, his entrepreneurial skills have taken root since he retired from football at just 27 in order to care for his sick sister.

In the past two decades, he has invented a football boot, created software for hotel businesses to monitor minibar thefts, made up a revolutionary system for coaching children, developed computer models for analysing football statistics and most recently, established himself as an award-winning photographic artist.

Bruce Grobbelaar may be considered more Rhodesian/Zimbabwean – but he was actually born in Durban. He moved from South Africa before he was two months old and spent time fighting in the Rhodesian Army, which shaped his outlook on football as a game to be enjoyed. Grobbelaar always played with a smile on his face and went on to be one of the club's most successful goalkeepers, making 628 appearances over 13 years.

Grobbelaar played for Durban City in the early years of his career and later discovered that their manager, Colin Addison, had tried to get him out of the Army halfway through his two years' national service. He moved to Canadian side Vancouver Whitecaps after being spotted at a training camp in South Africa. During his time at Anfield, Grobbelaar won six league championships, three FA Cups, three League Cups and a European Cup.

One of Grobbelaar's team-mates in the club's league and FA Cup Double-winning team of 1985/86, Craig Johnston, also had South African roots. He was born in Johannesburg but brought up in Australia and later went on to win Under-21 caps for England!. Towards the end of the 1990s, Liverpool paid Karlsruhe £1.8 million for striker Sean Dundee. He arrived with a reputation as one of the leading marksmen in the Bundesliga but struggled to repeat that form in the Premier League. His stay at Liverpool lasted a single season, in which time he made just a handful of appearances.

Cup final scorer Craig Johnston (front, second left) celebrates Double success in 1986

"The warmth of the man and his sheer personality was remarkable...it was a great honour for all of us to be there"

The Reds' most recent South African signing also had a difficult time adapting to English football. Mark Gonzalez was born to Chilean parents in South Africa as his father, Raul, was playing football there at the time. Liverpool had hoped to sign the winger from Albacete in 2005 but their application for a work permit proved an obstacle. It delayed the player making his Reds debut by a year, a season which he spent at Real Sociedad, proving a great success for the Spanish side. He finally received his permit in the summer of 2006 but struggled to shine at Anfield and, in June 2007, Gonzalez returned to Spain with Real Betis.

Other links with the rainbow nation saw two of Liverpool's greatest goalscorers, Roger Hunt and Ian St John, spend time playing with Cape Town club Hellenic in the early 1970s.

In 1994 the club made an historic trip to South Africa to take part in the United Bank Soccer Festival. The Reds flew out less than a fortnight after their league season had ended, taking on Aston Villa (2-1) along with South African sides Cape Town Spurs (3-0) and the Kaiser Chiefs (0-0). The highlight of the trip came ahead of the match against Cape Town Spurs at Newlands Cricket Club. Half-an-hour before kick-off the players and staff met president Nelson Mandela. Manager Roy Evans said after the game: "We were getting ready for the match when there was a knock on the door, and in he walked.

"It was a fantastic moment, and one that I think every one of us will remember for a long time. Mr Mandela had to be the number one man in the world at the time, and it was a great privilege to be introduced to him.

"The warmth of the man and his sheer personality was remarkable. He spoke to every one of us individually and seemed very knowledgeable, both about the game and about Liverpool Football Club. His enthusiasm was remarkable and he even put on a Liverpool shirt. It was a great honour for all of us to be there."

Nelson Mandela: Red for a day in 1994

More than 120 Liverpool-born first-team players have worn the red shirt

The Falcon pub in Southdene, scene of European Cup celebrations

Jamie Carragher: Bootle's Liverpool record-breaker

Huyton-born Steven Gerrard, inspirational captain

Scouse players, big contributors to the Reds' European Cup wins

FROM WALTON TO ISTANBUL

LOCAL BOYS MADE GOOD

Tommy Smith, Terry Mac, Fowler, Stevie, Carra... Growing up in town and living shoulder to shoulder with the fans, these lads don't have to be told what it means to wear the famous Liverbird upon their chest. More than 120 Scousers have lived the dream. We take a trip that's close to home – via the fields of Kirkby with Phil Thompson and the

LOCAL LADS LIVING THE DREAM

Liverpool may have been originally known as the 'Team of Macs', but there has always been something special about local players making the grade.

Supporters love to identify with one of their own and throughout the course of the club's history, Liverpool has been blessed with an array of Scouse talent. From the early days of pioneering players such as Jack Parkinson, Tom Bromilow, Walter Wadsworth and Alf Hanson to the modern-day backbone of Steven Gerrard and Jamie Carragher, fans have warmed to the men who have given their team a real Merseybeat.

Definitions of what constitutes a true Scouser vary, but there is no doubt that many have enjoyed being able to achieve the dream of playing for the club they grew up supporting. Using what is now seen as the Merseyside area as a criteria, more than 120 locals have gone on to represent the club at senior level. That local know-how has also made for a clutch of excellent captains – men who know the city and the club.

It is doubtful that any other city in the world has produced so many leaders with the qualities that Scousers possess. From Tom Bromilow to Tommy Smith, Phil Thompson and Steven Gerrard, each one has captured their own moment in history. They have inspired some great memories. From Thommo parading the European Cup around the Parc des Princes to Stevie G lifting the same trophy high into the Istanbul sky, everyone has their own memories of history-making Scouse skippers.

The current team contains two of the toughest Scousers in modern history – men who epitomise Scouse steel. Steven Gerrard and Jamie Carragher's exploits in a red shirt have made them revered figures on the Kop. So it was fitting when the pair were elected to Liverpool's Official Hall of Fame as the representatives for the decade 2000 to 2009.

Ian Callaghan, another Scouser who went on to become the club's record appearance maker, spoke of his pride at seeing the duo receive such recognition. Both men continue to make their mark. After enjoying a well-deserved testimonial in September 2010, Carragher is now in the top five in the list of the club's all-time appearance makers.

Gerrard, meanwhile, ensured that principal owner John W. Henry had quite a night when he first visited Anfield as the club's new chief. Having been unable to attend the Blackburn Rovers game in October due to illness, he was present for the UEFA Europa League tie against Napoli the following month. Liverpool trailed the Italians 1-0 at the break, resulting in manager

What's in a name?

Byrne

An Irish name, the Anglicised form comes from O'Broin, which itself probably comes from Bran. Btan, a son of the King of Leinster, died in Cologne in 1052.

The first recorded spelling of the family name may be that of Fiacha Mac Hugh O'Byrne, the military leader. This was dated 1544-1595 in the historical records of Dublin, during the reign of Queen Elizabeth I.

LIVERPOOL'S SQUAD OF SCOUSERS

Back in 2009, John Aldridge was asked to select a 16-man squad of Liverpool's other best Scousers. Here are the men who made his squad list:

Frank **LANE**

Chris **LAWLER**

Gerry **BYRNE**

Phil **THOMPSON**

Tommy **SMITH**

Jamie **CARRAGHER**

Ian **CALLAGHAN**

Steven **GERRARD**

Terry **McDERMOTT**

Jimmy **CASE**

Sammy **LEE**

Steve **McMAHON**

Steve **McMANAMAN**

Robbie **FOWLER**

David **FAIRCLOUGH**

David **JOHNSON**

Roy Hodgson asking substitute Gerrard to get ready to enter the action for the second period. The number eight produced a breathtaking 45 minutes to give the Reds a 3-1 win by claiming his second European hat-trick for the club.

All three goals showed off different attributes. The first summed up his grit and determination; the second his composure in dispatching a penalty; the third encapsulated his brilliance as he produced a world-class finish to put the seal on a night to remember. And for all Liverpool fans, the fact the goals were scored by one of their own made it that little bit sweeter.

What's in a name?

McDermott

Recorded as MacDermot, MacDermott, McDermot, McDermott and Dermot, this is a famous royal and noble Irish surname. It is said to stem from a clan claiming to descend from Dermot, the King of Connacht in the 12th century.

The first recorded spelling of the family name is shown to be that of Brian MacDermot who died at Moylurg, Ireland in 1592. It is not recorded whether he had a perm and a dodgy moustache.

THE JOE FAGAN PLAYERS' TREE
– July 1, 1983 to May 30, 1985

Fagan

Goalkeeper

*Bruce Grobbelaar 1981-1994,
Durban, South Africa

Defenders

Phil Thompson 1971-1983,
Kirkby, England
Phil Neal 1974-1985,
Irchester, England
Alan Hansen 1977-1990,
Sauchie, Scotland
Alan Kennedy 1978-1985,
Sunderland, England
*Mark Lawrenson 1981-1988,
Preston, England
Steve Nicol 1981-1994,
Ayrshire, Scotland
Gary Gillespie 1983-1991,
Stirling, Scotland
Jim Beglin 1983-1987,
Waterford, Republic of Ireland

Midfielders

Sammy Lee 1976-1986,
Liverpool, England
Graeme Souness 1978-1984,
Edinburgh, Scotland
Ronnie Whelan 1979-1994,
Dublin, Republic of Ireland
*Craig Johnston 1981-1988,
Johannesburg, South Africa
John Wark 1984-1987,
Glasgow, Scotland
Kevin MacDonald 1984-1988,
Inverness, Scotland
Jan Molby 1984-1995,
Kolding, Denmark

Forwards

Kenny Dalglish 1977-1990,
Glasgow, Scotland
Ian Rush 1980-1987;
1988-1996,
St Asaph, Wales
David Hodgson 1982-1984,
Gateshead, England
*Michael Robinson 1983-1984,
Leicester, England
Paul Walsh 1984-1987,
Plumstead, England

• Although born in different countries, players marked with an asterisk either went on to play international football
for another nation or were considered to be of a different nationality.

Players used: 21. **By position:** Goalkeeper: 1, Defenders: 8, Midfielders: 7, Forwards: 5.
By nationality: England: 6, Scotland: 7, Wales: 1, Ireland: 4, Zimbabwe: 1, Australia: 1, Denmark: 1.
Key: On the player information, the first date is the year the player signed for LFC and the second the date of his last senior appearance.

BORN IN WALTON: A BOOTROOM LEGEND

Joe Fagan had dreamed of playing in a red shirt, but was not deemed good enough by manager George Kay. After a career as a centre-half with Manchester City, he returned as a coach in 1958.

Fagan was born in Walton Hospital on March 12, 1921 and spent much of his childhood in Litherland, where his footballing ability was soon evident. At 14 he captained his school, St Elizabeth Central, to the Daily Dispatch trophy and, when not playing, he was a frequent visitor to Anfield.

In July 1971 he took charge of the reserves and, following Bill Shankly's surprise departure, was promoted to first-team trainer in July 1974. Becoming a key figure in the Liverpool 'bootroom', he became Bob Paisley's assistant in 1979 and after four years as his trusted right-hand man, was appointed first-team manager on July 1, 1983.

Following Paisley was tough, but Fagan commanded respect. He enjoyed an incredible first season, becoming the first British manager to win three major titles in one season – league, League Cup and European Cup.

Much changed in the summer of 1984 with skipper Graeme Souness leaving for Italy and Ian Rush out injured until October. At the end of that month, the European champions were in the bottom three. Things improved and the Reds went on a fine run to finish second, while reaching another European Cup final. Fagan had already decided the game against Juventus would be his last, but he was left devastated by the events at Heysel. It meant Fagan retired on a sad note – when things could have been so different.

A much-loved figure, the effect the disaster had on him was sad to see and he rarely made public appearances following his retirement. He died in July 2001 at the age of 80 following an illness.

What's in a name?

Fagan

This surname is of Irish origin, but the source is uncertain. The Gaelic form is 'O Faodhagain', but a personal name Faodghagan is not known, and so it may be a Gaelicized version of a surname of Norman origin.

A number of Irish bearers of this name are descended from Patrick Fagan, who owned estates in County Meath in the 13th century.

THOMMO'S KIRKBY PRIDE

It's difficult to imagine anyone being more proud of their roots than Phil Thompson. Does anyone not know his hometown? The man breathes Kirkby, bleeds Kirkby.

The first player-manager at Liverpool was Kenny Dalglish, right? Almost. Thommo was running a pub team in Kirkby when he was 21. The job and the people meant so much to him that he went to the pub the night after lifting the European Cup in 1981, with the trophy in tow. This gave many Liverpool fans two 'I was there' nights in a row.

Phil, who turned 57 in January 2011, was raised in the Southdene area of a town that was not much older than him. One of the new towns created after the war to house refugees from districts of Liverpool such as Scotland Road and Kensington, Kirkby struggled to assimilate so many people so quickly and provide a stable infrastructure and services. The social problems meant it had a poor reputation and received a negative press.

"It was a tough upbringing," Phil admits. "We used to get a lot of people knocking us. You just tried to rally round and stick together, because you were hammered left, right and centre. It was a tough place, you couldn't get away from that, but I just hated people knocking it. It was as though it was the only place on earth that had problems. I was very proud of the fact [I was from Kirkby] and I think a lot of people are like that.

"Times were hard, life was tough. Adversity drew people together and helped create a real sense of community. Very few were well-off and there was little to do for the youngsters but play sport, football above all. You didn't have much in those days, none of the extra-curricular activities that kids enjoy now. My whole life revolved around football."

Street games on a car-free Stone Hey Road or St Joseph's school field, which backed onto his home, were a daily way of life for Thompson and his mates. There was one ball between eight families, a plastic 'Fido'. It would often rip, forcing one lad to rush home, heat a knife on the gas stove and solder up the hole. The tell-tale smell and another ruined knife would ensure Phil felt the sharp end of his mother's tongue.

Although things were not easy, Phil had a happy childhood. "I came from a large family. There were three boys and four girls. We had a great time. Most families were like that, everybody got on well."

He won his first medal in a cup final at Millbrook Primary at the age of 11, but Phil's football really began to develop when he started attending Brookfield School (now Kirkby Sports College). Bob Downing was the PE teacher there for many years and his football sessions were always notable for enthusiasm and encouragement. When the bell rang, the teacher would be as disappointed as the pupils. The boys would often return to Brookfield after hours for a kick-around with Bob. The school is unique in having produced two European Cup-winning captains, Dennis Mortimer of Aston Villa emulating Phil's success in 1982.

Thompson regularly went back to Brookfield to see Bob, who oversaw the Sports College created there. When we took Phil back there a few years before Bob's retirement, Mr Downing was still relishing the job with all the enthusiasm of a newly-qualified teacher.

As Phil walked into the sports hall as the final session of the day drew to a close, the excited murmurs of "Thommo" among the first years drew Bob's attention to the famous visitor. As they exchanged greetings and 'How are yous', one little lad interrupted their conversation, turned to Bob and asked: "Is that Phil Thompson?" Phil was not impressed when he spotted two pupils who had 'forgotten' their kit. Pointing to Bob, he said: "That man used to whack me on the backside if I didn't have my gear."

Thompson paid tribute to his teacher: "We need more people like Bob Downing. He did everything he could and more for us."

What's in a name?

Thompson

An extended form of the surname Thomas, most Thompsons are to be found in the north of England. In England, the name Thomas was found only as the name of a priest before the Norman Conquest of 1066, but became one of the most popular male personal names afterwards, generating a wide variety of surnames.

One of the very earliest settlers in the New World was William Thompson recorded as 'living at Elizabeth Cittie, Virginea', before February 16, 1623.

'Times were hard, life was tough. Adversity drew people together and helped create a real sense of community'

As well as football, Bob encouraged Phil in athletics, and the gangly lad from Kirkby defeated all-comers to win the North of England Junior cross-country championship in Manchester.

Phil was a midfield player who could "run all day" then. He was not selected for Kirkby Boys at Under-11s, but did make it with the U14s and U15s. Wearing the navy blue blazer, with distinctive badge and tie, made him feel ten feet tall.

As his father, Owen, was away with the Merchant Navy, it was Phil's late mother, June, who devotedly followed his son all over the country, often getting up before dawn to join Phil in Cardiff or Durham. Owen was an Evertonian, so it was off his "mam" that Phil inherited his love for Liverpool and she was the one who took him to the match to begin with. The pair would watch from the paddock until Thompson was old enough to go alone, able to jump the railings from the boys' pen into the Kop.

Phil is eternally grateful for what his parents did for him: "They gave me a lot of support but I don't think they ever envisaged me going on to play for Liverpool. They pushed you without going over the top. It wasn't a case of 'You must do football' or 'You must do cross-country'."

Kirkby Boys was a great name in schoolboy football and produced a conveyor belt of players who progressed to a high level, Mortimer, Kenny Swain, Terry McDermott and Alan Stubbs among them. You had to have something about you to be selected and Phil still counts this achievement as one of his proudest.

"One of the great things about my life was playing for Kirkby Boys. Liverpool was your derby game and one of the highlights of my whole career was actually getting beat by Liverpool in the English Schools Trophy first leg at Kirkby 1-0, then we went to Penny Lane and defeated them 2-0. That was extremely pleasing. They were great days. There were so many kids in Kirkby. It had the highest birth rate in the country so you were always going to have talent coming out of Kirkby in abundance."

Phil became established in the Liverpool team in 1973/74, and was part of the side which won that season's FA Cup. He was the talk of The Falcon pub on Bewley Drive, which was then known to have red leanings. Many of his mates, including his two brothers, drank there. The regulars began to have kick-abouts on St Joseph's field and decided to get a team together. However, Falcon FC started poorly. At half-time in their second league match they were in trouble. Phil takes up the story.

"I was on the touchline watching. One of the players sidled over to me

Above: Back to school to meet now retired former teacher Bob Downing, a big influence on Phil's early career

instead of the manager; a great guy called Terry Campbell, who had been elected by the lads. Terry took the hump and rightly so. I was just chatting to them and said a couple of things. When the game finished – if I remember rightly we won 5-2 – the lads again came over to me to ask what I'd thought of the game, rather than Terry. Terry again took the hump and packed in. His time as The Falcon manager lasted all of two games. I didn't know but the lads must have all gone back to the pub and had a chat. They decided to ask me if I'd do it."

Thommo was taken aback but agreed, with the proviso: "If we're going to do this, we're going to do it properly. If you all want to get something out of it, let's give it a good go."

Returning to the appropriately named Windy Arbour fields in Northwood rekindles memories of a dozen blissfully happy years spent freezing to death on the touchline as The Falcon soared to success. It's also where he met his wife, Margaret.

Above: Outside Brookfield
High School, since re-named
Kirkby Sports College

Above: Phil re-visits Windy Arbour, Northwood, scene of some of The Falcon's successes

"The state some of the lads were in of a Sunday morning," recalled a laughing Thompson. "You could see them getting changed, still absolutely pissed. Although I had some fantastic times in my professional life, my hobby was The Falcon football team, I didn't play golf very much. Running The Falcon of a Sunday morning, besides playing football of a Saturday afternoon, was the highlight of my week.

"They were a great bunch of lads. I think people appreciated the time out that I had taken to be involved. There was a bond struck with spending a lot of time on the touchlines of Kirkby. It was a dream. In the Kirkby Newtown League we were the first team to ever win the treble and there were some fantastic Sunday League teams who came out of Kirkby."

Did it provide a good apprenticeship for his later role as assistant-manager at Anfield? "I think so. It's where I got my vocal chords from! It whets your appetite. We played in the right manner. It was nice that people would always talk about The Falcon as a footballing side.

"I always used to feel for the lads because all the other teams put in extra effort and were extra aggressive, because it was me running the team. I said: 'If you can't handle it, I'll call it a day because you lads have to go to work of a Monday morning'. They said no.

"It did become difficult if I had to leave one of my brothers out, that was always hard. But it gave me great enjoyment. I did have verbals on the line with opposition teams (*there's a surprise*) but there was always mutual respect at the end of the game."

For a few years Thommo would be Liverpool captain on a Saturday and Falcon manager on a Sunday. If he had picked up an injury and needed treatment, Phil would go to Melwood early so he would be able to get back to Kirkby for 11am. Of course, he would never be able to combine the roles now, given the regularity of Sunday fixtures.

Family Secrets

Arthur Berry

Liverpool-born Berry was a double-Olympic gold medal winner with England (representing Great Britain) in 1908 and 1912.

Berry had signed amateur forms for Liverpool in October 1907 and only figured for the first team on four occasions.

But he made an impact at Olympic level and was one of only two men to have been a member of both winning teams, Vivian Woodward being the other.

Berry was a bright man, studying law at Oxford. After quitting football he joined his family's law firm.

Tasting success: Thommo drinks to another Reds championship triumph

Family Secrets

Jack Cox

Liverpool-born Jack Cox, a winger who represented England, starred for the Reds from 1898 and 1909.

After hanging up his boots Cox went on to excel in another sport – bowls.

Cox was excellent on the bowling greens and in 1925 became the first man to win the Waterloo Cup and Talbot Cup in the same year.

A report of his triumph stated: 'By winning the Talbot bowling championship Jack Cox the popular Blackpool sportsman, accomplished the fine feat of bringing off the double having won the Waterloo final. He has thus made bowling history. Cox's record may probably never be equalled."

Opposite page, top: Phil's first football management role – The Falcon pub Sunday League side. Opposite page, bottom: Holding the European Cup aloft as Reds skipper – the trophy would soon depart the Parc des Princes, Paris for Southdene, Kirkby

Eventually, he had to relinquish the Falcon role after taking over Liverpool's reserves in 1986. Training demands for Monday games often meant he was required to be at Melwood on the Sabbath. The Falcon lads still played on in over-40s competition, which possibly also referred to their respective waist sizes.

Apart from running the football team, the main reason why Thompson's name will forever be linked to The Falcon's occurred on May 28, 1981. The night before Liverpool had beaten Real Madrid in Paris to claim a third European Cup. What followed next is established Kirkby legend. As the team toured the city on an open-top bus, Phil spotted a few of his Sunday League players below and yelled: "Get back to The Falcon", but admits now: "I didn't tell them why."

After winning the League Cup six weeks earlier, the trophy had been left on the team bus and Phil, as captain, was held responsible for the oversight. Club secretary Peter Robinson told him: "You were in charge, you should have taken care of the cup."

Thommo says: "I didn't need telling twice to take care of the European Cup. I put it in a big, red velvet bag, as there was no case. I put it in the back of my smart Capri and headed for The Falcon. We had a fantastic time. All the football lads headed back, all my family were there, and I walked in with the European Cup.

"It spread like wildfire throughout Kirkby. People were on the phone telling friends that Phil Thompson was in The Falcon with the European Cup. Lo and behold, everybody was thinking that they had enjoyed one drink too many and didn't believe them. Other people did head down there. It was a great story.

"Peter Robinson had to ring me the next morning because the world's press were waiting to take pictures of it. I'd told all the guys in The Falcon to bring their children down the next day so they could have their pictures taken. I stuck to my word and was there at 11am to have these pictures taken with the kids. I got down to Anfield about 12 o'clock. All the press were there and Peter Robinson. There was no rollicking, and Phil Thompson, bleary-eyed, returned the European Cup."

Phil doesn't live too far from Kirkby now, and is encouraged by the developments in the town, which include Liverpool's own Academy. "The number of new-build houses is incredible. Knowsley council have worked extremely hard. There is a David Lloyd centre and big businesses like QVC. The facilities are astonishing compared to when I was growing up." Yes, kids even have non-melt footballs these days.

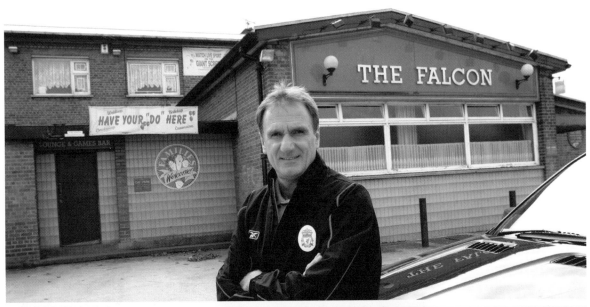

BOOTLE BOY – REMEMBERING HIS ROOTS

With a pint of Tennent's in hand, teeth like a row of vandalised gravestones and a Scouse accent so thick you could spread it on toast, this particular client of the Salisbury Hotel is surprisingly un-moved by the sight of Jamie Carragher wandering around the streets of Bootle on an average August afternoon.

"Alright Jamie kid," mumbles the stumbling patron with his ill-fitting Mizuno t-shirt and acid-washed jeans. "How's ye'arld fella?" Philly, Carragher's father, was once the landlord of the pub so his face is familiar – even in the midst of a stupor. "What's going on lad?" Liverpool's vice-captain responds. Then, whispering over his shoulder, he offers a revelation: "That's what happens if you spend too much time in The Solly..." Carragher, who lived out his childhood on these streets, classes Bootle as his manor. He grew up in the suburb, five miles north of Liverpool's city centre, living in a semi-detached house with his parents and two brothers.

While Carragher has since moved to nearby Blundellsands by Crosby Beach, he maintains a link with the area. His mother still resides here and if he ever has a drink (such occasions are rare), he frequents one of the watering holes around Marsh Lane, the thoroughfare that bisects the two places where Carragher first discovered football: the fields of St James' RC Primary School and the indoor concrete floors of the Brunswick Youth Club, universally known in Bootle as 'The Brunny.'

Today, it's the school holidays and his daughter Mia is spending her afternoon at the club, just over the road from The Solly, watching films with a group of other kids, most of whom live in the terraced houses on the streets that lead towards Seaforth Docks. Son James would also usually be here having a kick-about with his mates but instead is attending a David Campbell Soccer School.

For Carragher, it's the standard routine of shuttling his children around the borough. Such behaviour characterises him. Fans see the sportsman, the defender with close to 700 appearances for Liverpool, someone who in Istanbul threw a body burning with cramp into a tackle – for the club, for the city. Donating a cheque worth £8,000 to The Brunny in January 2010 towards the cost of a new minibus identifies the man – the father.

"The Brunny and Bootle generally is very important to me," he says. "I had a modest upbringing with good working-class people helping me out. I want my kids to have the same and that's why I bring them here. I benefited from having a place like this to go to because it kept me off the street."

What's in a name?

Carragher

Recorded in a number of spellings including (Mac) Caraher, (Mac) Carragher, Carah and Carrah, the surname of the Reds' vice-captain is more usually found without the 'Mac' or 'Mc' prefix. It is an Irish surname but also has close associations with Scotland.

As MacCarraher, it is recorded in the Hearth Tax Rolls of King Charles II in 1663, while in the modern forms it is recorded in the Famine Registers of 1846-1848. An example being 15-year-old Mary Carah, one of the first emigrants, who left on the ship John R Skiddy of Liverpool in 1846, bound for New York, USA.

Street skills: A rare
opportunity for Carra to
practise his keepy-ups

Some footballers might send their children to a more salubrious location during the holidays – a camp in southern France perhaps. Here, in Bootle, as you walk through the steel doors of The Brunny, youngsters enjoy sport in a humble but secure and supervised environment. Inside, Carragher's face is as recognisable to the five to ten-year-olds as it was to The Solly regulars over the road, such is his recurring attendance at the club.

With a group in the middle of a five-a-side game, Carragher asks one lad wearing a full Liverpool kit for a kick. "We're 'avin a match 'ere," seems to be the attitude, before he eventually relents, offering a pass.

Carragher believes that having a community facility such as The Brunny so close to his home helped him develop as a footballer naturally. Through his 23 Foundation charity, other kids might benefit from similar amenities like this around the city in the long-term.

"You've got to learn for yourself, haven't you? When you play street football, you learn to express yourself and make your own mistakes. As you get older, understandably, coaching becomes more important, but when you're a youngster you get an understanding of life by playing sport with other kids from the street. You need to find your own way because there is no set path towards becoming a footballer."

Carragher became a professional at Anfield after supporting Everton as a child. He was a regular at Goodison and travelled away with his dad – the staunchest of Blues – along with his brothers. In 1989 when Michael Thomas scored an injury-time winner at Anfield to deny Liverpool the title, he celebrated by applauding the lads who daubed the legend "Thank you Arsenal" on a pub wall.

"I was lucky that I followed Everton during one of the best periods in their history," he says. "They won the league twice, but when Everton weren't winning it, Liverpool were, so there was a healthy competitive rivalry between both clubs. Ian Rush seemed to score every time he played in the derby and he became a figure that I grew up really disliking because he was so good. I was a Blue and I'm not afraid to say that when I was a kid, I really hated Liverpool." Such was the Carragher family's resentment of all things Red, father Philly once embroiled himself in an argument with a certain Kenny Dalglish.

"I was playing for Bootle Boys against Crosby Boys, who had Kenny's son, Paul, in their team," Carragher recalls. "The scores were level in a two-legged semi-final, with the winners due to go through to play at Goodison Park. Then we got a penalty that was a little bit iffy. Kenny kicked off saying

it was a dodgy decision and he was giving the ref a load of stick. So my dad shouted to Kenny: 'You'd know about dodgy penalties wouldn't you – you get them all the time.' The argument went on for what seemed like ages and eventually, someone had to separate them."

When Carragher joined Liverpool's centre of excellence as a striker at the beginning of the '90s, Kenny Dalglish, remembering that exchange with the Philly, labelled him 'Sharpy' after Everton's Graeme Sharp.

"Everyone knew I was an Evertonian and I wasn't shy about it. I remember coming back on the bus from a game shouting 'get in' when I heard on the radio that Everton had scored a late equaliser. Ronnie Moran marched to the back of the bus to see who'd made the noise – he went ballistic."

More than a year after making his professional debut, Carragher celebrated Everton's escape from relegation in 1998 in the dressing room after Liverpool lost 1-0 at Derby County on the final day of the season. Everton had scrapped to a decisive 1-1 draw at home to Coventry City. Soon, though, his allegiances would change.

"When you walk into a football club full-time at 16, you are going to change a lot by the time you are 32. I have a family now and kids, which straight away makes you think differently about life. On the football side, all you want to do when you're a youngster is look after yourself by making sure you're in the team. You want the team to win, but most of all, you're a little bit selfish because you want to play well and make sure you carve a career for yourself. As you get older you take more responsibility and spend time worrying about the team. The major turning point for me was in 1999 when we lost to Man United in the FA Cup after two injury-time goals. I felt sick because we'd played well and surrendered the lead so late in the game."

Carragher went to a pub called The Chaucer to unwind. There aren't many areas in Liverpool that can be identified by either of the city's football teams. Marsh Lane is, however, one of them.

"Bootle is a bit of an Everton hotbed but I thought that people knew me well enough to leave me alone. I expected some banter but I expected them to leave it at that because they could see that I was totally gutted. Instead, I got a load of abuse and they treated me like any other Red. That was the end for me. The penny dropped. I left my pint and walked out.

"They hadn't done anything particularly wrong and most of the lads that were there are still my mates. But I'd been defending Liverpool against all of the jibes for quite a while by then and because I'd got so involved at the club, I finished with Everton that day."

Opposite page: From schoolboy to first-team scorer, (Clockwise from top left) in the Bootle Boys changing room; an early Anfield visit; Goodison winner; hailing a rare goal, on his Anfield debut; FA Youth Cup glory, 1996

THE FIRST STEPS TO CARRA'S GOAL

In 1988, Jamie Carragher had a moment of madness. The Everton-supporting youngster did the unthinkable and swapped Liverpool's centre of excellence for that of his boyhood heroes. It was an aberration that was to last just two weeks.

While no-one could doubt Carragher's commitment to the cause nowadays, at the time the lure of playing at Goodison Park turned his head. However, Everton proved to be a disappointment to him and the opportunity to see the likes John Barnes, Jan Molby and Kenny Dalglish every day inspired a change of heart.

"I couldn't believe it because Kenny Dalglish actually used to come and watch us train! I mean he was the Liverpool player-manager and he used to come and watch a bunch of kids train on a week night," says Carragher, with an air of disbelief that can still be heard in his voice today.

"I think it was because his son Paul used to train with us then too, but it was still great! He would come from Anfield in his suit and watch us train in a local gymnasium at seven or eight o'clock at night, which shows how dedicated he was to Liverpool Football Club at that time."

Carragher's path to becoming a Liverpool legend began as a six-year-old with his junior side Merton Villa, where he featured in a position that may shock those who have grown accustomed to his no-nonsense style of play.

"My first ever position playing football was right or left midfield because I was a lot younger than the other kids," he reveals. "I was probably six or seven playing Under-10s football for Villa so I think they tried to keep me out of the middle really, where it is a bit more physical."

The St James' Catholic Primary School pupil made an instant impression and his performances soon attracted the attention of Bootle Boys at the age of nine.

By this time he had converted into a centre-forward and in one season he even managed to fire an impressive tally of 38 goals! His passion for the game and ability with the football meant his coach at the time, Ian Chapman, had no doubt Carragher had the ability to make it in the game.

He said: "I used to call him Billy Whizz. He played with an infectious enthusiasm, wanting to take all the corners, throw-ins, free-kicks and do everything. He was the best player Bootle Boys have ever produced."

While many fans believe his first goal at Anfield came on his first start for Liverpool against Aston Villa in 1997, they may be surprised to see that it actually came years earlier during a regional youth cup final.

Above and opposite page:
'Carra's Lodge', home to
Jamie's mother in Bootle

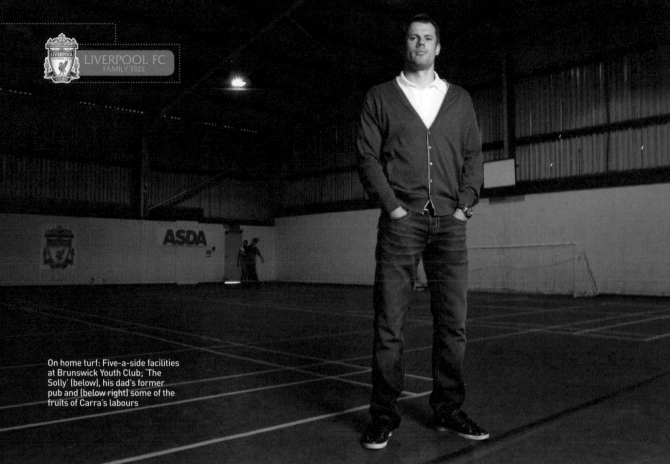

On home turf: Five-a-side facilities at Brunswick Youth Club; 'The Solly' (below), his dad's former pub and (below right) some of the fruits of Carra's labours

"I scored for Bootle Boys when I was about 10 or 11 at Anfield and it was at the Kop end as well," says Carragher fondly. "I cut in on my right foot and hit a shot that went right in the top corner, but the keepers were quite small then so it wasn't too difficult.

"I think we lost to Liverpool Boys 3-1. They always had the edge on us because they had about 300 other schools to pick from. We only had about 10 or 12 schools in Bootle so we did quite well, considering."

It was during his time with Bootle Boys that local scout Harry Hodges spotted him and recommended him to Liverpool.

"He picked up a few of us from Bootle Boys," he recalls. "I was about 12 at the time. He was the scout for the Liverpool area so he'd been watching Bootle Boys because the best players from all the schools in the area played for them. Four or five of us got invited to Liverpool and it went from there really."

Carragher's arrival at Liverpool did not prevent him from continuing to play for his local teams and during his final year at Savio High School, he had a trial with Sefton U14s.

But it was only a brief spell as his ability meant he was destined for greater things. The prospect of a career in football began to take shape when he was selected to go to the National School at Lilleshall.

TRIBUTE TO HARRY HODGES

In August 2006, the man who played a significant part in Jamie Carragher's road to stardom passed away.

Harry Hodges, who died at the age of 80, was the local scout who spotted Jamie when he was playing for Bootle Boys back in the late 1980s. While Carragher has since gone on to achieve success as one of Liverpool's brightest homegrown stars, he has never forgotten just what Hodges did for him.

"Well he passed away a while ago and I went around the house with some flowers for the family and it was a sad day," recalls Carragher.

"You know, I owe him a great deal and I still know his sons and his grandsons very well. It wasn't just me he spotted, I think he picked up Stephen Wright as well.

"He did a lot for Liverpool and obviously he was delighted with how I've done and I kept in touch with him for a long time. I was very disappointed to see him pass away but he always did a good job for the club – I'll remember him fondly."

Family Secrets

James Jackson

An all-action defender like Jamie Carragher, Jackson was also a man of the cloth.

He established himself in the Liverpool team towards the end of the 1920s and only missed two out of 126 First Division games from August 1928 until May 1930 while captaining the side.

He had three further seasons at Anfield before leaving to be ordained as a minister in the Presbyterian church in 1933. He had started his divinity studies at Aberdeen University, and continued them in Liverpool.

Because of his church connections, he was nicknamed 'The Parson' around the club.

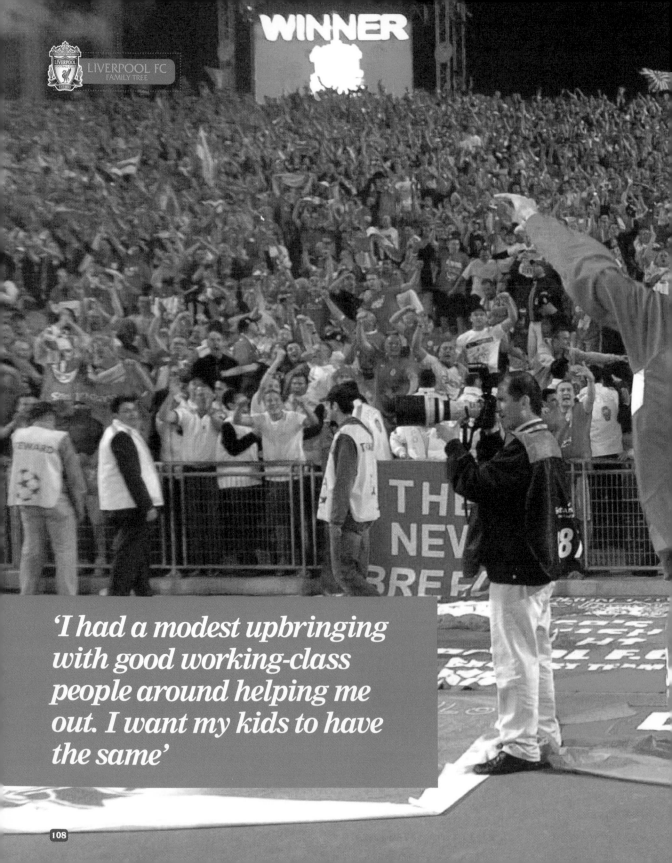

'I had a modest upbringing with good working-class people around helping me out. I want my kids to have the same'

MAJOR TROPHIES
ABOUT CULTURE
23
STEWARD
M'GLADBACH
77
BRUGGE
78
1981 1984
LIVERPOOL

THE MAKING OF A MODERN-DAY CAPTAIN

During the Second World War, the Liverpool suberb of Huyton suffered bombing from the Luftwaffe. Some Huytonians were killed or injured but the scale of destruction was nowhere close to that experienced by Liverpool, Bootle and Birkenhead.

Unlike Liverpool, schoolchildren were not evacuated from Huyton – but schools and homes were provided with air-raid shelters. Huyton was also host to three war-time camps: an internment camp, a prisoner of war camp and a base for American servicemen.

The internment camp, one of the biggest in the country, was created to accommodate those 'enemy aliens' deemed a potential threat to national security. First occupied in May 1940, the camp was formed around several streets of new, empty council houses and flats, secured with high-barbed wire fencing. The camp was sited in and around what became known as the 'Bluebell Estate' and many of the streets were given names of the great battles of the Second World War. It was on the Bluebell Estate that Steven Gerrard grew up.

After being born at Whiston Hospital in May 1980, Liverpool's future captain was taken to his new home on the Ironside street in the sprawling estate. It was on a patch of grass nearby that the young Gerrard played his first games of football, often with his brother Paul, and their mates.

His first school was St Michael's Primary, now known as Huyton-with-Roby Church of England Primary School. Once he was old enough to go to secondary school, he had a tougher choice to make. The more obvious options appeared to be Bowring Comprehensive School or Knowsley High. But in the end it was decided he would attend Cardinal Heenan's Catholic High School. It was a choice which pleased Gerrard as the school was well known for being strong at sport. It also meant he was eligible to play for Liverpool Boys rather than Knowsley Boys.

After brief spells playing with Denburn, who he helped to the Edgehill Junior League title, and Whiston Juniors, Steven was asked to attend training sessions with Liverpool's Centre of Excellence – the forerunner to the modern day Academy. Playing alongside fellow youngsters such as Michael Owen and Jason Koumas, he attended two evening training sessions a week at the Vernon Sangster Sports Centre with coaches Steve Heighway, Dave Shannon and Hughie McAuley all helping to take his game to a higher level. He left Cardinal Heenan with nine GCSEs to his name – a 'C' in English, six 'D's and two 'E's. But by then he had only one thing on his mind – carving out a career for himself in professional football.

What's in a name?

Gerrard

The Liverpool skipper's surname is of Old Germanic origin. It hails from a personal name introduced into Britain by the Normans after the Conquest of 1066. In the Old French its forms are "Gerard", "Gerart" and "Girart".

The name proved very popular and a large number of variants of it were forthcoming: Garrett, Garratt, Garred, Garrad, Jarratt and Jarad, to Garrard, Gerrard, Jarrard and Jerrard.

There are records of an Edward Garrard dating back to April 1635.

MAKING HIMSELF HEARD

Nowadays the Liverpool captain's armband has become synonymous with Steven Gerrard. His all-action style always marked him out as a leader.

"The first team I captained was my primary school team," he revealed. "I played two years up out of my age, up at my brother's age group. By the time I got to fourth year I'd been playing for the team for a couple of years already so that's probably why I got chosen to be captain. The teacher told the other lads I already had the experience of playing and gave me the captaincy.

"That was fourth year primary so I must have been about 10 or 11 at the time. Normally you would only play for the school team in the last year of primary school but I was always playing with my brother and his mates anyway so I was used to it. I was always trying to play with kids that were older than me. I always wanted to be like my brother, so any game in the street or on the field, most of the lads would be two or three years older than me. That was a big help at that age. It helped toughen me up and I became more vocal when I was playing with kids of my own age. I was probably a bit bossy if you like. I suppose I had the makings of a captain in me even at a young age."

While the young Gerrard was thrilled to be leading his school team, his dad was every bit as excited. He quickly made his son aware of the traditions of the great Liverpool leaders as he educated him in the art of captaincy. Gerrard recalls: "It's an honour to captain any team. My dad was buzzing when he found out I was captain of the school team. Straight away he was telling me about all the past captains of Liverpool and what you should do as captain. Sometimes I'd have a little moan at a few of the kids who maybe didn't have the same ability as me. My dad would pull me aside and tell me that as captain I should be helping those kids. From an early age I was getting the right pointers and advice from my dad about how to behave and conduct myself as captain of a football team.

"When I got the captaincy of Liverpool, I made a phone call to my dad and he was over the moon. But one of the first things he said to me was to make sure I spoke to Sami (Hyypia) about it. He told me he was made up for me and that I deserved it, but was also conscious of Sami's feelings. He'd been saying to me before I got the captaincy that if I kept playing as I was I had a big future at the club. He would tell me that he could see me becoming captain of the club one day. But I don't think anyone expected it to happen as soon as it did, when I was that age. I was only 23, which was young to be Liverpool captain."

Early days – opposite, top: The Bluebell estate, Stevie's old patch. Opposite, bottom: Lining up with his school team – one of the pupils donning the 'Candy' 'home kit, back row sixth from right

While Steven's dad remains a big influence, his teachers and coaches also played a key part in his development. He said: "As well as my dad, I would have my schoolteachers and the coaches at Liverpool, people like Steve Heighway, guiding me and teaching me about responsibility.

"Without wanting to sound too big-headed, I was always good in my own age group. When you're young, you can sometimes start taking that for granted and getting on other kids' backs who don't share that same ability. That's wrong and you learn that as you get older. But at the time I might have become frustrated because other lads may not see things I did on a pitch, or be on the same wavelength. Having the likes of Steve Heighway and all the coaches at Liverpool there to put an arm around my shoulder and teach me how to be more helpful on the pitch really helped my development."

Gerrard has admitted that he still recalls those early matches played on the pitches near Ironside with great fondness. And he says that in many ways, his approach to playing the game has not changed much over the years. "I don't think the way I play the game now and the way I played on the streets is too different because I have always wanted to win any game of football I play. I realise that a lot of people would give their left arm to be where I am now and that inspires you. I'm a fan myself and if things had worked out differently for me then I'd have been on the Kop with them. I know the levels they demand from the team because it's the same as I demand of myself.

"I think the desire to work hard is just the result of where I grew up and comes naturally to me. No-one can play at their very best every week but so long as the fans see people working hard and giving everything they've got then I think they will forgive your off-days."

Boy amongst men (opposite page, fron top): Stevie lines up with the Liverpool Boys side (back row, right); a very young future Liverpool captain celebrating success with the Reds' youth side

'*I realise that a lot of people would give their left arm to be where I am now and that inspires you. I'm a fan myself and if things had worked out differently for me then I'd have been on the Kop with them*'

Hero: Stevie strikes to save the
day against West Ham in the FA
Cup final at Cardiff in 2006

ETCHED IN REDS' FOLKLORE

Every family is proud of those members who go on to achieve good things. Measuring greatness is a subjective thing but when it comes to naming Liverpool's best-ever player, most followers seem to have narrowed it down to a field of two. Kenny Dalglish or Steven Gerrard? Take your pick.

Both men's contribution to Liverpool Football Club cannot be understated. Gerrard's story is the classic 'Boy's Own' tale of the local lad made good. His achievements are all the more satisfying as he learned his trade in the club's own youth set-up, going on to captain the Reds to Champions League glory.

Many experts have described Gerrard as the complete footballer. Technically gifted, his range of passing is second-to-none, his tough-tackling able to shake opponents and stir the Kop. His shooting skills have seen him move into the top 10 in the list of Liverpool's all-time goalscorers and his defensive awareness and covering provide vital protection to the Reds' defence. Mix in his incredible drive and determination, and you have the recipe for an incredible player.

A one-club man, his status has been enhanced by his ability to perform on the biggest stage. When Liverpool fans think back to the 'Miracle of Istanbul', Gerrard will be uppermost in their thoughts. His header brought the Reds back into the game and he then won the penalty that continued one of the most incredible fightbacks in footballing history. All this in the biggest club game in the world. His reward that night was the chance to lift the famous trophy high above his head – the defining moment of Liverpool Football Club's modern age.

Gerrard turns 31 in May 2011 and can reflect on numerous proud memories he has shared with his Liverpool family. After breaking onto the first-team scene in 1998 following an injury to Jamie Redknapp, it soon became clear that Liverpool had a star in the making on their hands. He played 50 games during the treble season of 2000/01 as the Reds ended the campaign with the League Cup, FA Cup and UEFA Cup in the trophy cabinet. After that, he produced a moment of magic without which Istanbul would never have happened.

In December 2004 Liverpool needed to beat Olympiakos in their final Champions League group game by two clear goals. As the match entered it's final five minutes with Liverpool just 2-1 up, their dreams of glory were fading fast. Then came the moment that mattered. Neil Mellor teed up Gerrard

for a half volley and he drilled home his long-range strike with power and precision. As the net at the Kop end rippled, the ground erupted in celebration. That goal ensured there would be plenty of other wonderful European nights ahead during the remainder of the season.

If that strike provided a dramatic finish, Gerrard's late intervention in the 2006 FA Cup final had an even greater touch of Hollywood about it. He had already scored in the Cardiff showpiece against West Ham but the Reds trailed the Hammers 3-2 going into the final minute. Despite struggling with cramp, Gerrard somehow rustled up enough energy to fire a brilliant long-range effort beyond goalkeeper Shaka Hislop and take the game into extra-time. There was no further scoring and the Reds captain duly slotted home one of the penalties in the shoot-out. Liverpool won 3-1 and Gerrard went on to lift another trophy.

His influence during the past decade has been immense. Idolised by the Kop, his efforts are also appreciated by his team-mates and managers. Kenny Dalglish knows a thing or two about helping Liverpool achieve success. He cannot speak highly enough of Gerrard's performances for the team. "Steven Gerrard is such a complete footballer that he can play comfortably in any position in the team, and he loves Liverpool so he's prepared to play wherever he is asked."

Dalglish, Gerrard's manager during the second half of the 2010/11 campaign, added: "He has been asked to play as a support striker and in the centre of midfield, but for me his best position is in a red shirt, on a football pitch with the ball at his feet. The rest comes naturally to one of the best players playing anywhere. Just give him a strip and let him play."

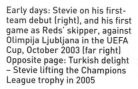

Early days: Stevie on his first-team debut (right), and his first game as Reds' skipper, against Olimpija Ljubljana in the UEFA Cup, October 2003 (far right) Opposite page: Turkish delight – Stevie lifting the Champions League trophy in 2005

1892: Liverpool FC plays
its first game. Ten Scots
are in the starting line-up

April 1939: Billy Liddell,
aged 17, signs for
Liverpool for £500

1951: Kenneth Mathieson
Dalglish born in Glasgow

1961: Ian St John and Ron
Yeats join from Motherwell
and Dundee United
respectively

1977: Alan Hansen plays his
first game for Liverpool, and
is followed shortly after by
Graeme Souness

FROM TEAM OF MACS TO GARY MAC

THE KOP'S GREAT SCOTS

**Liddell, Shankly, Dalglish, Souness, Hansen...
where would we be without the contribution of our legends from
north of the border? It all started when the first Reds' line-up
included 10 Scots and generations later, we would salute
another unexpected hero whose golden free-kick in Dortmund
brought us another trophy treble to celebrate**

(Above) The Team of the Macs line-up from 1892/93; back row, left to right: McQue, McCartney, Hannah, Ross, McQueen, McLean, McBride, Dick; front row, left to right: Wyllie, Smith, Miller, McVean, McQueen

Opposite page: Scottish defenders who have donned the red shirt down the years – Joe McQue (left, illustrated) and Ron Yeats (right)

THE TEAM OF MACS

Following the acrimonious 'split' with Everton, John Houlding was a man in a hurry. He wanted the new Liverpool Football Club to quickly establish itself as a direct rival to Everton and become one of the league's leading lights in the process.

As he set about that task, John McKenna was sent to Scotland in search of players capable of helping the club challenge for honours. To Houlding's fury, the new club had been turned down for membership of the newly-expanded Football League for the 1892/93 season. On the plus side, it allowed the band of new recruits time to bed down in the Lancashire League.

Among those newcomers was Andrew Hannah, who signed from Everton. The Renton-born player had starred for Everton in their 1891 league championship-winning season. He had been a captain of Everton and when he was appointed to the same role with Liverpool, he enjoyed the distinction of being the only man to lead both clubs at Anfield. Alongside Hannah, Scottish international Duncan McLean – another ex-Everton player – was brought in alongside Celtic reserve Joe McQue.

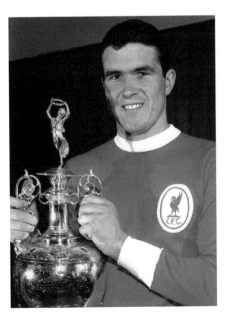

The McQueen brothers Matt (who went on to become a key figure in the club's early history) and Hugh arrived from Leith Athletic. John McCartney, Tom Wyllie and Malcolm McVean, who all hailed from north of the border, also joined and so the club was dubbed 'The Team of Macs'.

Indeed, 10 of Liverpool's 11 players who lined up for their first Lancashire League fixture in September 1892 against Higher Walton (an 8-0 win) were Scots. Joe Pearson, signed from West Derby, was the exception.

The recruitment policy was not popular among the local Press. It was speculated that the club's wage bill for that first season would be in the region of £15,000, and there was consternation at the fact that most of the recipients would be Scotsmen.

In the course of time such attitudes softened. Liverpool has long been noted for its similarities to Glasgow and it is not just because of Shankly's legacy that the club has enjoyed strong links with Scots.

Indeed, many have worn Liverpool's colours in senior competitive football. Of those were some of the best players to don the famous red shirt: Billy Liddell, Ron Yeats, Ian St John, Graeme Souness and Alan Hansen and, of course, the man who is considered by many the finest of them all, Kenny Dalglish.

In the town where I was born

Harthill, Scotland
(The McQueen brothers)

Located half-way between Glasgow and Edinburgh, Harthill is the home of Scotland's first motorway service station, which was built next to the M8 in 1978. It incorporated a landmark motorway footbridge and was known as Harthill Services until 2006, when it was redeveloped and renamed Heart of Scotland Services. A modern replacement footbridge was constructed at the site in 2008, costing £5m.

Scotland's 'Turnpike' system was first established in 1767, with the main route between Edinburgh and Glasgow passing through Harthill. By 1780, the 'Edinburgh to Glasgow Flyer' stagecoach would pass through Harthill up to 20 times a day with many travellers stopping at the town's 'Halfway House' – now a private dwelling at Polkemmet Country Park – while horses were changed and watered.

KING IN THE MAKING

The date of March 4 is a significant milestone in the history of Liverpool Football Club.

It was the day Emlyn Hughes made his Reds debut in 1967, the day Everton were thrashed 4-0 in 1972 and CSKA Sofia seen off 5-1 in 1981. But the most significant thing that happened to the club on that date occurred 220 miles away in 1951 – the birth of Kenneth Mathieson Dalglish.

Dalglish was born in Glasgow, a city which bears many similarities to Liverpool. A port situated on the River Clyde, it is the third most populous city in the UK. The future Reds' legend spent his formative years in Dalmarnock, a district to the north of the Clyde with Parkhead, the stadium where he would first make a name for himself, located nearby.

Before long the family were on the move, setting up home at Milton, a district to the north of the Clyde. Building on Milton started in the late 1940s, as part of a general post-war construction programme by Glasgow Corporation to deal with the housing shortage and slum clearances.

Kenny's family lived on an estate in the district and it was here that he took part in his first football with a team called Milton Milan, who played on spare ground at Egilsay Street. Another Milton graduate was Ian Ross, three-and-a-half years Kenny's senior, who later played for Liverpool.

In his autobiography, Dalglish admitted that he spent most of his waking hours consumed by football. His father Bill was an avid Glasgow Rangers supporter and would take his son to Ibrox on a regular basis. It was there that the youngster encountered his early heroes. Powerful South African centre-forward Don Kitchenbrand, who netted 38 goals in 51 matches for Rangers, was one of his first favourites. Others included midfield marvel Jim Baxter and talented inside-forward Ian McMillan, who Gers fans nicknamed 'the Wee Prime Minister'. Another favourite was Denis Law, the skilful forward who Dalglish idolised after seeing him play for Scotland at Hampden Park. Years later, Law's number eight shirt would take pride of place in his home after he obtained it following a testimonial match between Celtic and Manchester United.

A pupil at Milton Bank Primary School on Skerray Street, Dalglish attended Sunday School but claimed religion held little interest to him. Although he followed Rangers, that naturally came about through taking the lead of his father. He was a member of the Boys' Brigade at Possil Park,

an area which became one of the poorest in the United Kingdom following the closure of the Saracen Foundry – a major employer where ornamental ironwork was manufactured – in 1967.

Dalglish later moved on to complete his education at High Possil during which time he played for the Possil Park YMCA team based at Peters Hill Drive. It soon became clear that Dalglish possessed above-average ability and he had hopes of representing the Scotland Under-15s and U16s teams, after playing against them for a Glasgow city side in trial matches.

Despite initially missing out on selection, he was later called up to play for Scotland U16s against Northern Ireland at Glentoran's ground The Oval. He was then selected against England – a particular thrill as the match was played at Ibrox, the ground where he had watched most of his football. The game ended in a 1-1 draw.

His talents meant that suitors were starting to circle and in August 1966 he was invited to trials at Liverpool and West Ham United. He met the great Bill Shankly during his spell at Melwood. Indeed, Shankly and Reuben Bennett even gave the 15-year-old a lift back to the YMCA where he was staying, before asking him to extend his trial for an extra couple of days.

However, Kenny's strong pull for watching Rangers was underlined when he told Shanks he had to return home. The premise was that he wanted a couple of days at home before travelling back south to trial for Ron Greenwood's West Ham. That was something of a half-truth. His main eagerness to head back north was that Rangers were playing Celtic in an Old Firm clash later that week, and he wanted to be present.

Throughout the 1966/67 season it was assumed that Dalglish would sign for the blue half of Glasgow. At the time, Kenny's bedroom was within a goal-kick of Rangers' Govan training ground.

However, for whatever reason, the expected approach never materialised. At the time Dalglish was playing for Glasgow United, a team so strong that Celtic regularly asked them for friendly fixtures so that they could run the rule over prospective signings.

On one such occasion, Celtic boss Jock Stein and his assistant Sean Fallon were in attendance and Dalglish caught their eye. Following further discussions, Kenny must have been left bewildered when a representative from Celtic called round to the family home to secure an agreement for his signature. For one thing, he hurriedly considered removing the pin-up posters of his Ibrox favourites from his bedroom wall! His previous

Below: Denis Law – a hero to the young Kenny Dalglish – scores for Scotland against England at Hampden Park in April 1966

THE KENNY DALGLISH PLAYERS' TREE
– May 30, 1985 to February 21, 1991

Players

Goalkeepers

*Bruce Grobbelaar 1981-1994,
Durban, South Africa
Mike Hooper 1985-1993,
Bristol, England

Defenders

Phil Neal 1974-1985,
Irchester, England
Alan Hansen 1977-1990,
Sauchuie, Scotland
Alan Kennedy 1978-1985,
Sunderland, England
*Mark Lawrenson 1981-1988,
Preston, England
Steve Nicol 1981-1994,
Ayrshire, Scotland
Gary Gillespie 1983-1991,
Stirling, Scotland
Jim Beglin 1983-1987,
Waterford, Republic of Ireland
Mark Seagraves 1983-1986,
Liverpool, England
Gary Ablett 1983-1992,
Liverpool, England
Brian Mooney 1983-1986,
Dublin, Republic of Ireland
Barry Venison 1986-1992,
Consett, England
Steve Staunton 1986-1991
and 1998-2000,
Drogheda, Republic of Ireland
Alex Watson, 1988-1989,
Liverpool, England
David Burrows 1988-1993,
Dudley, England
Nick Tanner 1988-1992,
Bristol, England
Glenn Hysen, 1989-1992,
Gothenburg, Sweden

Midfielders

Sammy Lee 1976-1986,
Liverpool, England
Ronnie Whelan 1979-1994,
Dublin, Republic of Ireland
*Craig Johnston 1981-1988,
Johannesburg, South Africa
John Wark 1984-1987,
Glasgow, Scotland
Kevin MacDonald 1984-1988,
Inverness, Scotland
Jan Molby 1984-1995,
Kolding, Denmark
Steve McMahon 1985-1991,
Liverpool, England
Nigel Spackman 1987-1988,
Romsey, England
*John Barnes 1987-1997,
Kingston, Jamaica
Ray Houghton 1987-1992,
Glasgow, Scotland
Mike Marsh 1987-1993,
Kirkby, England
Steve McManaman 1990-1999,
Liverpool, England
Jimmy Carter 1991-1991,
Hammersmith, England

Forwards

Kenny Dalglish 1977-1990,
Glasgow, Scotland
Ian Rush 1980-1987;
1988-1996,
St Asaph, Wales
Paul Walsh 1984-1987,
Plumstead, England
Alan Irvine 1986-1987,
Broxburn, Scotland
John Durnin 1986-1988,
Liverpool, England
*John Aldridge 1987-1989,
Liverpool, England
Peter Beardsley 1987-1991,
Newcastle, England
Ronny Rosenthal 1990-1993,
Haifa, Israel
David Speedie 1991-1991,
Glenrothes, Scotland

Players used: 40
By position: Goalkeepers: 2
Defenders: 16, Midfielders: 13
Forwards: 9
By nationality: England: 19,
Scotland: 9, Ireland: 6, Wales: 1
Zimbabwe: 1, Australia: 1,
Denmark: 1, Israel: 1, Sweden: 1
Key: On the player information,
the first date is the year the player
signed for LFC and the second
the date of his last senior
appearance.
* Although born in different countries,
players marked with an asterisk either
went on to play international football for
another nation or were considered to
be of a different nationality.

What's in a name?

Dalglish

With various off-shoots of the name including Dalglesh, Dagleas and Dagless, Daglish is of Scottish origin and is locational from a place "above the sources of the Tinna Water in the parish of Ehrick, Selkirk". It was first recorded in 1383 in the form Dalglas and derives from the Gaelic "dail", field and "glas", green.

It appears that some early individuals of the family were connected with disturbances of the peace and got on the wrong side of the law. George Dalgleish, confidential sevitior of the Earl of Bothwell, was executed for participation in the murder of Lord Darnley in 1567.

The first recorded spelling of the family name was that of Symon de Dagles, which was dated 1407.

affiliations were not held against him by Fallon and though it would not have been something Dalglish could ever have foreseen, he signed for the Parkhead club.

Kenny's main ambition was to succeed in professional football and if that meant it was to be with Celtic, his attitude was 'so be it'. But, as they say, you never forget your first love. Dalglish's story has parallels with Jamie Carragher's in that whereas Carra continued following Everton after signing for Liverpool, so Dalglish would keep a keen eye on Rangers' fortunes. Indeed, he would still go to watch Gers' matches when he had no Celtic commitments.

A team-mate at Glasgow United, Danny McGrain, was in the same boat. He was also taken on by Celtic and the two became great mates, with Kenny later being best man at McGrain's wedding. McGrain, who would go on to make more than 650 senior appearances in Celtic colours, used to join Dalglish in taking the bus from Argyle Street – a thoroughfare that stretches almost two-and-a-half miles – in the city centre, out to Celtic Park.

The North Lanarkshire new town of Cumbernauld was created in 1956 as an overspill for Glasgow. Its name comes from the Scots Gaelic *comar nan allt*, which translates as 'the meeting of the waters'. This is because from its high point, streams flow west to the River Clyde and east to the River Forth. With a chronic shortage of housing in the aftermath of the Second World War, five new towns were designated, the others being East Kilbride, Glenrothes, Livingston and Irvine.

In recent times a popular advertising campaign promoting the town, located 10 miles outside the city centre, had the rhyming sign-off: 'What's it called? Cumbernauld.' Now home to Scottish Third Division side Clyde, who moved to the Broadwood Stadium in 1994, the town's early days saw the formation of a junior football club. Cumbernauld United were founded in 1964 and it was at their Guys Meadow stadium that Celtic's hierarchy decided that a young Dalglish should cut his teeth, sending him out on loan for the 1967/68 season.

It proved an invaluable experience. Dalglish later likened the standard as the equivalent of playing for a club in the current Blue Square Premier set-up. The talented teenager quickly found out that opponents weren't afraid to play him if they couldn't play the ball! Nonetheless, his talent ensured he stood out. After scoring four on his

Four Cumberland United players hold up their mascot, Fiona Gibb, in 1967/68. Dalglish, then 17, is on the right of the picture

debut, he finished the campaign with 37 goals to his credit.

While playing for Cumbernauld, Dalglish would train at Celtic on two evenings a week whenever fixtures permitted. In the meantime, it had been advised that Dalglish should learn a profession in case things didn't work out in a sport where the prospect of a serious injury is always present.

The trade that awaited him was that of a joiner and he would regularly work through the day before travelling to training in the evening. His experience of an eight-hour day job afforded him valuable knowledge of a different workplace, and he went through the usual initiations of being asked to find a left-handed screwdriver, and to request a long weight.

It wasn't long before he took the next step in his footballing career. After his successful season with Cumbernauld, Dalglish hoped that he would be able to sign full-time terms with Celtic. Jock Stein initially felt he would be better served by another season playing regular junior football, but relented

"His talent ensured he stood out. After scoring four on his debut, he finished the campaign with 37 goals to his credit"

Cutting a dash:
Kenny takes his eye
off the ball in this
shot, taken in 1975

following further discussions with Dalglish and his father. The teenager signed professional forms and became part of the Celtic reserve team.

Featuring other talented prospects such as McGrain, David Hay and Lou Macari, the team became nicknamed "The Quality Street Gang" after a newspaper headline stuck. The 1968/69 season saw Dalglish gain experience of reserve-team football and, working under the astute management of Stein, his game continued to develop.

In September of that term, 17-year-old Kenny was given his first taste of senior football when he was named on the bench for the League Cup tie at Hamilton Academicals. He made his debut as a second-half substitute, coming on to replace Charlie Gallagher. There were no more first-team outings that season but after starting the following campaign in the second string, his big day came on October 4, 1969, when Stein deemed him ready to make his league bow for the Hoops.

Raith Rovers were the visitors to Parkhead, and an excited Dalglish took his place in the starting line-up in the number four jersey. He made a fine start, producing an encouraging performance as he linked well with Tom Callaghan in the midfield. He also provided the assist for the last of Celtic's goals – scored by John Hughes – as Stein's side ran out handsome 7-1 winners. Dalglish went on to make a total of four appearances that season and five in the following campaign, but his prodigious talent was being noted by the shrewd Stein.

Sadly, Dalglish's footballing journey has taken in some devastating days. For the Old Firm clash at Ibrox on January 2, 1971, Kenny was part of the travelling Celtic party but when he was not named in the matchday squad, he was given a ticket for the away end. Tragically, a major disaster occurred towards the end of the game. With Celtic leading 1-0, Rangers supporters started to leave the stadium. But as they heard the roars that followed Colin Stein's late equaliser, many turned to go back into the stadium – and met other fans coming out by stairway 13. The incident led to 66 deaths, with more than 200 others injured. Most of the fatalities were caused by compressive asphyxia. It happened at the opposite end to where Dalglish was standing, and he knew nothing of the tragedy at the time.

Back on the pitch, he was continuing to impress the Celtic management and towards the end of that season, was selected to play in a testimonial match for Frank Beattie at Kilmarnock. Dalglish helped Celtic to another 7-1 victory, just as he had on his league debut. This time, he scored six of the seven goals! He was now ready for a regular run in the team at Parkhead, a stint that would put him on the path to becoming a Liverpool legend.

THE KENNY DALGLISH PLAYERS' TREE
– January 8, 2011 to February 2, 2011

Players

Goalkeepers

Jose Reina 2005-present,
Madrid, Spain

Squad

Peter Gulacsi 2007-present,
Budapest, Hungary
Dani Pacheco 2007-present,
Malaga, Spain
Brad Jones 2010-present,
Armadale, Australia
Danny Wilson 2010-present,
Livingston, Scotland
Paul Konchesky 2010-present,
Barking, England
Joe Cole 2010-present,
Islington, England
Andy Carroll 2011-present,
Gateshead, England

Defenders

Jamie Carragher 1996-present,
Liverpool, England
Daniel Agger 2006-present,
Hvidovre, Denmark
**Fabio Aurelio 2006-2010,
2010-present,**
Sao Carlos, Brazil
Martin Kelly 2007-present,
Bolton, England
Martin Skrtel 2008-present,
Handlova, Slovakia
Glen Johnson 2009-present,
London, England
Sotirios Kyrgiakos 2009-present,
Trikala, Greece

Midfielders

Steven Gerrard 1997-present,
Whiston, England
Lucas Leiva 2007-present,
Dourados, Brazil
Jay Spearing 2007-present,
Wallasey, England
Raul Meireles 2010-present,
Porto, Portugal
Maxi Rodriguez 2010-present,
Rosario, Argentina
Jonjo Shelvey 2010-present,
Romford, England
**Christian Poulsen
2010-present,**
Asnaes, Denmark
***Milan Jovanovic
2010-present,**
Bajina Basta, SFR Yugoslavia

Forwards

Dirk Kuyt 2006-present,
Katwijk, Holland
**Fernando Torres
2007-2011,**
Madrid, Spain
Ryan Babel 2007-2011,
Amsterdam, Holland
David Ngog 2008-present,
Gennevilliers, France
Luis Suarez 2011-present,
Salto, Uruguay

Players used: 21
By position: Goalkeepers: 1
Defenders: 7, Midfielders: 8
Forwards: 5
By nationality: England: 6,
Denmark: 2, Slovakia: 1, Brazil: 2
Portugal: 1, Argentina: 1,
Serbia:1, Holland: 2, Spain: 2,
France: 1, Uruguay: 1, Greece: 1
Key: On the player information,
the first date is the year the player
signed for LFC and the second
the date of his last senior
appearance.

* Although born in different countries,
players marked with an asterisk either
went on to play international football for
another nation or were considered to
be of a different nationality.
* Although born in the country then
known as Yugoslavia, Milan Jovanovic is
a full Serbian international

133

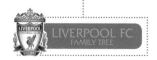

ALEX WALKS TALL

There was an authoritarian presence about Alex Raisbeck, one of the key figures in Liverpool Football Club's early history.

The Scot was one of seven brothers who either became footballers or soldiers, and there was a sense of the military about the way he carried himself both on and off the pitch. Although he was not especially tall at 5ft 10ins, the man from the village of Polmont in Stirlingshire was as commanding a centre-half as you could wish to see.

An inspiration to his fellow team-mates, he moved to Anfield in May 1898 while still

a teenager. Having started his professional career with Hibernian, he played only eight games for Stoke before Liverpool boss Tom Watson paid £350 for his services. Despite his small stature for a central defender, Alex was a dominant influence, whose timing and athleticism enabled him to reach the ball before taller opponents. Raisbeck was a natural leader and he captained the team to their first Football League Division One title in 1901 – and lifted the championship again five years later.

It came as no surprise that Raisbeck harboured managerial ambitions and after a spell in charge of Hamilton Academicals, where he had ended his playing career, he returned south of the border to take over at Bristol City – leading them to two Division Three (South) titles. He had been tipped to succeed David Ashworth as Liverpool manager in 1922/23, but Matt McQueen was the directors' choice.

After spells in charge of Halifax Town, Chester City and Bath City, Raisbeck did return to Liverpool in a scouting capacity in 1939, serving the club in that role until his dying day in March 1949.

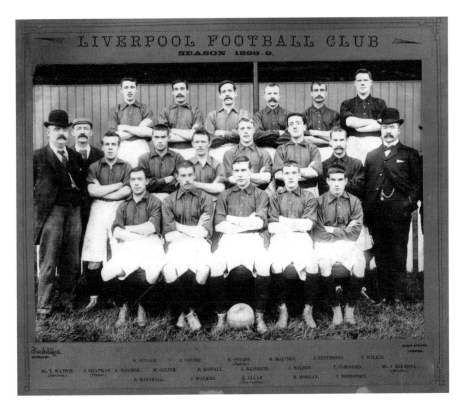

LIVERPOOL FOOTBALL CLUB

SEASON 1898-9.

W. DUNLOP.   A. GOLDIE.   M. STORER.   M. McQUEEN.   J. STEVENSON.   T. WILKIE.
(Captain.)

Mr. T. WATSON   J. CHAPMAN   A. McGOWIE.   M. GOLDIE.   R. HOWELL.   A. RAISBECK.   G. WILSON.   T. CLEGHORN.   Mr. J. McKENNA
(Secretary.)   (Trainer.)   (Director.)

R. MARSHALL.   J. WALKER.   G. ALLAN   H. MORGAN   T. ROBERTSON.
(Vice-Captain.)

Left: A squad photo from
1898/99. Matt McQueen
is third from right on the
back row; Alex Raisbeck
is fourth from right on the
middle row.
Below, left: A Liverpool
team line-up from the
1930s. Matt Busby is stood
fourth from the right

What's in a name?

Busby

Sir Matt Busby is probably the most famous 'Busby' Britain has ever had! The surname is thought to be of early medieval English or Scottish origins (the county of Renfrewshire). Its north England roots are thought to emanate from a place near Yorkshire, which was so-called after a nearby bush shrub farm.

It is also thought that the village of Bushby in Leicestershire may also have given rise to some instances of the surname.

BUSBY – UNITING NORTH-WEST REDS

On March 12, 1946, Liverpool paid Manchester City £8,000 for Alexander Matthew Busby. With the Reds deep in the relegation mire, manager George Patterson needed to strengthen his half-back options so he brought in the 26-year-old, an inside-forward who had found success at half-back when playing there in an emergency.

Busby had played in the 1933 and 1934 FA Cup finals for City but after over 200 appearances for the Maine Road outfit, his career was on the slide. A leg injury had kept him out for almost a year and with his wife Jean suffering from a serious illness, Busby had become unhappy in Manchester. City were looking to sell so when Liverpool came in the move suited all parties.

"In March 1936, when I asked Manchester City to release me, I would have been content to join any club in England," he recalled in *Matt Busby – My Story*, which was serialised by the *Liverpool Echo* in 1957.

"Liverpool arrived with an offer, which was accepted, and I was happy at the prospect of moving to Merseyside, even though Liverpool were having a bad time being threatened with relegation to the Second Division. They signed me to assist in the fight against relegation, also appointing Mr George Kay from West Ham United as manager at about the same time.

"George Kay's appointment was not made a day too soon, because the affairs of Liverpool Football Club were at a very low ebb, with a lack of discipline being responsible for many of Liverpool's problems."

Liverpool's 1936 team weren't exactly unruly, but Busby reckoned they lacked leadership. "The training routine was slipshod, players lacked the sort of supervision which I consider essential in every club, and the Anfield Road ship would most certainly have foundered on the relegation rocks without a strong man at the helm.

"George Kay was such a man, but he had to work very hard to pull the club out of trouble. The players were there, great players most of them, but many were obviously past their best."

Busby's Liverpool debut came in a 1-0 defeat at Huddersfield and he made 11 appearances in total that season, scoring the first of three goals for the club a month later in a 2-2 draw against Blackburn.

The Reds won just three of their final 20 games that season – one was Busby's home debut against Leeds – and stayed up by just three points. It all got too much for Patterson who had been suffering from stress (and was evidently unable to control his players) and a serious illness forced him to quit as manager, with Kay taking over. Busby became an integral part of Kay's team over the next three seasons and, along with Tom Bradshaw and

Jimmy McDougall, was part of an all-Scottish half-back line.

According to *lfchistory.net*, that half-back line "certainly ranks with the best the club has ever had in those three positions at any one time in its history," while the *Liverpool Echo* rated Busby as "the greatest and most classic half-back in these islands." The Liverpool number 4 also became a firm favourite on the Kop.

Born in Orbiston, Lanarkshire, Busby came from a working-class mining background. He worked hard on the pitch and his attacking runs from right half-back were a feature of his game, as was his passing ability. On the day he signed for the Reds, the *Liverpool Echo* described him as "one of the cleverest constructors in the country" – and he lived up to that billing. It was said that Busby was one of the first players who could accurately pass a ball along the ground without looking at his intended recipient.

"It would land within an inch of the required spot," wrote the *Liverpool Echo's* 'Stork' in 1948, "usually just in front of the forward who could take it in his stride." The newspaper also reported that "he is one of the best trappers of the ball the game has known because he 'kills' the ball dead, yet when it suits him he can 'kill' the ball and propel it with one and the same notion." It sounds like the kind of pass Steven Gerrard would be proud of.

Busby was also noted for his unusually running style and was said to "run with a crouch, well over the ball." The Kop loved him and the feeling was mutual. Even after 11 years of being manager of Manchester United, Busby talked about Liverpool supporters, and the Kop, in glowing terms.

Table manners: Liverpool players treated to a hotel meal with Busby front, fourth right

Sir Matt Busby, pictured in Liverpool strip during 1936 tour games in Belgrade

"Liverpool have solid support and encouragement from some of the finest followers in Britain," he wrote. "The Spion Kop is famous, as certain football reporters have discovered when an ill-chosen word in their writings has brought upon their heads a storm of abuse from those behind the goal.

"That Anfield Spion Kop is one of Liverpool Football Club's most precious possessions and I am certain matches have been won through the vocal efforts of its regular patrons. Only a man who has worn the red shirt of Liverpool, when the home team is attacking the Kop goal, knows and appreciates the value of the Kop supporter.

"The deafening roar that accompanies every attacking move carries sufficient volume to cause all but the most experienced of defences to panic and make mistakes. I know this is true because I have played at Anfield – for and against Liverpool – and I know which side I would rather be on!" For the manager of Manchester United to say he would rather be on the Kop's side than against it, after 11 years as United boss, is as good as tribute to football's most famous stand as you will ever find.

Even in his playing days it became clear that management was going to be a natural progression for Busby and in 1938 he played a significant part in the Anfield arrival of a player who, in the eyes of those who watched him, was the greatest to ever wear Liverpool red. Without Matt Busby, the great Billy Liddell may never have become a Liverpool player.

"As a Liverpool player I still retained many connections with Manchester City and my playing colleagues at Maine Road. Alex Herd and I, as playing colleagues, used to play a lot of golf together in Scotland during the close season and I saw no reason why my move to Merseyside should interfere with such enjoyable summertime activities.

"One day Alex did not turn up for his round and when I went in search of him I was told that he had taken Willie McAndrew, the Hamilton Academicals manager, in his car to see a 15-year-old boy called Liddell playing football for Lochgelly Violet. No business was done with Hamilton because Billy Liddell's parents wanted some assurances about their son's future in the game and Willie McAndrew's club were not really in a prosperous enough state to make lavish promises in that line.

"When Alex told me the story, I telephoned George Kay at Anfield and suggested he might succeed where Hamilton had failed. He did, and Billy Liddell became a Liverpool player, a very fortunate day for Liverpool."

A year later and Liverpool enjoyed another fortunate day when they signed a 20-year-old half-back called Bob Paisley from Bishop Auckland. Busby, who by now had been appointed Liverpool captain, took the youngster

from the North East under his wing and the pair became life-long friends as well as team-mates. Nobody could have foreseen that they'd also win four European Cups between them in the future.

Unfortunately for both Busby and Paisley the onset of World War Two meant they never got to play together for Liverpool in a competitive fixture. Football ground to a halt in 1939/40 and on October 11 a notice in the *Liverpool Echo* stated that Busby would not be available for future matches as, 'he has been appointed sergeant-instructor to the Army Physical Training School and leaves for the South tomorrow.'

Busby never played a competitive game for Liverpool again with his 125th and final appearance coming against Chelsea at Anfield nine days earlier. Between 1939 and 1945 Busby did make 26 war-time appearances for the Reds, and also guested for seven other clubs, but by the time the war was finished Busby was considering his next career move. Aged 35, his best days were behind him and he sought a move into management.

"Like most demobilised soldiers, I was at a loose end, wondering how I could pick up the peace-time threads after six years in Khaki," he wrote. "I suppose I could have continued playing for a year or two but that would have served no purpose other than delaying the day when I should have to think of doing something apart from my football, for my bread and butter.

"The stark truth that has to be faced was that I was out of a job, although there were openings in the game on which I could count for my employment, but my problem was deciding which job offered the best prospects for my future and that of my family.

"I was anxious to become a manager, but I had to make certain I did not join a club prepared to install me as a mere figurehead, ready to tolerate my presence, for a couple of seasons, before showing me the door. I wanted a good club, not necessarily a First Division outfit, but a club that would give an opportunity to a man willing to work for the success of that club."

Liverpool weren't about to axe Kay, but they had long recognised Busby's potential as a future manager. In June 1944 the *Liverpool Echo* reported that when football resumed Busby would continue as skipper and 'when the time comes for his retirement from the more active side of the game he will be appointed to a position on the coaching staff.' Liverpool's board offered Busby a five-year deal to stay at Anfield, but he was still desperate to go straight into management. Inevitably, other clubs came in for him.

"Liverpool were very keen to retain my services as a coach, and it seemed their offer of a five years' contract with the probability of promotion during that time, provided me with my main requirement…security," he wrote. "I

In the town where I was born

Orbiston, Bellshill,
(Sir Matt Busby)

A town in North Lanarkshire, Scotland 10 miles south east of Glasgow, Belshill has a population of around 30,000.

Settlers first resided in the area in the mid-17th century, when a stone quarry was founded but the area only really developed 200 years later when large coal and iron deposits were discovered nearby. A number of mines opened, even attracting immigrants from as far afield as Lithuania.

The local maternity hospital specialised in dealing with infection diseases during World War I and has been the birthplace of other famous names including politican Robin Cook, singers Sharleen Spiteri and Sheena Easton plus a number of footballers past and present including Ally McCoist. It closed down in 2001 to make way for new housing.

Belshill also has a public leisure centre named after Sir Matt.

Family Secrets

Jim Harley

The Reds have employed some pacy players over the years, but few were as quick as Jim Harley.

One of many players to have had their careers cut short by the Second World War, Harley was a member of the 1946/47 squad that claimed the club's fifth league championship.

His sprinting skills paid off in other avenues, too. The Fife-born full-back once won the Powderhall Handicap, a well-known sprint in Scotland, which had been contested since 1870.

agreed verbally to accept but before signing a contract I had a chat with the directors so as to leave no doubts in their minds that my hopes in soccer were centred on a managerial job, despite my keenness on coaching."

Clearly Busby didn't get the reassurances he craved because on February 14, 1945, it was reported in the *Liverpool Echo* that Liverpool had 'decided to release Matt Busby from his engagement as post-war coach' because he was 'in negotiation with a Scottish club for a managerial position.'

It was thought that the Liverpool chairman, William McConnell, had persuaded his fellow directors to let Busby go back on the verbal agreement even though the board did not know which clubs he was talking to. The board agreed, and McConnell wished him well.

"It is with the deepest regret that the Liverpool club loses one of the finest sportsman that ever graced a football field," said McConnell. "He reminds me of the quotation 'I dare do all that may become a man; who dares do more is none'." What he didn't know was that Busby was actually talking to Manchester United.

After hearing that Liverpool had released him, United chief scout and long-time acquaintance Louis Rocca wrote to Busby saying that they were looking for a manager and the Liverpool skipper, who was still registered as a player at Anfield, returned to Manchester for talks.

"The (Liverpool) directors' plan was that, besides coaching, I could take some of the weight off George Kay," he recalled. "I was considering this offer, when quite unexpectedly I was informed that Mr J W Gibson, then chairman of Manchester United, would like to see me. The sequel was that the club offered me the manager's position at Old Trafford, thus providing me with the opening I had been seeking."

Busby accepted the job and in October 1946, when he was finally demobilised by the army, was officially appointed as manager of Manchester United. The news didn't go down well at Anfield.

"When I told the Liverpool directors of my decision they did not take it very well. In fact, although I was as happy as a player could be at the club, the one black spot on my career there concerned the unfortunate events surrounding my departure.

"Liverpool seemed to think I was going to Old Trafford in the capacity of player-manager and there were suggestions about demanding a transfer fee from United, but I had no intention of trying to combine the two jobs.

"Having agreed terms with Manchester United and finally severed what had been a very happy association with Liverpool, I was asked by George Kay to return for one sentimental visit – to play in an exhibition game.

Nearing the end of the week George Kay again telephoned from Anfield and said: 'There has been a change of mind here. The directors don't want you to play'.

"I discovered later that the board were upset because I was joining Manchester United, and they had taken the decision to cancel my sentimental journey. It hurt me to think that after nine of the happiest years of my life – even the war years – the directors of my club could turn against me simply because I preferred to be manager of Manchester United instead of coach of Liverpool." And that is where Matt Busby's Liverpool story ended.

You can only speculate as to what would have happened if he had stayed on at Anfield and eventually succeeded Kay as Liverpool manager instead of Don Welsh. If he had, and made as good a job of it as he did at Old Trafford, then the chances are that there would have been no job going for Bill Shankly in 1959. Maybe Shanks would have ended up at United instead?

Busby went on to be hugely successful at United winning five titles, two FA Cups and the European Cup in 1968. Building his team after the devastation of the Munich Disaster in 1958 – a tragedy that almost claimed his own life – was testament to his managerial ability and strength of character.

"When you think about it, it was only right that United, under Matt, should be the first English club to win the trophy," said Bob Paisley, who invited his friend onto the Reds' open-top bus after the 1983 Milk Cup final success shortly before his own retirement.

Legends, friends: Sir Matt Busby and Bob Paisley saluted Liverpool and Manchester United fans following the 1983 Milk Cup final at Wembley

"There was the style with which his teams played – and the character of the man, shown at its greatest when he and the club fought back after the tragedy of Munich."

History tends not to remember the Matt Busby Liverpool story in full. It doesn't remember his service as a player. It doesn't remember his love of Liverpool fans. It doesn't even remember that he got offered a better job at a time when the country was rebuilding after World War Two, a time when you took whatever the best job going was. It simply remembers that he committed the cardinal sin of leaving Liverpool for Manchester United.

THE PRICE OF A FOOTBALL GENIUS? £3 A WEEK

When candidates are discussed for the title of 'Liverpool Football Club's greatest player', Billy Liddell's name is guaranteed to be one of the first mentioned.

Liddell was born in Townhill, a mining village just north of Dunfermline in Fife, Scotland, in January 1922. He was the eldest of six children born to father James, who worked down the pit, and mother Montgomery. The Liddell family was part of a religious community and Billy's Christian beliefs were core to how he conducted his life. In his 1960 autobiography, *My Soccer Story*, Billy wrote: 'It was a struggle making ends meet, and many were the sacrifices my parents made for their children. In 1936 my father's wage as a mineworker was £2 5s a week. Life was pretty tough, and the family's main diet was porridge (with salt, of course), Scotch broth (kait we called it) and bread. Plenty of bread.'

The young Billy was a precocious footballer and student, with mathematics his speciality in the classroom. His parents insisted that he didn't neglect his studies at Dunfermline High School while his football progressed, and Billy was happy to comply with their wishes. He played for Kingseat Juveniles before being taken on by Lochgelly Violet, who were also based in Fife. He came to the attention of Liverpool manager George Kay in 1938 after a tip-off from the Reds' Scottish defender Matt Busby, who would go on to achieve fame at another north-west club.

Kay visited the Liddells to persuade them that Liverpool was a suitable destination for their eldest. They insisted Billy be allowed to continue his accountancy studies, and be given a suitable job in the city. Kay agreed to the request without hesitation.He moved in July 1938, aged 16, having been bought for £500, before officially becoming a professional on April 17, 1939. Considering his future achievements, Liddell's first pro deal was far from lucrative. The contract records his weekly wage as being £3, with a £1 bonus for Central League appearances "and a further £1 extra in the first team".

Because of the advent of war in September 1939, Liddell's official debut was delayed until January 5, 1946 when he was part of the Liverpool team who defeated Chester City 2-0 in the FA Cup, five days before his 24th birthday. Billy served with the RAF during hostilities, but did appear for Liverpool in war-time matches.

The early years of his career were spent on the wing but he moved to centre-forward in the mid-1950s. Despite his belated bow, Liddell still managed to make 534 first-team appearances between 1946 and 1960, scoring 228 goals. The statistics cannot do justice to his brilliance and bravery.

Family secrets

Billy Liddell

Known for his sporting attitude and impeccable conduct while playing, Liddell's generous and altruistic nature was demonstrated after his playing days were over. He did voluntary work at local boys' clubs, served as a justice of the peace and was bursar of Liverpool University. Billy died in July 2001, aged 79, having suffered from Alzheimer's Disease in his final years.

Over 50 years after he last wore a red shirt, Liddell's deeds live on, both in his home village and at Anfield. In 2009 the Townhill Sports Complex was renamed in his honour, with a memorial garden also created. A plaque listing his achievements is placed outside the entrance to the Anfield museum.

THE MEN WHO MADE THE DIFFERENCE

In retrospect, the summer of 1961 proved hugely significant for Liverpool as two of the club's most famous players were recruited by Bill Shankly from his native Scotland.

Ron Yeats and Ian St John joined a team who were then still languishing in Division Two. Yeats was recruited from Dundee United, while St John came from Motherwell. In *Liverpool: A Complete Record* the pair were described as "the cornerstone upon which many future Liverpool successes were built".

Dubbed a "colossus" by Shankly when he signed the central defender, Yeats was a rock at the heart of the Reds' defence through the 1960s, captaining them back into the First Division as they were promoted in his first season at the club.

Within four years Yeats had lifted two league championships and the FA Cup – the first time it had been won in the club's history. He remains Liverpool's longest-serving skipper, moving on to Tranmere Rovers in 1971. Yeats was running a fruit and vegetable stall in Kirkby when he was brought back to Anfield in 1986 by player-manager Kenny Dalglish, who made him chief scout – a position he retained until his retirement in 2006.

If Yeats was a commanding presence in defence, Ian St John wasn't short of strength in attack – despite being only 5ft 7ins tall.

His power, determination, close control, skill and eye for goal made him a hero of the Kop, most notably when he scored the extra-time winner in the 1965 FA Cup final win over Leeds United at Wembley.

St John was a perfect foil for Roger Hunt and helped create many of his strike partner's goals during a memorable era for the Reds.

Other Scottish players who wore the red shirt during the 1960s and 1970s included striker Bobby Graham, Brian Hall (who continues to work for the club as head of public relations), Tommy Leishman, Gordon Wallace, Ian Ross, goalkeepers Tommy Lawrence and Bert Slater, plus Peter Cormack.

RICH PICKINGS NORTH OF THE BORDER

The three great Scots Kenny Dalglish, Graeme Souness and Alan Hansen emerged as Anfield legends during the 1970s and 1980s, establishing a legacy that would extend far beyond the decade.

Dalglish and Souness would go on to manage the club, while Hansen would become captain and settle in Merseyside, becoming a widely respected media pundit. Liverpool, however, nearly missed their chance with the elegant central defender from north of the border.

Hansen travelled to Liverpool for a trial aged just 15 but didn't make an impression on the watching scouts, and later received the standard rejection letter, signed at the time by the club's chief scout Geoff Twentyman.

He revealed: "I remember it as if it was yesterday. First of all, I didn't really want to be there. I was only a boy and it seemed like a long way from home. Liverpool looked after me really well but I had a little corn on the little toe of my right foot and I was in agony for four days. On the last day, we had a friendly against a local non-league side. I was playing in the middle of the park and I just remember getting kicked everywhere. The first challenge came in and someone whacked me and after then, I couldn't get my game together."

Years later, it was only Twentyman's vision that saw the club renew their interest. The classy, languid ball-playing abilities of Hansen proved a perfect fit for the Reds' passing game and he moved to Anfield for £100,000 in 1977. *'Looks the best CH (centre-half) in Scotland. Worth buying now'* read the entry in one of Twentyman's scouting books in 1975/76.

Above: Geoff Twentyman, the scout who brought so many players to the club, including Alan Hansen. To the right is an extract from Twentyman's scouting diary. On the opposite page, Hansen celebrates after scoring the winning goal against AZ Alkmaar in the 1981/82 European Cup

Hansen added: "None of the scouts reckoned I was any good. I remember playing in a trial game at Under-18 level and I felt that I gave one of the best passing displays that I ever had at any time. But I never got through the trial. I was told later that I never got in because they felt I didn't run round much, which is absolutely stupid.

"All the way through my days at Partick, people felt that. Everyone seemed to think that I was a good player on the ball but I was a bit slow. That reputation stuck in Scotland. Then, when I went to Liverpool, my game was set up for the way they played and Geoff realised that."

Twentyman's judgement proved astute and Liverpool reaped the rewards as 'Jocky', as he was fondly nicknamed by the Kop, went on to win eight league titles, three European Cups, three League Cups and two FA Cups during a glittering Kop career.

Scotland, indeed, was a rich hunting ground for Liverpool Football Club during the 1970s and 1980s. Twentyman's scouting books reveal a host of big names that the club was keeping a close eye on – from Hansen to Andy Gray and Davie Cooper.

Others, who would go on to wear the red shirt included John Wark, Gary Gillespie and a young talent from Ayr United called Steve Nicol.

What's in a name?

Hansen

A European surname, it can be derived from the father or mother. The male version comes from "Hann", a German-Flemish short form of Johann, itself from the Hebrew "Yochanan", which translates as "Jehovah has favoured (me with a son)."

LABOURER WHO BUILT A BIG REPUTATION

Other Liverpool Scots had higher profiles – but few were as enduring and effective as Steve Nicol, a brilliant footballer whose versatility allowed him to make important contributions in several positions during 13 years at Anfield.

Born in Irvine, a new town on the North Ayrshire coast of the Firth of Clyde, Nicol's football career began with Ayr United, making his debut in 1979 and racking up 70 league appearances over the next two years. At the time, he was a part-time player and occasional building labourer.

Nicol was still a teenager when Bob Paisley signed him for £300,000 in October 1981. He made four first-team appearances the following season, before establishing himself as a regular starter in 1983/84. His first Anfield goal came in a 3-0 Merseyside derby victory over Everton that season, a campaign that climaxed with the European Cup final against Roma in Rome. Following a 1-1 draw, Nicol missed Liverpool's first penalty in the shoot-out but the Reds still managed to prevail as the Italian side failed with two of their attempts. His performances almost led him to being named PFA Young Player of the Year but he was just pipped by Luton Town's Paul Walsh, who soon after became a team-mate at Anfield.

Whether he played right-back, left-back, in the centre of defence, in midfield or up front, Nicol could excel. He would do far more than fill-in. As time went on, full-back became his most frequent home, particularly after Phil Neal's departure in 1985.

The Liverpool team of 1987/88 were often sublime but frequently it was Nicol who stood out, notably with a televised hat-trick in a 4-0 win at Newcastle United. The following season, 1988/89, he was named the Football Writers' Footballer of the Year, deserved individual recognition for a man who always put the team first.

In the 9-0 demolition of Crystal Palace in September 1989, Nicol was the only man to score twice, netting the first and final goals of the night. He went on to win another league championship medal in 1989/90 and the FA Cup in 1992, before making his final appearance in a red shirt in 1994.

John Wark was the club's top scorer in 1984/85, the midfielder hitting 27 goals in all competitions. Signed from Ipswich Town in March '84, he played enough games to win a championship medal at the end of that season. He would also help the club to the Double in 1985/86, before injury curtailed his Anfield career. He returned to Portman Road in early 1988.

Gary Gillespie enjoyed an eight-year stint at Anfield, having been Joe

Fagan's first signing in 1983. A back-up for the first half of his Liverpool career – although he did pick up European and League Cup winners' medals, the Stirling-born defender played enough games to land a First Division championship medal in 1985/86 – hitting a hat-trick against Birmingham in the process. He also won titles in 1988 and 1990, as well as the 1989 FA Cup before leaving for Celtic in the summer of 1991.

Kevin MacDonald, born in Inverness, arrived a year later than Gillespie, the midfielder joining after impressing at Leicester City. Although never a regular in his five years at the club, he helped the Reds to Double success in 1986, before a broken leg curtailed his opportunites, eventually departing for Coventry in 1989.

Left, clockwise from top: Steve Nicol, Gary Gillespie and John Wark; three Scots who shone for the Reds in the 1980s

SOUNESS: SILK AND STEEL

A magnificent amalgamation of silk and steel, Graeme Souness was one of the classiest midfielders ever to wear the red shirt.

Born in Edinburgh, he was brought up in the Saughton area of the city and played for North Merchiston and Tynecastle Boys Club as a youngster. His professional career began in England with Tottenham Hotspur, after being signed by their legendary manager Bill Nicholson.

The teenage Souness was living in a strange city but he didn't feel overawed; instead, he regularly told an increasingly exacerbated Nicholson that he was better than established players such as Alan Mullery, Martin Peters and Steve Perryman. Nicholson did not agree, and moved Souness on, as far away from London as possible. Thus Souness found himself at Middlesbrough, having played only one first-team game at Spurs.

His impressive performances earned him a move to Liverpool in January 1978, where manager Bob Paisley saw him as a replacement for Ian Callaghan. Souness settled immediately, scoring a brilliant volley against Manchester United in February and creating the winning goal for Kenny Dalglish in the European Cup final against Bruges at Wembley. Fearless, ruthless and with a temperament that relished any kind of confrontation on the pitch, Souness was the pivot of Liverpool's play; his passing, vision and close control were excellent, and he possessed a powerful shot.

He was fundamental to the league championship wins in 1979 and 1980, plus the European Cup success of 1981. However, in 1981 Liverpool's league performances dipped and with the Reds languishing in 12th place in Division One at the turn of 1982, Paisley turned to Souness, making him club captain in succession to Phil Thompson.

Liverpool's form improved immediately and they stormed through the field to claim the title again, while the League Cup was also won. That particular double was repeated in 1982/83, while 1983/84 proved to be the club's most successful. The title was won for the third season in succession, while Souness scored the winner in the League Cup final replay victory over Everton at Maine Road. His last act as a Liverpool player was to skipper the side to a fourth European Cup, secured in an intimidating atmosphere against Roma in Rome as the Reds won on penalties following a 1-1 draw. As you would expect, Souness coolly converted his spot-kick.

That summer he left Anfield for Sampdoria and it took a while for Liverpool to adjust. He returned as manager in 1991 and won the FA Cup in 1992 but during his time in charge, the quality of the squad declined and so did the team's performances, prompting his departure early in 1994.

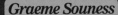

THE GRAEME SOUNESS PLAYERS' TREE
– April 16, 1991 to January 31, 1994

Graeme Souness

Goalkeepers

*Bruce Grobbelaar 1981-1994,
Durban, South Africa

Mike Hooper 1985-1993,
Bristol, England

David James 1992-1999,
Welwyn Garden City, England

Defenders

Steve Nicol 1981-1994,
Ayrshire, Scotland

Gary Gillespie 1983-1991,
Stirling, Scotland

Gary Ablett 1983-1992,
Liverpool, England

Steve Staunton
1986-1991 and 1998-2000,
Drogheda, Republic of Ireland

Barry Venison 1986-1992,
Consett, England

David Burrows 1988-1993,
Dudley, England

Nick Tanner 1988-1992,
Bristol, England

Glenn Hysen, 1989-1992,
Gothenburg, Sweden

Steve Harkness 1989-1999,
Carlisle, England

Barry Jones 1989-1991,
Prescot, England

*Rob Jones 1991-1998,
Wrexham, Wales

Mark Wright 1991-1997,
Dorchester, England

Torben Piechnik 1992-1993,
Copenhagen, Denmark

Stig Inge Bjornebye 1992-1999,
Elverum, Norway

Dominic Matteo 1992-2000,
Dumfries, Scotland

Neil Ruddock 1993-1997,
Wandsworth, England

Julian Dicks 1993-1994,
Bristol, England

Midfielders

Ronnie Whelan 1979-1994,
Dublin, Republic of Ireland

Jan Molby 1984-1995,
Kolding, Denmark

Steve McMahon 1985-1991,
Liverpool, England

*Ray Houghton 1987-1992,
Glasgow, Scotland

*John Barnes 1987-1997,
Kingston, Jamaica

Mike Marsh 1987-1993,
Kirkby, England

Steve McManaman 1990-1999,
Liverpool, England

*Don Hutchison 1990-1994,
Gateshead, England

Jimmy Carter 1991-1991,
Hammersmith, England

Mark Walters 1991-1995,
Birmingham, England

Michael Thomas 1991-1998,
Lambeth, England

Jamie Redknapp 1991-2001,
Barton-on-Sea, England

Istvan Kozma 1992-1992,
Paszto, Hungary

Paul Stewart 1992-1993,
Manchester, England

Phil Charnock 1992-1992,
Ormskirk, England

Nigel Clough 1993-1995,
Sunderland, England

Forwards

Ian Rush 1980-1987;
1988-1996,
St Asaph, Wales

Peter Beardsley 1987-1991,
Newcastle, England

Ronny Rosenthal 1990-1993,
Haifa, Israel

David Speedie 1991-1991,
Glenrothes, Scotland

Dean Saunders 1991-1992,
Swansea, Wales

Robbie Fowler 1992-2001
and 2006-2007,
Liverpool, England

Players used: 42
By position: Goalkeepers: 3,
Defenders: 17, Midfielders: 16,
Forwards: 6.
By nationality: England: 24,
Scotland: 5, Wales: 2, Ireland: 3,
Zimbabwe: 1, Denmark: 2,
Israel: 1, Sweden: 1, Jamaica: 1,
Hungary: 1, Norway: 1.
Key: On the player information,
the first date is the year the player
signed for LFC and the second
the date of his last senior
appearance.
* Although born in different countries,
players marked with an asterisk either
went on to play international football for
another nation or were considered to
be of a different nationality.

GARY MAC – FABULOUS FOOTBALLER

For someone who was only at the club for two years, Gary McAllister is one of the most celebrated players in Liverpool's history.

A championship winner at Leeds United, he was already well into his 36th year by the time Gerard Houllier brought in the Motherwell-born midfielder from Coventry City on a free in summer 2000. Despite his advanced years, McAllister proved to be an extremely shrewd recruit.

McAllister wasn't able to get a first-team run until mid-October because of a red card on his full debut at Arsenal, and his wife being diagnosed with a serious illness. Once established, McAllister was fulcrum of the Reds' midfield in the memorable treble-winning season and a positive influence on a young Steven Gerrard.

He scored in five consecutive games in April and May, including the unforgettable last-minute free-kick at Goodison Park and the winning penalty against Barcelona in the UEFA Cup semi-final. He was also on target in the final against Alaves, and took the free-kick that Delfi Geli headed past his own keeper for the decisive Golden Goal in extra-time.

McAllister's first-team appearances became infrequent in the latter half of the 2001/02 season, but he was afforded a tremendous reception when he said goodbye to Anfield on the final day of that campaign. The man was sheer class.

Right: Gary McAllister celebrates the League Cup and FA Cup final wins at the Millennium Stadium in Cardiff. Opposite page: Overjoyed to be holding the UEFA Cup following the incredible final against Alaves

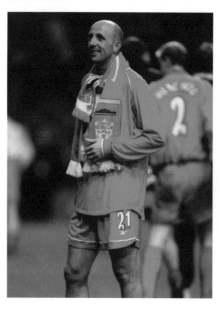

John McKenna: A
sporting leader

Stevie Heighway
on the wing and the
Anfield Irish influence

The Beglins: A
footballing family

Ian Rush and the
Welsh dragons

Roy Evans – the last of
the bootroom boys

FROM KOP CELTS
TO BOOTROOM BOSS

CELTIC COUSINS, BROTHERS,
FATHERS AND SONS

The roots under the fields of Anfield Road will
bleed to red, white and green in homage to the
men from Ireland and Wales who
have represented the club with
distinction. From Stevie Heighway
on the wing to Rushie's legendary
deeds, the Celtic influence has
burned bright. It's in our genes.

Elisha Scott: Irish
record-breaker

THE IRISH AT ANFIELD

Just as the city of Liverpool seems to have always possessed an Irish presence, the same is true of LFC. After Everton moved away from Anfield in 1892 John Houlding, the ground's owner, set about establishing a new club to play there. As we know he did so, with the organisation eventually becoming the famous Liverpool FC.

Houlding, a brewer by trade, achieved this goal thanks to the help of business associate WE Barclay and the arrival of Irishman John McKenna on to the committee of the newly-founded organisation. McKenna, known as 'Honest John', originally hailed from County Monaghan in Ulster and had moved to Merseyside at the age of 19.

Through his interest in various sports and involvement in the Anglican community he became friendly with Houlding, who had no hesitation in appointing him as secretary of the new outfit. Despite that title McKenna played a major role in managerial duties, working closely with Barclay. Together they won the Second Division title in 1894 and 1896. After the latter of those achievements Tom Watson, the man who had led Sunderland to the title three times, arrived to take over team affairs on McKenna's recommendation. Under his charge the title came to Anfield twice.

That successful appointment was an example of the foresight McKenna brought to the club. The man from across the Irish Sea went on to become Football League president for two decades and also had two separate spells as chairman at Anfield before he passed away in 1936.

Since the days of McKenna a flurry of Irishmen, or players with Irish roots, have followed the same path. Legendary goalkeeper Elisha Scott was born in Belfast and, after making his Reds' debut in 1913, didn't retire until he'd completed his 468th and final appearance for the club 21 years later. Scott was a member of the title-winning sides of 1922 and 1923. He was joined in that line-up by less well-known Wexford-born winger Billy Lacey.

Following their impact it would not be until the 1970s that someone with Irish links again appeared for the Anfielders. Steve Heighway may have only spent his childhood in Dublin, but he wore the green shirt with pride and accumulated an enviable collection of silverware during his time with Bill Shankly and Bob Paisley's all-conquering teams. League, European, FA and UEFA Cup medals all came his way as he won a place in the hearts of the Kop – and his feats are still celebrated in song today.

When Steve's playing days came to a close another Irishman began to break through in the shape of Ronnie Whelan. As Kenny Dalglish said in typically understated manner: "He came over from Ireland as a young boy at 18 years of age, scored on his debut against Stoke City and just carried on from there. A good goalscorer, good passer and good runner. A determined and hard midfield player who was very underrated." Just like Heighway, Whelan won it all – and even wore the skipper's armband on that emotional day in 1989 when the post-Hillsborough all-Merseyside FA Cup final produced a fitting tribute to those who had tragically passed away.

For a period during the 1980s, Liverpool seemed to become a home for Irish players. At various times in the decade Dubliner Whelan was joined by Mark Lawrenson, Michael Robinson, Jim Beglin, John Aldridge, Steve Staunton and Ray Houghton, all of whom picked up at least one championship medal in what was an exceptional period of success. Of those half a dozen names, Beglin and Staunton hailed from Waterford and Dundalk respectively, with the rest of the group qualifying for an Irish passport through their ancestors.

By the time Whelan left the club in 1994 a new breed of Irish Reds were on their way, starting with Phil Babb. The former Coventry centre-half was born in London, and had impressed for Eire at the USA World Cup.

Steve Heighway: Irish star who enjoyed a glittering career for the Reds

Lawrenson

Staunton

Aldridge

Such displays led to Roy Evans purchasing him for a fee of £3.6m, making him the most expensive defender in the country at the time. Unfortunately Babb could never justify such a label and eventually left after 170 games and largely unfulfilled promise.

Mark Kennedy and Jason McAteer arrived during the following year. Both had stood out during cup runs for Millwall and Bolton respectively, yet neither would go on to establish themselves as Liverpool greats. Dublin-born Kennedy, 19 when he signed, only played 21 games before moving on to join Wolves. McAteer, a Republic of Ireland international through family having been born in Birkenhead, started in brighter fashion, operating as a wing-back in Evans' entertaining 3-5-2 formation. He played 40 games in his debut season, but a broken leg and a change of management saw his chances limited. He eventually departed in 1999.

It would not be until 2003 that an Irish presence again appeared on a Liverpool team-sheet, and it only became a reality after much speculation. Gerard Houllier had long been listed as one of Steve Finnan's admirers and he finally brought the Limerick-born full-back to the club that summer. Injuries hampered his initial progress, but when he found full fitness and form the number three provided a consistent and reassuring presence at right-back. Even Rafa Benitez went out of his way to praise the defender, who claimed Champions League and FA Cup medals before going to Espanyol as part of the deal that brought Albert Riera the other way.

That same pre-season had witnessed the arrival of one of Finnan's international colleagues, Robbie Keane. A boyhood Liverpool fan who had been on trial there as a teenager before opting to join Wolves, the Republic of Ireland's all-time top goalscorer appeared to be a shrewd acquisition. But it wasn't until October that Keane found the net, in a Champions

Babb

Whelan

Houghton

League encounter with PSV. His maiden league strike didn't arrive until the following month. Despite giving everything for the cause, the forward was in and out of the side and it was clear Benitez was having second thoughts about the number seven. After rumours of a potential departure, he rejoined Spurs only six months after moving to Merseyside.

At the time of writing (February 2011) there is no Irish player amongst the senior squad at Anfield. That lack of presence on the field is never reflected in the stands though.

If anything, it's the opposite. When you glance at the Kop on matchdays, flags bearing allegiance to Ireland can usually be seen. Home or away, there always seems to be a few voices from Ireland and Northern Ireland mixed in with the Scouse army wherever they travel.

That Irish contingent is sure to remain part of the LFC family forever, a vital component of what makes the Kop so special.

'Home or away, there always seems to be a few voices from Ireland and Northern Ireland mixed in with the Scouse army ... sure to remain part of the LFC family forever'

THE LFC IRISH CONTINGENT

Northern Ireland

Willie Donnelly 1896-1897,
Magherafelt, Northern Ireland

Sam English 1933-1935,
Coleraine, Northern Ireland

David Hannah 1894-1897,
Raffrey, Northern Ireland

William Hood 1937-1937,
Belfast, Northern Ireland

Billy McDevitt 1923-1924,
Belfast, Northern Ireland

David McMullan 1925-1928,
Belfast, Northern Ireland

Billy Millar 1928-1928,
Ballymena, Northern Ireland

Elisha Scott 1912-1934,
Belfast, Northern Ireland

Sammy Smyth 1952-1954,
Belfast, Northern Ireland

Republic of Ireland

John Aldridge 1987-1989,
Garston, Liverpool

Phil Babb 1994-2000,
Lambeth, London

Jim Beglin 1983-1987,
Waterford, Republic of Ireland

Steve Finnan 2003-2008,
Limerick, Republic of Ireland

Steve Heighway 1970-1981,
Dublin, Republic of Ireland

Ray Houghton 1987-92,
Glasgow, Scotland

Robbie Keane 2008-2009,
Dublin, Republic of Ireland

Mark Kennedy 1995-1998,
Dublin, Republic of Ireland

Bill Lacey 1912-1924,
Dublin, Republic of Ireland

Mark Lawrenson 1981-1988,
Preston, England

Jason McAteer 1995-1999,
Birkenhead, England

Brian Mooney 1983-1986,
Dublin, Republic of Ireland

Richie Partridge 2000-2007,
Dublin, Republic of Ireland

Darren Potter 2004-2005,
Liverpool, England

Michael Robinson, 1983-1984,
Leicester, England

Steve Staunton 1986-1991 and 1998-2000,
Drogheda, Republic of Ireland

Ronnie Whelan 1979-1994,
Dublin, Republic of Ireland

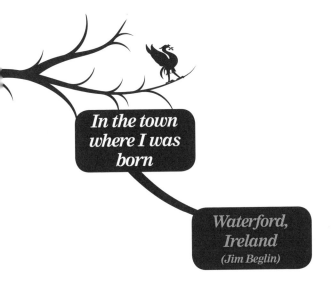
In the town where I was born

Waterford, Ireland
(Jim Beglin)

Waterford boy: Jim, a winner age 12

What's in a name?

Aldridge

This name is derived from several sources. The Olde English pre-Seventh century name "Aedelric" is one source, the town of Aldridge in Staffordshire (which is recorded in the Domesday Book) another, while a third alternative is Aldridge Grove in Buckingham.

The original name came from 'adel' meaning noble and 'ric'- a ruler (noble ruler), and in ancient times it was one of the most popular given names.

Variants of the name include Aldrich or Oldridge.

Waterford Crystal is a brand of crystal glassware for which the city is world-renowned.

George and William Penrose formed the first crystal business in the city in 1783 and although their company closed in 1851, Waterford's reputation for fine glass continued, leading to Charles Bacik establishing a glassworks in the city in 1947. Production of crystal glassware at a factory in Waterford ceased in 2009 after Waterford Wedgwood went into receivership, but Waterford Crystal is still produced in other European locations – and a new Waterford Crystal visitor centre was opened in June 2010.

The most recognisable landmark in Waterford is Reginald's Tower – the oldest urban civic building in Ireland. Founded by the Vikings between 856 and 914AD, the early fort that stood where the tower is situated formed the apex of the triangular Viking settlement in the city. In 1170, the Anglo-Normans attacked Waterford and the capture of the tower heralded the fall of the city. The Irish-Viking ruler of Waterford, Ragnall MacGillemarie, was held prisoner there and from that the tower received its name.

Every August, on the Bank Holiday weekend, the Spraoi Festival is held in Waterford city centre. Showcasing national and international street art and world music, the three-day festival has become hugely popular and attracts audiences of over 80,000 to Waterford.

Houghton

A place name in various counties with a range of different old English origins. In Lancashire and west Yorkshire, it translates to 'place on a hill-spur' or 'place in an enclosure' while in east Yorkshire it also meant 'place where ale-hoof (ground ivy) grow'.

In some cases it is thought that the first element of the name could also relate to the name of an Anglo-Saxon owner, Hofa.

What's in a name?

Beglin

Recorded in many spellings including Beglan, Baglan, Baglin, Bagline, Bagling, and Baglon, Beglin is an Irish surname which developed from the ancient Gaelic O' Beigleighinn.

'Beag' translated as little and 'leighinn', as a scholar, thus meaning 'the descendant of the little scholar'. It is a rare name found mainly in County Westmeath and County Longford. The surname was said to have first been recorded in the famous register known as 'Petty's census of Ireland 1659'.

THE BEGLINS – A FOOTBALL FAMILY

For Irish youngsters, identifying an English team to follow often appears to be a random choice, with paternal and sibling influence having little or no effect. Jim Beglin's family was typical of football-lovers in Ireland. Dad supported Liverpool; eldest son followed Manchester United; middle son preferred Chelsea while youngest son was an Evertonian.

The middle son was Jim himself, drawn to the London Blues by their appearance in the 1970 FA Cup final when he was an impressionable six years old. While young Jim didn't inherit his father's love of Liverpool, genetics surely had something to do with his all-too-brief football career. Dad Thomas played for Waterford (the Beglins' local club) and Sligo Rovers in the League of Ireland. "From when I was young, I was aware that there was football around me," explained Beglin. "I remember as a very, very young kid being taken to watch my dad wind down his career with local football sides."

Thomas, an attacking midfielder and striker, was a different character to his calm and composed son. "His only problem was that he couldn't keep his mouth shut and was often getting into trouble. He could be excitable. I can remember going to see Waterford as a kid playing in a cup semi-final on neutral ground in Dublin. My dad got into a pushing match with an opposition supporter. He was very, very passionate – an all or nothing type of character."

Beglin was brought up in Gracedieu, Waterford City, the largest city in the south-east of Ireland. He was the third of six children, three boys and three girls. The eldest, Eddie, was a Manchester United fan, the youngest brother, Tom, an Evertonian.

"Football was huge in the family. If look back at any photographs, nearly every one taken of me when I was younger has a ball in the shot. We were all footy-mad." The love of football covered both sides of the Irish Sea. "It was a big thing to follow our local team, Waterford, because in the '70s, as I was growing up, they were winning the league every other year. If not the strongest side in Ireland, they were one of the strongest through that decade. I loved following them and we used to go to quite a few of their away games as well.

"The home ground was Kilcohan Park, which also had a greyhound track. It is still used for greyhounds but Waterford no longer play football there – they are a division down and are based at the regional sports centre. Kilcohan Park was almost Wembley for me and I dreamed of playing on it to emulate my heroes. I managed to do that eventually through De La Salle College, my secondary school."

When Beglin was a boy, 'soccer', as it's generally known in Ireland, came third in the sporting hierarchy behind Gaelic football and hurling, but his school, thankfully, didn't view it with a sniffy attitude. "Even though soccer always played second fiddle to the Gaelic games, particularly hurling, there was still plenty for us to play. We had a brilliant new gymnasium built so there were five-a-side competitions and they were very competitive. For us, Waterford was a good soccer city."

Beglin did dabble in Gaelic games but much preferred the football codes to hurling. "I took a liking to the Gaelic football but hurling was very physical, very tough. I did play when I was very young but I remember thinking: 'This is not for me'. I preferred to play Gaelic football or soccer. I remember the school arriving to pick me up at the house for a hurling game and I told my mother: 'Tell them I'm not here; I don't want to play.' She said: 'Get out there; don't embarrass the family.'"

Beglin's early football heroes came from watching Waterford in the flesh. His interest in English football grew as television coverage expanded. "In the early to mid-70s we began to get 'Pipe' television so we could watch ITV Wales, for example. *The Big Match* was shown on a Sunday afternoon and I loved things like that. I had a voracious appetite for football, or soccer. I also remember going to the Theatre Royal in Waterford to watch World Cup reels. It was packed while we watched a film of the World Cup in Mexico in 1970. When I was very young I can recall my father sat in the kitchen at home, listening to Radio 2 and the great Peter Jones as he commentated on the big match on a Saturday afternoon."

Dad was listening out for Liverpool's fortunes, but son was more interested in a London club. "I honestly don't know what triggered it. Maybe it's because they were playing Leeds in the cup final and Chelsea would have been underdogs. Something made an impression on me and I decided to support Chelsea. I stuck with them and they became my team.

"Unfortunately, he's passed away now but my favourite player was Ian Hutchison, the guy with a long-throw. I fancied myself as a left-winger when I was younger. That's where I played in my local teams early on. There were pictures of me when I was very young with a Chelsea kit on and the number 11 on my shorts. I had a relative who would sew on the numbers."

He did get the ferry to England with his father to watch First Division football but unfortunately never made it to Anfield. "I saw Manchester United beat Derby 3-0 when I was about seven or eight. My father's group

What's in a name?

Staunton

This English surname is nearly always held by Irish people. It is understood to be one of the first English surnames in Ireland, with the first settlers arriving in Connaught after the Anglo-Norman invasion of Ireland in 1170.

Subsequently the Stauntons held the baronies of Clanmorris and Carra and many adopted the gaelic 'MacEvilly', which translates as 'The son of the knight'. However, in the 16th century the MacEvillys reverted to being called Staunton, to the point where MacEvilly or Evilly are now rare surnames. The name's old English meaning is either 'The stony farm' or possibly 'Stan's farm'.

Villages called Staunton are found in several English counties. The first recording of such a village is probably 'Stantune' which was listed in the rolls of Herefordshire in the year 958.

What's in a name?

Whelan

Recorded in many spellings including Wheelan, Whalen, Whelan, Whelehan, Welan, Weallan, Wealleans, Feolande, Fyland, O'Phelane, Phelan and others, this is an Irish name.

It is the developed form of the ancient pre-10th century Gaelic name O' Faolain, meaning a male descendant of Faolan, itself a personal name meaning 'Young wolf'.

Historically, the family tends to have settled in the counties Waterford, Kilkenny, Wexford and Carlow.

of friends at work supported different teams. My elder brother experienced more journeys and he got to go to Anfield, not just Old Trafford. All that fed my appetite, it made me even keener to be a footballer."

Beglin says it didn't really register with him that he possessed above-average ability when he started to play competitive football as a boy. "I remember being picked out for Under-10s and being told I was going to be in the team. Under-10s were created around the time I was that age. Initially the youngest age group was U12s and I went for a trial with them when I was eight. I played in an U12 team with my brother, who is four years older than me. The team was called Crusaders and it was my first experience of a local competitive team. They were pretty hopeless. I was a midget as well; I didn't start stretching until I was in my teens."

He played for a team called Bolton Wanderers initially before moving to Bohemians. "There have been a few lads who made it as professional footballers who played for them, including John O'Shea and [Scunthorpe's] Eddie Nolan. Bohemians have been the strongest club in Waterford over the years.

"I obviously had some ability and as I came through the years, I evolved from wanting to be an attacking player into someone who attacked from a defensive position. Bit by bit I moved from outside-left to left-half and I ended up playing local football at U14s and U15s at centre-back. When I moved into professional football my team in Dublin, Shamrock Rovers, had a problem at left-back and I was placed there. That was it – Liverpool signed me as a left-back and I never got away from there."

As with most teenage boys who are striving to become a professional footballer, Beglin's school work suffered. "I was a decent pupil – I did enough to get by. My older brother went on to become a teacher and he was much more studious than me. I always did my homework but I didn't put the hours in because I was sport-mad and would play pitch-and-putt, tennis, squash, basketball and even dabbled in athletics. I was desperate to get out and not be stuck inside reading books.

"In the last couple of years at secondary school, my work began to suffer because I was being called up for various things. I got the chance to represent my province, Munster, and Johnny Giles and Eamon Dunphy were watching that day. I impressed them because the next thing I knew I was called up for an Ireland U17s tournament in Cannes in France. On the back of that I was offered professional terms with Shamrock Rovers. That was all before my final exams. I can remember my parents being on my case about making sure I didn't neglect my schoolwork."

Beglin completed his leaving certificate, the main qualification in Ireland, shortly before his 17th birthday. Two weeks later he became a professional footballer. "I suppose there was a bit of apprehension but it was very exciting at the same time. I was delighted to be chasing my dream.

"When I joined Shamrock Rovers in Dublin, part of the deal was for me to go to college and re-sit my leaving certificate. I was taking honours papers in all subjects to try and qualify myself for university. Because I was a full-time pro I was exhausted. I was trying to go to college in the afternoons and I couldn't cope. I found myself getting more and more behind. I stopped attending because it was too much for me."

Dublin, the capital city, was 100 miles from the comfort of home and Beglin is grateful that he got used to fending for himself before he moved to England. "It made me grow up and opened my eyes. I matured quicker and it gave me independence. I came from a relatively small place in Waterford and the Dublin lads were much more streetwise and switched on. It was a hell of a learning curve. It was basically sink or swim, as with a lot of dressing rooms. You have to harden yourself to the Mickey-taking and not let anything get in the way of your goal. I always say Dublin gave me great grounding for that.

"I was lucky in that I was only 100 miles away from home. Even though they were trying to break me in and get used to life on my own, if I really felt that I needed a hug from my mother and father, I could sneak home on the train for 24 hours and Shamrock Rovers would never know. I'd come back, reassured, and everything would be fine. From 16 to 19 I was learning my trade and being given a chance to get experience and mature, while only being up the road from home, not stuck at a big club totally homesick in England – as had happened to a lot of Irish lads."

Above left: Jim lines up with Waterford Under-15s at a tournament in Germany, 1977 (front row, right).
Above right: De La Salle Waterford U16s, 1978 (Jim is back row, third right)

Early days at Shamrock Rovers

Beglin in action for the national side

The Shamrock Rovers manager when Beglin became a professional (1980) was Johnny Giles, not long retired as one of Ireland's greatest players. He had a very positive influence on his young recruit. "I had a fantastic grounding. He was a superb coach and a hard taskmaster. A lot of what Johnny Giles preached was what was being done at Liverpool anyway. On day one in front of my parents he said it wasn't all about running out in a lovely strip of a weekend – he said there was a lot of hard graft and blood, sweat and tears."

Beglin was placed in digs with another Shamrock Rovers player. By his own admission, it wasn't a "raving success". He explained: "The guy I was sharing digs with was a bit mad. It ended up coming to a head with the family we lived with. They were used to having students who spent an awful lot of time out of the place. Once we got pre-season out of the way, we had afternoons free so we'd take over the house. It created tension. We weren't rowdy but they found that their privacy was invaded too much. One evening they said to us that we had to leave.

"The other player had a girlfriend in Dublin so he was fine and I was lucky that my brother was there as a trainee teacher. We ended up finding our own flat. Subsequently, my sister Barbara arrived in Dublin and ended up securing a beautiful apartment but she needed help so myself and another couple of players moved in with her and a couple of her mates."

Beglin's performances in the League of Ireland quickly earned him recognition and English clubs regularly watched him. "When I picked up the paper on a Sunday, there was always a reference to 'such-and-such a scout was watching Jim Beglin'. I felt that something was going to happen."

It did happen and at a convenient time for Beglin. His club was owned by the Kilcoyne family, who wanted to create a team that would dominate in Ireland and prove competitive in European competition. It wasn't to be and during the 1982/83 season they ran into financial difficulties. "Johnny Giles had left – he was managing Vancouver Whitecaps and us but then he went full-time to the Whitecaps. The full-time system at Shamrock Rovers began to break up. I had started a commercial course with Aer Lingus and I was a week into that when I got word that I was going to Arsenal."

Beglin was delighted but there was a twist ahead. "Shamrock Rovers were playing in my home town, Waterford, on a Sunday and I was due to travel on the Sunday night. I played at Waterford and on the way back to Dublin the chairman pulled me aside and said: 'Look, for whatever reason Arsenal have changed their mind and they don't want you to go over.'

"It was disappointing because I knew everything was unravelling in terms of the full-time set-up at Shamrock Rovers. It was a case of 'what are you going to do from here?' I was expecting to have to get a job and play football on a part-time basis. Within a week of that, Liverpool wanted me over on a month's loan."

It was a lifeline but Beglin was well aware this could be his only opportunity to fulfil his dream. "There was an Irish lad called Ritchie Bayly who went over just before me and was being spoken of as the next Liam Brady. He was fantastically talented – great feet and wonderfully skilful – but it didn't work out for him at Liverpool. I remember thinking, 'Bloody hell – this is my last throw of the dice.' I'd like to think it wasn't but it felt like that at the time. The fear of failure drove me on because I didn't want to go home. There were a few lads who had gone to England to try and make it and ended up coming home. I didn't want to be one of those guys. Thankfully, within 10 days of joining Liverpool, Bob Paisley wanted to sign me. I played two reserve games and they liked what they saw. I became his last signing in April '83."

On and off the pitch, he was prepared for the move. "This was now the next step. I'd always hoped to use Dublin and Shamrock Rovers as a springboard to English football. Thankfully that turned out to be the case. In terms of moving to another country, I was ready for it. It was a totally different environment and a much bigger club but I knew what it was all about by then. I'd been hardened to the professional side. I was very lucky to have had Johnny Giles as a coach. He really prepared me for what was to come in England."

Beglin didn't have far to travel to work when he first moved over. "I stayed on Anfield Road at Mrs Pike's, right beside the ground. I could fall out of bed and I was in the ground. I was in there with a guy called John McGregor, who ended up going on to play for Rangers. John would have

On target at the Kop end in the 1985 European Cup semi-final against Panathinaikos

Lost in blue: Taking on Everton during the 1986 FA Cup final

had a good chance of making it with Liverpool but he got a very bad knee injury in a reserve game against West Brom. In those days, if you did your cruciate you were really up against it. He was never the same after that and once I got my injury, neither was I."

His first season, 1983/84, was spent with the reserves, playing alongside the likes of Paul Jewell, Gary Gillespie and Phil Thompson – who had lost his first-team place. "I was quite shy and was never the loudest person. I kept my head down, listened and spoke when I was asked to. Once you get to know the lads, you feel more at ease. There was a little resentment as when I joined there were a few lads who were about to be moved on. There were one or two characters that were a bit difficult but I kept my head down and focused on what I needed to do. Thankfully things began to take off and I made an impression."

He made his first-team debut in November 1984 in a 1-1 draw with Southampton, before establishing a regular place towards the end of that season, appearing in the ill-fated European Cup final at Heysel. The following season he became first-choice left-back in succession to Alan Kennedy, helping the Reds to the memorable Double of league championship and FA Cup. It was a bitter-sweet achievement for Beglin, who mourned the loss of his Liverpool-supporting father, Thomas, three years earlier.

"Just before I returned for pre-season training ahead of the 1983/84 season, my father died in the July. He had a heart condition and he had to go to Dublin for regular checks. I was going to see him in hospital on my way to the airport but he passed away. He was over with me on the weekend

Beginning of the end: A serious Injury in this League Cup Merseyside derby in early 1987 all but ended Jim's professional career

I signed for Liverpool. When Liverpool played Aston Villa towards the end of the 1982/83 season and Bob Paisley was given the league championship trophy, he was there too.

"It was hard initially when I went back to Liverpool but I knew my family all supported me and they told me that he'd want me to go on to make everyone proud. It's unfortunate that he never got to see me play for the first team. I always regretted that and it all came to a head at Stamford Bridge after we won the league. I remember crying in the dressing room. I was gutted that he wasn't there. To go and win the league like that was for him. It was very emotional for me that day.

"The following week I was very sad but against Everton in the FA Cup final it was wonderful because I knew I had a huge amount of family and friends in the crowd at Wembley. It was brilliant to celebrate with them that night – before we finished up at Stringfellows!"

In familiar surroundings, covering the Reds for Radio 5 Live in 2004

Beglin could be excused bitterness at what happened less than a year later – a horrific broken leg sustained in a League Cup tie at Goodison Park that hastened the end of his career. He was only 23 and although he did play again for Leeds United, Blackburn Rovers and Plymouth Argyle, he wasn't right and the attempted comeback was curtailed. Instead, he is thankful for what he was able to achieve in the short time available to him.

"When I look back on it now, I consider myself very fortunate because I could have broken my leg before I experienced all the big occasions I enjoyed with Liverpool. It was the best, absolutely awesome. To do the Double in '86 before I suffered the injury was brilliant. I was devastated with what happened but to experience those highs with Liverpool Football Club was just fantastic. I'll forever be grateful."

Beglin admits that despite growing up in Ireland, he was initially oblivious to just how popular Liverpool were in his native country. "When I signed for Liverpool, I wasn't fully aware of how big it was in Ireland. I soon realised. All of a sudden, people in my hometown were asking about coming over.

"From my memories of Liverpool Irish players there was Stevie Heighway, Mark Lawrenson, Ronnie Whelan and Michael Robinson. There were other young Irish lads at the club who didn't go on to make the first team, like Ken DeMange and Brian Mooney. All that was a big help for me.

"Liverpool are absolutely loved in Ireland. There's a huge, huge following and they still come over in their droves. A lot of people say that Manchester United have a slight edge now, probably because of their recent success in the '90s and into the noughties, but the Liverpool following is huge."

Dean Saunders:
Record buy

BLOOD REDS

There have been plenty of blood brothers in the Liverpool family down the years and a few father-and-son combinations to have worn the famous red shirt during the course of the club's proud near 120-year history.

The first brothers to play for the club were the McQueens. Matt McQueen, who would go on to have a significant impact in the club's early history, arrived from Scotland only two months into Liverpool's first season. He played in a number of different positions during the successful inaugural season in the Football League, even taking over from first-choice goalkeeper William McOwen on five occasions.

After finishing his playing career, he qualified as a referee. When manager David Ashworth surprisingly left in 1923, McQueen took over. His brother Hugh had arrived at Anfield in 1892. A winger whose greatest assets were his speed and crossing ability, he scored 17 goals in 61 appearances during a spell with the club of just under three years.

The next brothers to represent the Reds were the Goldies. Archie Goldie was another of numerous Scots to represent Liverpool in its early years. He was bought to strengthen a squad which had been relegated in 1895, and helped to immediately restore the club to the top division. Archie spent five years at Anfield and was joined in the side for half that period by his brother Bill, also bought from Scottish club Clyde.

Around the time of the First World War, two sets of brothers represented the club. Walter Wadsworth was a commanding centre-half who was at Anfield for seven seasons immediately following the end of the conflict. When the club first won and then retained the league championship in 1922 and 1923, Wadsworth was an integral part of the team. His brother Harold was a left winger who was on the Reds' books for five years in a period just after the war.

More controversial were the Miller brothers. Tom Miller, along with three other Liverpool players – Thomas Fairfoul, Bob Pursell, Jackie Sheldon – plus three Manchester United players were found guilty of fixing a game between Liverpool and United on Good Friday 1915. Bookies had put up to 8-1 against United winning 2-0 – which is how the game ended.

Miller was given a life ban from football but this was lifted in recognition of his subsequent service to his country in the war. He remained a Liverpool player after league football resumed. He scored 13 goals in 25 starts in the 1919/20 season, as Liverpool finished fourth and reached the fourth round of the FA Cup. Miller started the following season well by scoring three goals in his first two games, but ironically, given the Good Friday scandal, moved to Manchester United in September 1920. His brother John appeared for the Reds in inter-war games and went on to play eight times upon the resumption of league football. The Miller brothers appeared in the same Liverpool team together on three occasions.

Other family links have seen fathers and sons, grandfathers and grandsons in action for the Reds. Versatile performer Bill Jones made 277 appearances after signing from Hayfield St Matthews in 1938, and was in the Liverpool team for the club's first Wembley FA Cup final against Arsenal in 1950. Forty-two years later, his grandson Rob was in the Liverpool team that won the FA Cup for the fifth time after a 2-0 win over Sunderland. He made 243 appearances for the Reds after signing from Crewe Alexandra in 1991, and also went on to play for England.

Liverpool's first father-and-son combination were Roy and Dean Saunders. Roy was a left-half who played 146 matches, despite struggling to secure a starting place because of the excellence of wing-halves and future managers Phil Taylor and Bob Paisley. In 1991 his son Dean, a striker, joined the Reds from Derby County for a then club record fee of £2.9 million. He stayed for just over a year, scoring 25 goals in 61 appearances.

The most recent father-and-son connection is provided by Paul and Thomas Ince. England international Paul had two seasons at Anfield after joining from Inter Milan in 1997, while Thomas made his senior debut as a substitute in the Carling Cup tie against Northampton in September 2010.

One other family link was provided by the Fagans. Although he never played a first-team game for the club, Joe served Liverpool in numerous capacities before overseeing a highly successful two-year stint as manager between 1983 and 1985. His son Chris, a full-back, played twice during the 1970/71 season. He made his senior debut in a League Cup tie against Mansfield Town, before starting a Division One match at Manchester City that ended in a 2-2 draw.

A couple of other notable father-son combinations didn't quite manage to follow in the footsteps of their famous fathers by representing the first team. Kenny Dalglish's son Paul was on the club's books, but left without making a senior appearance. The same was the case with Phil Neal's son Ashley, but he did make history by scoring the last Liverpool goal in front of the standing Kop. He converted a penalty against Nottingham Forest in a reserve-team game that ended in a 2-2 draw in April 1994.

Phil Neal: Famous LFC father

Joe Fagan: Never played

171

What's in a name?

Hateley

An English locational surname, recorded as Hateley, Hately, Hatley, Hattley and others.

It is said to come from the now lost medieval village of Hateley Heath, in the town of West Bromwich, although some also believe three villages called Hatley in Bedfordshire are possible sources of the name.

The meaning is said to be 'the farm on the top of a hill', from the pre-sixth century 'hatt - leah', with hatt meaning a hill top and leah, an area of ground fenced for agriculture.

Jones

The second most popular surname in Britain stems from the first name Ioan, one of the Welsh forms of the Christian name John.

In Wales, Jones is the most common surname with around one in 10 people having the name in 1890. Another form of John, Evan, is responsible for the surname Evans.

LIVERPOOL'S WELSH CONNECTION

The Welsh Dragon has breathed fire into Liverpool on more than a few occasions in the club's history – and the principality gave the Reds its most lethal finisher.

There have been quite a few Welsh favourites at Anfield – most notably of course the club's greatest goalscorer. Superlatives flow when discussing Ian Rush, a man whose prowess in front of goal is surely unmatched in the modern era.

Signed from Chester City in the summer of 1980 for £300,000, Rush, born in St Asaph and a boyhood Evertonian, proved to be the bargain of the century. He broke into the team towards the end of 1980/81 (starting the League Cup final replay) and fully established himself the following season, scoring 30 goals by the end of that campaign, as the Reds were crowned champions.

From then on it was goals, goals and more goals for Rush. His partnership with Kenny Dalglish was magnificent during a wonderful era for the club. There are so many Rush moments, it's difficult to know where to start.

Everton suffered more than anyone, notably when he put four past them in a 5-0 Goodison demolition in November 1982, plus the FA Cup final braces in 1986 and 1989. His most prolific season was 1983/84 when he fired 47 in all competitions as Liverpool completed the treble of league, League Cup and European Cup.

His departure to Juventus in 1987 was mourned but Reds' fans were delirious when he returned 12 months later, marking the start of another goalscoring spree as he teamed up with the likes of John Barnes and Peter Beardsley for the first time. Rush helped bring another league championship to Anfield in 1990, the FA Cup in 1992 and the League Cup in 1995, by which time he was club captain. He left in 1996 having scored 346 goals in 660 first-team appearances.

In the 1970s Liverpool had another Welsh striker who brought goals and trophies to the club. John Toshack, from Cardiff, proved the perfect foil for Kevin Keegan and their understanding was often described as telepathic as the Welshman's head frequently created chances for Keegan. That's not to underestimate Toshack's own eye for a goal, with 23 scored in 1975/76 as the Reds won the league and UEFA Cup.

Toshack left in 1978 to become Swansea City player-manager. Three years later the Swans were Liverpool's opponents in the first league game at Anfield following Bill Shankly's death. During the minute's silence before the game, Toshack removed his Swansea tracksuit top to reveal a Liverpool

Rush: Welsh goalscoring legend

John Toshack: 1970s striking hero

shirt. He later moved abroad to manage clubs including Real Sociedad and Real Madrid with success, before becoming Wales boss in 2004, a role he held for six years.

Another Welsh favourite in the 1970s was Joey Jones, whose approach and attitude made him hugely popular on the Kop. He only made 97 first-team appearances, but the Llandudno-born left-back had quite an impact in a relatively short time. Signed from Wrexham in the summer of 1975, Jones made 13 league appearances in his debut season before becoming first-choice in 1976/77, winning the league championship and appearing in the FA Cup final.

Jones will always be associated with the European Cup final in Rome as it was there that he found himself immortalised in one of the fans' most famous banners. *'Joey made the Swiss roll, ate the frogs' legs, now he's munchen Gladbach'* appeared on the terraces in the Olympic Stadium and instantly wrote itself into Liverpool legend. It proved prophetic too as the Reds won 3-1 on a glorious evening. His appearances became more sporadic after that and Jones rejoined the Red Dragons in October 1978.

Going further back in club history Liverpool had two Welshmen who made big contributions to the team in the first full league season after the Second World War. Goalkeeper Cyril Sidlow and full-back Ray Lambert both picked up league championship medals in 1946/47, and were part of the team who reached the FA Cup final in 1950.

More recently Dean Saunders was a club record signing when he joined from Derby County in 1991, although his stay was short and he moved on to Aston Villa a little over 12 months later. Wales international goalkeeper Paul Jones made two loan appearances in 2004, when Jerzy Dudek and Chris Kirkland were both injured.

Craig Bellamy had a short and eventful spell at Anfield when Rafael Benitez signed him in the summer of 2006. He scored nine goals in his single season, most famously the equaliser in the 2-1 victory over Barcelona in the Nou Camp. In February 2011, he remained the last Welshman to wear the red shirt.

What's in a name?

Saunders

The Saunders surname is actually born out of the name Alexander, meaning 'defender of men'.

The shortened Scottish form of Alexander is Sandy and the surnames Saunders, Sanders and Sandison.

For many nameholders however, the origin is old English and locational from Sanderstead in Surrey. This place was recorded in the Anglo-Saxon Chronicles of the year 871 as 'Sondenstede' – 'the house on the sandy land'.

THE ROY EVANS PLAYERS' TREE
– January 31, 1994 to November 12, 1998

Evans

Goalkeepers

*Bruce Grobbelaar 1981-1994,
Durban, South Africa

Mike Hooper 1985-1993,
Bristol, England

David James 1992-1999,
Welwyn Garden City, England

Brad Friedel 1997-1999,
Ohio, USA

Defenders

Steve Nicol, 1981-1994,
Irvine, Scotland

Steve Harkness, 1989-1999,
Carlisle, England

*Rob Jones, 1991-1998,
Wrexham, Wales

Mark Wright, 1991-1997,
Dorchester, England

Stig Inge Bjornebye, 1992-1999,
Elverum, Norway

Dominic Matteo, 1992-2000,
Dumfries, Scotland

Julian Dicks, 1993-1994,
Bristol, England

Neil Ruddock, 1993-1997,
Wandsworth, England

*Phil Babb, 1994-1999,
London, England

John Scales, 1994-1996,
Harrogate, England

Jamie Carragher, 1996-present,
Liverpool, England

Bjorn Tore Kvarme, 1997-1999,
Trondheim, Norway

Midfielders

Ronnie Whelan, 1979-1994,
Dublin, Ireland

Jan Molby, 1984-1995,
Kolding, Denmark

*John Barnes, 1987-1997,
Kingston, Jamaica

*Don Hutchison, 1990-1994,
Gateshead, England

Steve McManaman, 1990-1999,
Liverpool, England

Jamie Redknapp, 1991-2001,
Barton-on-Sea, England

Michael Thomas, 1991-1998,
London, England

Mark Walters, 1991-1995,
Birmingham, England

Paul Stewart, 1992-1993,
Manchester, England

Nigel Clough, 1993-1995,
Sunderland, England

Mark Kennedy, 1995-1998,
Dublin, Ireland

*Jason McAteer, 1995-1999,
Birkenhead, England

David Thompson, 1996-2000,
Birkenhead, England

Patrik Berger, 1996-2003,
Prague, Czech Republic

Paul Ince, 1997-1999,
Ilford, England

Midfielders

Oyvind Leonhardsen,
1997-1999,
Kristiansund, Norway

Danny Murphy, 1997-2004,
Chester, England

Forwards

Ian Rush, 1980-1987,
1988-1996,
St Asaph, Wales

Robbie Fowler, 1992-2001,
2006-2007,
Liverpool, England

Lee Jones, 1992-1996,
Wrexham, Wales

Stan Collymore, 1995-1997,
Stone, England

Michael Owen, 1996-2004,
Chester, England

Karlheinz Riedle, 1997-1999,
Simmerberg-Weiler, Germany

Players used: 39. **By position:** Goalkeepers: 4, Defenders: 12, Midfielders: 17, Forwards: 6. **By nationality:** England: 21, Scotland: 3, Wales: 3, Republic of Ireland: 3, USA: 4, Zimbabwe: 1, Czech Republic: 1, Denmark: 1, Germany: 1 **Key:** On the player information, the first date is the year the player signed for LFC and the second the date of his last senior appearance. * Although born in different countries, players marked with an asterisk either went on to play international football for another nation or were considered to be of a different nationality.

What's in a name?

Evans

Translates to son of Evan, one of the Welsh forms of John.
This gave rise to the other equally popular surname Jones.
It is claimed in some sources that Evan sometimes absorbed the Romano-British first-name Eugenius or 'well-born'.

McManaman

Recorded in several spellings including MacMenamin, McMenamin, MaMacManaman, McManamon, Marmion and O'Merry, this is an anglicised ancient Irish surname. Its original meaning is uncertain. Some believe it comes from the Gaelic "Mag Giolla Mheidre", meaning "the son of the merryman", but this is disputed. The surname is popular in Donegal and West Tyrone.

THE LAST OF THE BOOTROOM GRADUATES

From the latter part of Bill Shankly's reign, through the eras of Bob Paisley, Joe Fagan, Kenny Dalglish and Graeme Souness, there was a shrewd constant at the club: Roy Evans. Considered indispensable by them all, Evans moved through the Anfield ranks until he took the top job in 1994.

His playing career was short, but he was persuaded to hang up his boots at the age of 25 to become a coach at the club. It was a decision he debated – but never regretted.

Evans, born in Bootle, joined the club in 1964, beginning as an amateur. A left-footed defender/midfielder, he made only 11 first-team appearances appearances between 1970 and 1974. By his mid-20s, a crossroads was approaching when manager Bill Shankly unexpectedly announced his retirement. An opportunity to join the coaching staff arose but Evans was not sure it was the right time.

"It did shock me and I turned it down about four or five times," he admitted. "At the age of 25 you are not thinking of being a coach. People like Joe Fagan, Tommy Smith and Ronnie Moran talked me into it. They said: 'You may as well have a go at it, you can always go back to playing if you want'. I was only playing about three games each season because the standard was so high. Playing is always the best thing but it was a great second career."

He had no coaching qualifications, but did possess plenty of enthusiasm. Paisley was the new manager and agreed that Evans should take charge of the reserves. He was largely given free rein to select his own team and implement his own tactics. Seven Central League titles between 1975 and 1983 suggest he did pretty well.

"We had a hard core of kids who were decent players and we also had what we called the 'big heads' from the first team. My job was to put my arm round them sometimes and talk to them if they were out of the team and unhappy. Sometimes I would kick them up the backside and encourage them to work hard to get back in. It was a good learning curve for me because I was dealing with top players and young lads as well. It was probably the best job of all; there was no pressure on it."

Completing the bootroom quartet of Paisley, Joe Fagan and Ronnie Moran, Evans was also encouraged to have his say on first-team affairs. "We were a team behind the team. My opinion was as good as anyone else's. It was important to them that I became involved. We used to mix it round in training sessions. It was great experience from day one for me."

He stepped up to become first-team coach when Joe Fagan replaced Paisley as manager in the summer of 1983. He stayed in that role for 10 years until being promoted to assistant-manager at a time when Graeme Souness' hold on the managerial position was shaky. Early in 1994 Souness was sacked, and Evans stepped up to the top job.

He was hugely honoured. "I felt it was the right time. I felt confident enough in my own ability. I'd worked with some great people and I had the respect of the lads. My only regret is that we never won enough for the team we had."

The 1995 League Cup was his sole honour as boss.

Evans' sides were capable of thrilling football; Robbie Fowler, Steve McManaman and Jamie Redknapp were at their best as Liverpool players under him, while he was also able to unleash a 17-year-old Michael Owen on the Premier League.

Liverpool threatened to win the championship in 1996 and 1997 but, all too often, defensive frailties cost them vital points against modest opposition. Evans felt they needed "one or two experienced players" to go that extra step.

He added: "It was a young side. We struggled to get a back four that was solid. We didn't have that dominant figure at the back to control things. That was how Shanks started, with Ron Yeats. We couldn't find one at the time. I really enjoyed seeing the young players progress and I certainly enjoyed the way we played, but would have liked to do a bit more in terms of trophies."

The beginning of the end for him at Liverpool was the arrival of Gerard Houllier in the summer of 1998. Installed as joint-manager alongside Evans, it was a doomed experiment and one where Evans was always going to be the fall guy.

Roy admitted: "In hindsight, it wasn't the greatest idea. The joint-manager thing was done for the right reasons but we ended up doing the same job. Nobody has made it work and we couldn't. The players felt they had two bosses. It was silly things, 'What time is the bus due?' 'Two o'clock' or 'half past two.'"

Evans' involvement in football has been limited since he left Liverpool. He had a short spell as joint caretaker-manager at Fulham with Karlheinz Riedle, was director of football at Swindon Town and then assisted John Toshack when the former Liverpool striker was Wales boss.

One of the game's good guys, his contribution to the Reds' success over many decades should never be underestimated.

What's in a name?

Fowler

This is an occupation term or nickname for a bird-catcher.
In the medieval period a fowler would have been an important position, and all major houses would have employed one.
Fowl denoted a bird of any kind in Old English, not just the barnyard or game varieties.

Owen

Michael Owen became one of Liverpool's best goalscorers during his seven years with the club.
The Owen surname hails from the Welsh Christian name Swain, most likely to have been connected with the name Ewan. This in itself was developed from the Latin Eugenius (Eugene).
During the last 700 years Owen has been one of the most popular Welsh names, probably second only to Jones within the country....

Hordes of Norwegian Kopites fly into Liverpool each matchday to follow the fortunes of their beloved Reds

Bob Paisley's Reds are reigning league champions as John Arne Riise is born in Alesund, Norway

Liverpool manager Joe Fagan signs Jan Molby from Ajax in 1984

A young boy grows up in the tiny village of Voikkaa in Finland. He lives 200 yards from a football pitch and grows to love the game

Sami Hyypia signs in at Anfield in 1999 and goes on to become a Liverpool legend, making 464 appearances

FROM STROMSGODSET TO VOIKKAA
A SCANDINAVIAN ODYSSEY

Liverpool have long had a famous link with Scandinavia from record European scorelines to legends like Sami Hyypia, who learned his trade in a tiny Finnish village and emerged as one of the club's modern-day giants. The Anfield scouting net has been thrown far and wide across northern Europe in recent decades with stars like John Arne Riise providing an extra sense of identity for the thousands of Norwegians who follow the Reds... ooh aah!

LIVERPOOL HEARTS

History shows that there are many historic links between Merseyside and Scandinavia.

Various place names have Viking origins and indeed, the famous Liverpool dish Scouse is said to be derived from the Norwegian sailors' name for a thick, meaty stew, lapskaus. These days, however, the boats have mostly made way for budget airline flights as thousands of loyal supporters make the pilgrimage to Anfield on matchday.

Liverpool have fans all over Scandinavia but especially so in Norway. The Norwegian fan base which was celebrated in 2010 with the publication of the official book *Liverpoolhjerter (Liverpool Hearts)*. The author Ragnhild Lund Ansnes grew up at the very top of Norway in Alta, only a couple of hours drive from Europe's northernmost point on the mainland, and in her own words "always thought football was over-rated".

She first learned about the lure of the Reds through her Liverpool-mad husband and what followed was a remarkable journey that gave her a fascinating insight into the passions that drive Kopites far and wide.

Ragnhild even revealed how the unforgettable drama of Istanbul interrupted her honeymoon. The events of May 25, 2005 unfortunately clashed with a flight to the island of Tobago which was a major problem for her husband, lifelong Kopite Jostein.

"In the air, the pilot told us it was still 3-3, and that the match was heading into extra-time," said Ragnhild.

"We were blissfully ignorant of Jerzy Dudek's miraculous double-save from Andriy Shevchenko. When we landed, it was still 3-3 and the penalty shoot-out was next.

"With the mobile attached to his ear, he wandered around the airport arrival hall aimlessly, without noticing anything or anyone around him. When they won, the guards started shaking with laughter as my husband slid across the floor on his knees and let out a lengthy "YEEEEEEEEAH!". We were let out first from the arrival hall, past the queue, without even showing our passports. And nine months later... we were a part of the birth boom in Liverpool when our first child arrived!"

Jostein is far from the only dedicated Norwegian Red. Tage Herstad hails from Florø on the west coast of Norway and lives with his wife Kamilla and their two little children, Tia Louise and William Shankly. Ever since Tage was a little boy and Norwegian television broadcast a live game from England every Saturday, he has been following Liverpool FC.

The Kop family: Massed ranks of Reds in Oslo,
left; lifelong Kopite Jostein's home in Norway
– complete with Liverbird – and (bottom) the
tension of the Istanbul shoot-out

What's in a name?

Dudek

*The name Dudek
will always be a
part of Liverpool
history after keeper
Jerzy's heroics in
Istanbul, 2005.*

*It is a popular
Polish surname
which means
'hoopoe'.*

*The hoopoe is a
colourful bird with
a distinctive crown
of feathers which
can be found across
Afro-Eurasia.*

Family trip: Scandinavian
Reds were among the many
who made the journey
to Istanbul

Norwegian Reds: (Right) Tage
Herstad and friends following
the Reds on the road and
meeting former England boss
Graham Taylor (second left).
Below: spreading the message
with Ragnhild in Norway with
former boss Roy Evans and
legends Bruce Grobbelaar and
Phil Neal

He hasn't missed one single game home or away for over seven years. "Some people love fishing, others wood work, some geography and others football. To me, Liverpool FC has become an addiction I can't cure. LFC is everything to me, and the club is my life."

Tage lives for the Reds and is friends with many of the former players like David Fairclough and Bruce Grobbelaar (who is also the Godfather of his son William Shankly). Tage says the interest for LFC is growing among his fellow Norwegians. Every year an increasing number of Norwegians travel overseas to see Liverpool play.

"The Norwegian Supporters' club (LFCSCSB) has over 36,000 paying members. It is crazy! On top of that you have neighbours, friends, parents and grandparents also interested in LFC. There must be around 3-400,000 Norwegians supporting the Reds (and there are only 4.9 million inhabitants in total), by coming to Liverpool, watching the Reds on TV or following their results and news from Merseyside in the papers or on the internet."

For many Scandinavian Kopites, our many historic triumphs in Europe have undoubtedly played a big part in their love of Liverpool. As the modern game has changed, the presence of men from their home countries wearing the famous red shirt has also added to the attraction of coming to Merseyside. Danish trio Daniel Agger, Christian Poulsen and Martin Hansen retain the link today but many others have followed the same path.

FROM RIISE TO HYSEN – FISHING FOR TALENT

The club has enjoyed some famous meetings with Nordic sides on the field. Liverpool played their first European tie against Icelandic side Reykjavik in 1964 and achieved their club record victory against Norwegians Stromsgodset 10 years later, when they recorded an 11-0 win at Anfield.

Of all the Scandinavian countries, Norway has produced the most first-team players for the Reds, with half-a-dozen having donned the Liverbird upon their chests by the end of 2010.

Two of the club's most consistent left-sided performers over the last two decades have hailed from Norway. Most recently, John Arne Riise served the club for seven seasons, winning three European honours and three domestic trophies. A bargain buy from Monaco in 2001, he was known for his ferocious left foot which he used to score the majority of his 31 goals for the club, including a thunderbolt against Manchester United at Anfield which was the catalyst for a popular chant among the Kop faithful to the tune of Bruce Channel's 1960s hit, *Hey! Baby*.

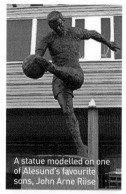
A statue modelled on one of Alesund's favourite sons, John Arne Riise

Salmon fishing: Vegard Heggem

Leonhardsen

Bjornebye

Riise eventually made his way to the banks of the Mersey from the seaport of Alesund in Norway. While Shankly was helping Liverpool net trophies in the 1960s, Alesund was enjoying its status as one of the main herring fishery stations in the country. Riise's home town is also renowned for its Art Nouveau architecture though the style of the statue called 'The Football Player' is somewhat different. Said to be modelled on the Reds' red-headed Norwegian, it can be found outside Alesund's Color Line Stadion.

One of Riise's predecessors on the left flank will be remembered more for his crosses setting up goals. Elverum-born Stig Inge Bjornebye, son of skier Jo Inge (who competed in the 1968 and 1972 Winter Olympics), made 184 appearances in eight years at the club. His best form came as the Reds challenged for the title in the 1996/97 season, but he became surplus to requirements under the stewardship of Gerard Houllier.

The late 1990s saw an influx of Norwegian arrivals at Anfield. Vegard Heggem promised much but his Liverpool career did not hit the heights that it might have done due to a string of injuries that forced him to retire early, but he was a skilful right-sided player who earned a cult hero status with fans.

'Vedgy', as he was popularly known on the Kop, returned home after his playing days and is now in charge of the family business. On his website, he explains: "In 2003 I headed back to my roots at Rennebu in Central Norway and took over the family farm 'Aunan'. The leap from Anfield to Aunan farm was quite considerable! Although I had been preparing for retirement from professional football, it was quite a change. The move from being a high-profile professional footballer to an entrepreneur and farmer has dramatically tested my practical ability to adapt to new circumstances.

"Traditional farming at Aunan has come to an end and neighbouring farmers rent the fields and grassland. The focus has changed to adventure activities and salmon fishing – a major beat on the famous Orkla River being an important part of my heritage.

"Salmon fishing has been a part of my upbringing, close to an obsession. A number of comfortable lodges have been built on the riverbank and the restored potato store has become a restaurant, seminar and training centre. My dream, and hope, is that the concept at Aunan will provide those who come with special memories."

Another Norwegian, Bjorn Tore Kvarme, made a relatively solid start to life at Anfield, but gradually lost form while Oyvind Leonhardsen's seven goals in 49 appearances wasn't enough for Gerard Houllier, who sold him to Tottenham. Finally, young defender Frode Kippe, from Oslo, played just twice in the first team in four years at the club before returning to Lillestrom, the club from whom Liverpool had signed him in 1998.

In the town where I was born

Elverum, Norway
Stig Inge Bjornebye

The town's coat-of-arms were granted in 1988 and feature a gold-coloured owl set against a red background. The owl was chosen as a symbol of wisdom due to the number of schools in the area; it also has its wings raised and an aggressive poise to represent the fighting spirit of Norwegian people.

Elverum and Liverpool have a musical connection thanks to The Wombats. The band were formed in 2003 when Scousers Matthew Murphy and Dan Haggis met Elverum-born bass-guitarist Tord Øverland-Knudsen. Their 2007 album 'A Guide to Love, Loss & Desperation' reached number 11 in the UK charts while their single 'Let's Dance to Joy Division' won Best Dancefloor Filler at the 2008 NME awards.

In the town where I was born

Hvidovre, Denmark
Daniel Agger

A suburb of Copenhagen situated 9km outside the city centre, Hvid means 'white' in Danish. The town gets its name from a white church which could be seen there.

The town's slogan – 'New angles on the future' – emphasises it as a place in constant development, striving for balance between business and personal life.

It is home to one of North Europe's biggest business parks, Avedøre Holme, and Fimbyen – a former military base – now a film studio complex.

Local team Hvidovre IF, formed in 1925, have been Danish champions three times and cup winners once. They play at the 15,000-capacity Hvidovre Stadium with their most famous former player being Peter Schmeichel.

A GREAT DANE CALLED JAN

Jan Molby is widely regarded as the first of Liverpool's successful overseas outfield imports of the modern era, and was the first Nord to wear the red shirt.

The cultured midfielder enjoyed a dozen seasons at Anfield, enthralling fans with his sublime skills, fantastic vision, pinpoint passing and powerful shooting. He was a key part of the Reds' 1986 Double-winning team.

Molby, originally born and raised in the seaport of Kolding, has now settled on Merseyside and is a popular figure, who continues to be closely involved with the fortunes of the club. He is a much in-demand after-dinner speaker where he regales fans with tales from the old days in his now characteristic accent, which combines thick Scouse with native Danish.

Another Dane, Christian Poulsen, became the 13th Nordic player to represent Liverpool in a first-team game when he made his debut against Trabzonspor in August 2010. Poulsen is the fourth Dane to have appeared for the Reds, following in the footsteps of Molby and defenders Torben Piechnik and Daniel Agger. Piechnik was not such a success, playing just two dozen games for the club after being signed by Graeme Souness from FC Copenhagen on the back of some impressive displays during Denmark's triumphant Euro 1992 campaign. He was released by Roy Evans after a disappointing spell of just over a year at Anfield.

Agger has been far more impressive in the Liverpool defence. Signed by Rafa Benitez from hometown club Brondby in January 2006, he quickly became a crowd favourite at Anfield with his calm defending and composure on the ball.

Two ages of Jan: In the thick of it during the 1986 FA Cup final (above), and flanked by team-mates during his testimonial 11 years later

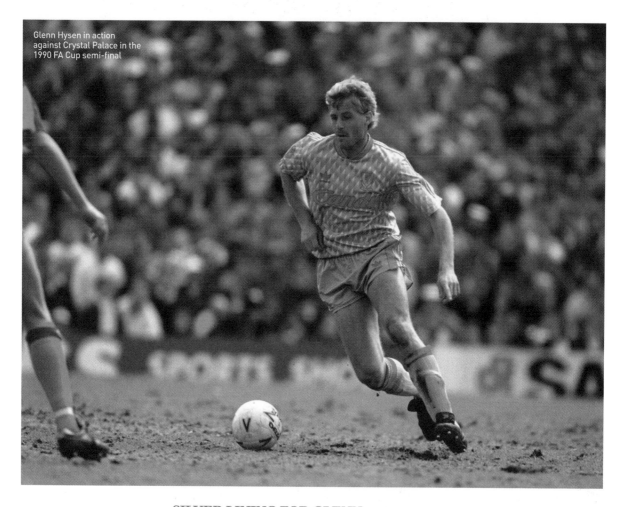

Glenn Hysen in action against Crystal Palace in the 1990 FA Cup semi-final

SILVER LINING FOR GLENN

To date, only one Swede has played for the Reds. Defender Glenn Hysen was brought in by Kenny Dalglish in the summer of 1989.

Hysen arrived from Italian side Fiorentina with an impressive CV. He was captain of the national side and twice a UEFA Cup winner during a successful spell at hometown club IFK Gothenburg.

Most of Hysen's best performances were in his first season under Dalglish, where he won the league championship, but appearances were sparse under Graeme Souness as he left the club with just under 100 appearances to his name.

JARI, OH JARI JARI, OH JARI JARI...JARI LITMANEN
**Completing the complement of Nordic players are a pair of Finns –
two of the greatest players the country has produced.**

Jari Litmanen, born in the southern city of Lahti, is Finland's most
capped player and all-time leading goalscorer. His free transfer move from
Barcelona in 2001 was seen as a real coup by the then Liverpool manager
Gerard Houllier.

With nine goals in 43 games Litmanen's return was decent, but niggling
injuries and being behind the English trio of strikers in Robbie Fowler,
Emile Heskey and Michael Owen in the pecking order meant the nine
times Finnish Footballer of the Year would make a return to Ajax in the
summer of 2002.

Jari Litmanen converts from the
spot against Roma

Sami Hyypia though would play more than 450 games for the club over 10
seasons, captaining the side alongside Fowler in a treble-winning season.
He went on to win every major club honour at Anfield, apart from the
league title and Club World Championship. The legendary centre-back is
regarded as one of the club's greatest ever players and remains among the
best overseas signings since the formation of the Premier League.

Both players had stints under former Reds' boss Roy Hodgson. Litmanen
had a brief spell at Fulham in 2008, while Hodgson, who lists the Finland
national side as one of his previous roles, admitted he attempted to
bring Hyypia back to the club in a player-coach capacity soon after his
appointment as Liverpool manager in the summer of 2010.

As well as managing Finland, Hodgson also had plenty of experience
coaching in domestic football in the Nordic nations. Swedish side Halmstads
were the first of the Nordic clubs he managed, leading them to the league
championship in 1976 despite the side being tipped for relegation.

Following a spell at Bristol City, he returned to Sweden to take over at
Orebro, where he would again win the league. Five successive Allsvenskan
titles were won at Malmo from 1985 to 1989, before spells in Switzerland,
Italy and England preceded a move to FC Copenhagen in Denmark, who he
guided to the league title in 2001. Hodgson also managed Norwegian club
Viking Stavanger during the 2004/05 season.

SAMI – A NATURAL-BORN FOOTBALLER

"Let me write that down for you," Sami Hyypia says for the umpteenth time, grabbing the biro. **"Finnish spelling is never straightforward." Hyypia, Liverpool's longest-serving foreign player since goalkeeper Bruce Grobbelaar, is one of the most genuine players you are ever likely to meet.**

Whether it's out of respect for his friends and former team-mates or out of courtesy in an attempt not to make the writer look foolish, he takes time to scrawl the names of the people that have most influenced his career. "I have been very lucky throughout my life and have been given the kind of breaks that not a lot of people get – so I need to appreciate the roles of everyone who has helped me."

The Finn has travelled a long way from his snow-bound upbringing in Voikkaa, a village with a population of less than 2,000 on the outskirts of Kuusankoski, a paper-mill town 100 miles north east of Helsinki. In one year alone Kuusankoski produces 1.4 million tonnes of paper, which was exported to more than 60 countries. The town is now regarded as the paper capital of Scandinavia.

"But Voikkaa is quite a remote place and the kind of village where everyone knows one another," insists Hyypia, who moved there a year after his birth when his father, a paper merchant, relocated from the southern outpost of Porvoo. Although his father has since retired, his mother still works as a banker in their adopted hometown.

"Voikkaa wouldn't exist if it wasn't for the paper mills and small industries," Hyypia continues. "When people think of Finland, sometimes they think of Lapland. But I can assure you that Voikkaa is very different to that perception.

"You have to remember that there are only three major cities in Finland that you can compare to those in England. They are Helsinki, Tampare and Turku. Finland is quite rural compared to other countries and hasn't adopted urbanisation so a lot of children like me grow up in small villages or the countryside."

In a nation which, in 2009, had just three juvenile offenders locked up behind bars (compared to 3,000 in the UK), Finland has never been a place that has bred mischievous adolescents and Hyypia, like the rest of the population, enjoyed a grounded childhood of education and sport.

"Both of my parents were decent players and I lived 200 yards from a pitch so football was always there. My mum was a very keen goalkeeper and I always used to go and watch her play. I would have a kick-around with

Sami celebrates a goal against
Arsenal with Fabio Aurelio and
Martin Skrtel in pursuit

all of the substitutes while the match was going on to keep warm because
it was very cold.

"I was pretty good at school too. I never really had to stress about results
and exams because I was naturally quite good at academics. That helped
me with football because there was never any pressure on me to make sure
I made it at a professional level because I always thought there would be
another profession out there for me if I didn't.

"Maths was my favourite subject and I enjoyed languages too. Before I
left school, I could speak a bit of three different foreign languages – English,
Swedish and German. It made life easier to learn Dutch when I went to play
in Holland."

Cup success with Mypa –
Sami is crouching, back,
eighth from left

Making an impact in
Holland with Willem II

Early days at
Anfield

Hyypia began playing organised football from the age of seven after being inspired by Liverpool and more specifically a Welsh striking legend. He revealed: "There was more English football on telly when I was growing up than there was Finnish football, so I never supported any Finnish teams. Every Saturday, I would watch and because Liverpool were the best team in England and playing the best football, they were on every single week.

"I really liked the way Ian Rush played. It wasn't just the way he scored all the goals, it was the way he worked so hard and fought for the team. He worked harder than any other player on the pitch and deserved every success he achieved because of it. He was a great example to young players like me because it showed me that if I worked hard on the pitch, I would get the absolute maximum from my game. When he came to Liverpool to coach the strikers under Gerard (Houllier), I was really nervous about meeting him for the first time. It really made me realise then how far I had come from Finland.

"Football was still only a hobby for me though when I was growing up. It was the number one sport for me but I also enjoyed ice hockey and cross-country skiing. In the winter, I'd usually leave football alone because it was quite difficult trying to play underneath half a metre of snow. I still follow ice hockey now and watch the NHL whenever I can because there are quite a lot of Finnish players playing in it.

"I think it was important in my development as a footballer to learn and understand other sports. All of them help each other in some small way – for example, you need a lot of stamina in cross-country skiing just to compete. That can only help you in football because although I have never been the fastest, I have never been substituted in my life because of fatigue."

Hyypia's all-round attributes meant that he never tied himself down to a position in his early days, only becoming a centre-back when he signed youth forms with local Ykkonen [second tier] side, Kumu, at the age of 17. "I played through the spine of the field through my teens. I had a go in each position. I probably enjoyed playing centre-midfield the most because I scored quite a lot of goals from there, but I was never a natural striker.

"Even at an early age when I wasn't as tall, I always had the physical attributes to be a defender. I didn't really start growing until I was 15 or 16, but I was a bit taller than other players. I never obsessed myself with football, though, and by the time I signed for Kumu – who were in the Second Division – everything started to fall into place.

"I had a lot of other interests in my life and never really idolised any team or player. It was only when I started playing men's football for Kumu

In the town where I was born

Porvoo, Finland

Six towns in Finland were established in the middle ages. Porvoo, at the junction of the river Porvoonjoki and the Gulf of Finland, was the second.

The town is known as 'Borga' (castle river) in Swedish, receiving its name from a castle built overlooking it.

Porvoo Cathedral was the site of the opening of the first 'Diet of Finland' in March 1809 when the country was declared an autonomous Grand Duchy by Alexander I during the Finnish war.

The expression 'Porvoon mitta' is linked to a story of the bailiff of Porvoo, who used to collect taxes – but then alter the collection box with a false bottom when delivering the proceeds to the King. He pocketed the difference and lived lavishly. It means 'plentiful supply' in the modern day.

A youthful
Sami in action
for his country

that I started taking football really seriously. I was lucky to play with a defender called Esa Pekonen. He'd played a few years in Sweden with AIK Stockholm and returned home to finish his career. I learnt a lot off him because he was a Finnish international and a role model to a lot of young players. I saw what he had achieved in his career and wanted to emulate it. But I never thought I'd end up achieving what I did."

Hyypia believes the second pivotal moment that aided his development as a player came once again by chance when he was midway through pre-season training with Kumu.

"It was winter time and we were playing a friendly game indoors," Sami explains. "They didn't have the synthetic surfaces in Finland like they do now in England. It was all thin carpet and I would finish training sessions with deep cuts all over my knees. Luckily though, on this one occasion, the Finnish Under-18s side were camping for a few weeks near where we were playing and had arranged to train shortly after our friendly match had finished.

"Before the game, our coach was speaking with the national team coach by chance and told him to keep an eye on me. I played the game and did quite well, then straight after the match had finished, the national coach came to the changing rooms and asked my coach if I could come back the following day and train with the national squad.

"I would say that was my biggest break in football because in Finland the bigger teams in the top league aren't really interested in players that haven't represented the national team at some level. It is also very difficult to get into the national team unless you play for one of the big teams, so it's a vicious circle. From then on, I was playing at a good standard with international games and other teams started to notice me. This moment really kick-started my career."

But before Hyypia's career could really begin, he had to embark on national service with the Finnish army. "I never seriously believed I would go and play abroad, but just in case I did, I completed my national service when I was still young. Some of the younger players coming through now are facing problems because they have been abroad for years but are being told by the government that they have to come back at inappropriate times. Most people have to do half a year, but they can't just say to the club who they are contracted to and who pay their wages that they are going home for half a year and to be happy with that.

"I could see that this might be a problem in the future if I ever did move abroad and so decided to get it out of the way as quickly as possible after I finished my studies. I was there for 11 months in total. We had to sleep in the woods in a little tent night after night and walk miles and miles for food and water. It was for conditioning.

"I had to shave all my hair off too for the first time. Beforehand, I had long hair like a mullet at the back, but the army wouldn't allow that. I kept the short hair for years after – but now the longer look is returning. It was a tough time, but looking back, it was a good experience for me. It would be a good experience for any young man."

Upon his return to football, Hyypia was spotted by MyPa-47 boss Harri Kampman after impressing in the Kumu team alongside cousins Mika Hernesniemi and Toni Huttunen. "We were all brought up in Voikkaa so for a village with so few people to have three footballers play in the top league of Finnish football is quite something. Me and Toni signed for MyPa, and Mika went elsewhere. Toni stayed at MyPa for the rest of his career, apart from a very short spell at Falkirk more than 10 years ago.

"It was an easy decision to leave Kumu. MyPa were the biggest relatively

The Kop offer
their salute

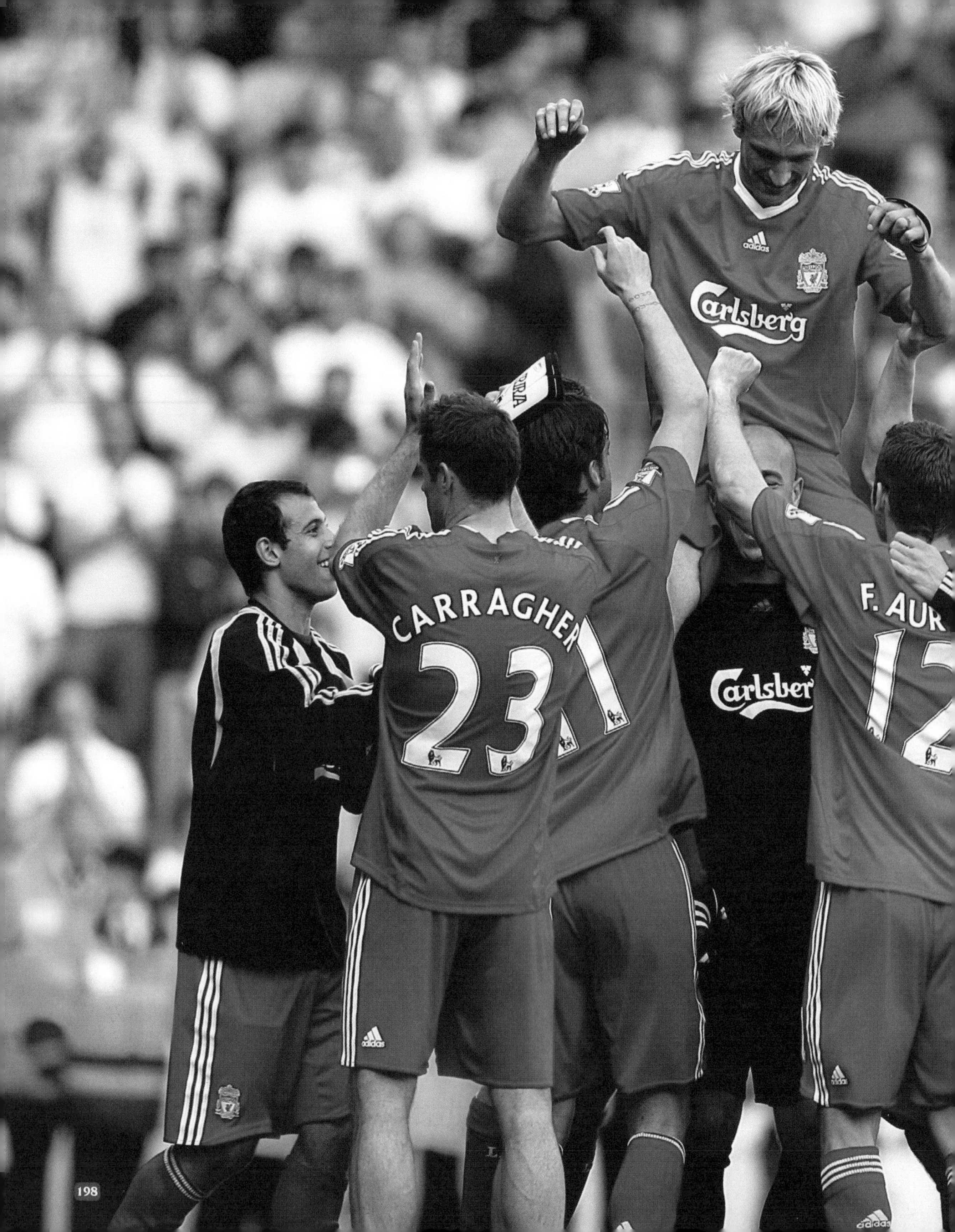
Carlsberg
CARRAGHER
23
F. AUR
Carlsber

Fond farewell:
Sami's Liverpool
team-mates give
thanks following
the defender's
final appearance
in a red shirt,
at Anfield v
Tottenham
Hotspur, May
2009

"...I had no regrets. If I didn't move away when I did, my chance to play in Europe and in England with Liverpool may have passed me by"

local team around and a family club, where everyone was together in defeat and victory."

During his four years at MyPa of Anjalankoski, another club spawned from a paper town in the south of Finland, Hyypia helped his team to three second-place finishes in the Veikkausliga – each time finishing behind champions HJK Helsinki. He did win the Finnish Cup on two occasions, however, featuring in the same side as Jari Litmanen when MyPa defeated FF Jaro in 1992 immediately before Litmanen was sold to Ajax.

"Jari scored in the cup final and that made Ajax move for him. He was a brilliant player even then," Hyypia says with a humbling smile. "I already knew about him before I signed for MyPa, but I didn't know just how good he actually was. Seeing him in training and in games was special for me because it is not very often that a player in Finland can say that he was a team-mate of the country's greatest ever player at such a young age."

Then, three years later, it was Hyypia's turn to score a winner in the cup final. "It turned out to be my last game. We won 1-0 and I scored with a header at the front-post. I didn't know I was leaving at the time so it was a real high point for me. The cup final was at the end of October then by February I'd moved to Holland."

Hyypia left MyPa barely a year before his former club drew Liverpool in the European Cup-Winners' Cup, with the Reds eventually winning through to the second round, 4-1 on aggregate.

"I remember watching the game on my TV in Holland. But I had no regrets. If I didn't move away from MyPa when I did, my chance to play in Europe and in England with Liverpool may have passed me by."

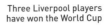

Three Liverpool players have won the World Cup

1998: Gerard Houllier joins the club – French revolution begins at Anfield

Rafael Benitez's Spanish influence brings success at home and abroad

Double Dutch: Westerveld and Meijer are the club's first imports from the lowlands

The Reds' Italian trio endure mixed success

OUR WORLD FAMILY

REDS' GLOBAL APPEAL

The growing global influence at the club is reflected by the breadth of nationalities to have represented Liverpool FC. A trend of the Premier League era, the club has also benefited from the continental working methods of Gerard Houllier and Rafael Benitez – both of whom maintained the club's traditions and continued the success. We celebrate the overseas players who have worn the red shirt, and the unique club of LFC World Cup winners

WORLD CUP TREE
– 1950 - 2010 –

1950
Laurie Hughes 1943-1957,
Liverpool, England

1958
Alan A'Court 1952-1964,
Rainhill, England
Tommy Younger 1956-1959,
Edinburgh, Scotland

1966
Roger Hunt 1958-1969,
Golborne, England
Ian Callaghan 1960-1978,
Liverpool, England

1978
Kenny Dalglish 1977-1990,
Glasgow, Scotland
Graeme Souness 1978-1984,
Edinburgh, Scotland

1982
Phil Thompson 1971-1983,
Kirkby, England
Phil Neal 1974-1985,
Irchester, England
Alan Hansen 1977-1990,
Sauchie, Scotland
Kenny Dalglish 1977-1990,
Glasgow, Scotland
Graeme Souness 1978-1984,
Edinburgh, Scotland

1986
Steve Nicol 1981-1995,
Ayrshire, Scotland
Jan Molby 1984-1995,
Kolding, Denmark

1990
Ronnie Whelan 1979-1994,
Dublin, Republic of Ireland
Gary Gillespie 1983-1991,
Stirling, Scotland
Steve McMahon 1985-1991,
Liverpool, England
**Steve Staunton 1986-1991;
1998-2000,**
Drogheda, Republic of Ireland
*John Barnes 1987-1997,
Kingston, Jamaica
Peter Beardsley 1987-1991,
Newcastle, England
*Ray Houghton 1987-1992,
Glasgow, Scotland
Glenn Hysen, 1989-1992,
Gothenburg, Sweden

1994
Ronnie Whelan 1979-1994,
Dublin, Republic of Ireland
**Stig Inge Bjornebye
1992-2000,**
Elverum, Norway

1998
**Steve McManaman
1990-1999,**
Liverpool, England
**Stig Inge Bjornebye
1992-2000,**
Elverum, Norway
Paul Ince 1997-1999,
Ilford, England
Michael Owen 1996-2004,
Chester, England
**Oyvind Leonhardsen
1997-1999,**
Kristiansund, Norway
Brad Friedel 1998-2000,
Ohio, USA

2002
Michael Owen 1996-2004,
Chester, England
Dietmar Hamann 1999-2006,
Waldasson, Germany
Emile Heskey 2000-2004,
Leicester, England
Jerzy Dudek 2001-2007,
Rybnik, Poland
*Abel Xavier 2002-2004,
Nampula, Mozambique
El Hadji Diouf 2002-2005,
Daqar, Sénegal

2006
Jamie Carragher 1996-present,
Liverpool, England
Steven Gerrard 1997-present,
Whiston, England

2006 (cont)
Harry Kewell 2003-2008,
Smithfield, Australia
Xabi Alonso 2004-2009,
Toloso, Spain
Luis Garcia 2004-2007,
Badalona, Spain
Peter Crouch 2005-2008,
Macclesfield, England

2010
Jamie Carragher 1996-present,
Liverpool, England
Steven Gerrard 1997-present,
Whiston, England
Dirk Kuyt 2006-present,
Katwijk, Holland
Daniel Agger 2006-present,
Hvidovre, Denmark
Fernando Torres 2007-2011,
Madrid, Spain
Javier Mascherano 2007-2010,
San Lorenzo, Argentina
Martin Skrtel 2008-present,
Handlova, Slovakia
Glen Johnson 2009-present,
London, England
Maxi Rodriguez 2009-present,
Rosario, Argentina
**Sotirios Kyrgiakos
2009-present,**
Trikala, Greece

NOTES: Salif Diao did not sign a contract with Liverpool until after the 2002 World Cup.
Milan Jovanovic didn't sign officially for Liverpool until after his 2010 World Cup participation.
Players marked with an asterisk represented a different country in the tournament than the nation they were born in.
On the player info, the first date is the year the player signed for LFC and the second the date of his last senior appearance.

WORLD CUP WINNERS

Five members of the Liverpool family have sampled the feeling of receiving the highest honour in the international game. However, only two of them have actually played in the final – Roger Hunt in 1966, and Fernando Torres 44 years later.

Three others – Ian Callaghan, Gerry Byrne and Pepe Reina – can lay claim to World Cup winners' medals, although of the three, only Callaghan played any part at the finals (winning one cap against France during the group phase in '66), Byrne and Reina having to make do with non-playing roles as part of squad in 1966 and 2010.

Members of the Reds' squad have competed in the World Cup finals on a regular basis since Laurie Hughes represented England in the 1950 showpiece event in Brazil.

Hunt played all six of England's games in 1966, the centre-forward progressing from Cheshire League football with Stockton Heath to parading the famous Jules Rimet Trophy around Wembley Stadium.

Hunt was a key figure in Alf Ramsey's line-up from the start of the competition. He started all three of his country's group games, scoring in the 2-0 win against Mexico before grabbing both England's goals in the 2-0 win over France. Hunt also started the quarter-final against Argentina and the semi-final against Portugal, before starting the final against West Germany.

Liverpool had to wait 44 years for their next active World Cup winner. Torres played a lesser role in Spain's 2010 success than Hunt did in England's 1966 triumph. However, the striker was a vital squad member as the Spanish team followed up their Euro 2008 victory be taking the game's highest prize for the first time in South Africa.

Torres went into the tournament looking to shrug off an injury which had sidelined him for the final month of the Premier League season. After making a sub appearance in the opening group game against Switzerland (a shock 1-0 loss), he started the next two matches as the Spanish saw off Honduras and Chile.

Coach Vicente del Bosque also started Torres in the next two matches against Portugal and Paraguay, but introduced him as a substitute in the semi-final win over Germany. He also came off the bench as a late sub for David Villa in the final against Holland – for whom Dirk Kuyt started – playing a part in the extra-time winner by Andres Iniesta.

One other Liverpool player has appeared in a World Cup final: Dietmar Hamann was a runner-up with Germany in 2002.

Below: Roger Hunt (1966) and Fernando Torres (2010), winners of the ultimate prize in international football

HOULLIER – FRENCH REVOLUTIONARY

When Gerard Houllier decided to study in Liverpool for a year as part of his degree in English, he had little idea of the impact it would have on his future employment.

A keen football fan, as a student he spent 1969/70 working as an assistant at Alsop Comprehensive School. While there he attended his first Reds' match on September 16, 1969 – a 10-0 thrashing of Irish team Dundalk in the Inter-Cities Fairs Cup. A strong bond with Liverpool FC was born that night as he watched Bill Shankly's side.

Born in Thérouanne within the Nord-Pas-de-Calais region of France, Houllier returned to teaching in France before starting his management career at Le Torquet Athletic Club in 1973. After three years there, he spent the next six at Nœux-les-Mines as head coach, winning two consecutive promotions into Ligue 2 before moving to Lens in 1982. He also took them to promotion and qualification for the UEFA Cup before landing a plum job with Paris Saint-Germain in 1985. He duly guided PSG to the French title the following year.

In 1988, Houllier was appointed technical director and France assistant under Michel Platini. He became boss in 1992, but resigned a year later after France failed to qualify for the 1994 World Cup. He remained as a technical director and when France won the World Cup in 1998, many in the camp paid tribute to Houllier's contribution.

Below: Gerard Houllier, who helped transform the Reds both on and off the pitch

He initially joined Liverpool as joint-manager with Roy Evans in the summer of 1998, but the partnership didn't work out and after just a dozen league games, Evans stood down, allowing Houllier to assume sole command. Liverpool ended that season in seventh and though they improved in 1999/2000, defeat at Bradford City on the final day meant they narrowly failed to qualify for the Champions League.

The following season would be Houllier's finest hour at the helm as the Reds finished third to reach Europe's highest-prized competition. But it was in the cup competitions that the Reds really excelled, winning a treble of the League Cup, FA Cup and UEFA Cup.

The improvement continued in 2001/02 as Liverpool finished second to Arsenal in the Premier League, and hopes were high that the long wait for the title may soon be over. Ultimately that summer's transfers failed to pay off and though they landed the League Cup again, the Reds' league form deteriorated and they had to settle for fifth. Despite finishing a place higher in 2003/04, it was decided that the club needed a change of direction and Houllier left the club by mutual consent.

GERARD HOULLIER TREE
– November 12, 1998 to May 24, 2004

Players

Goalkeepers

David James 1992-1999,
Welwyn Garden City, England
Brad Friedel 1997-1999,
Ohio, USA
Sander Westerveld 1999-2001,
Enschede, Holland
Pegguy Arphexad 2000-2002,
Guadeloupe, France
Jerzy Dudek 2001-2007,
Rybnik, Poland
Chris Kirkland 2001-2004,
Leicester, England
Patrice Luzi 2002-2004,
Ajaccio, France
Paul Jones 2004-2004,
Chirk, Wales

Defenders

**Steve Staunton 1986-1991
and 1998-2000,**
Drogheda, Republic of Ireland
Steve Harkness 1989-1999,
Carlisle, England
Stig Inge Bjornebye 1992-1999,
Elverum, Norway
Dominic Matteo 1992-2000,
Dumfries, Scotland
* Phil Babb 1994-1999,
London, England
* Jason McAteer 1995-1999,
Birkenhead, England
Jamie Carragher 1996-present,
Liverpool, England
Bjorn Tore Kvarme 1997-1999,
Trondheim, Norway
Stephen Wright 1997-2002,
Liverpool, England
Vegard Heggem 1998-2000,
Trondheim, Norway
Rigobert Song 1999-2000,
Nkenlicock, Cameroon
Sami Hyypia 1999-2009,
Porvoo, Finland
Stephane Henchoz 1999-2004,
Billenz, Switzerland
* Djimi Traore 1999-2006,
Laval, France
Frode Kippe 1999-2001,
Oslo, Norway
Markus Babbel 2000-2002,
Munich, Germany
Christian Ziege 2000-2001,
Berlin, Germany
Gregory Vignal 2000-2003,
Montpellier, France
John Arne Riise 2001-2008,
Molde, Norway
* Abel Xavier 2002-2002,
Nampula, Mozambique
Jon Otsemobor 2002-2003,
Liverpool, England
Steve Finnan 2003-2008,
Limerick, Republic of Ireland

Midfielders

Steve McManaman 1990-1999,
Liverpool, England
Jamie Redknapp 1991-2001,
Barton-On-Sea, England
Patrik Berger 1996-2003,
Prague, Czech Republic
David Thompson 1996-2000,
Birkenhead, England
Paul Ince 1997-1999,
Ilford, England
Oyvind Leonhardsen 1997-1999,
Kristiansund, Norway
Steven Gerrard 1997-Present,
Whiston, England
Danny Murphy 1997-2004,
Chester, England
Jean-Michel Ferri 1998-1999,
Lyon, France
Dietmar Hamann 1999-2006,
Waldasson, Germany
Vladimir Smicer 1999-2005,
Vernerice, Czech Republic
Layton Maxwell 1999-1999,
St Asaph, Wales
Gary McAllister 2000-2002,
Motherwell, Scotland
Nick Barmby 2000-2002,
Hull, England
Igor Biscan 2000-2005,
Zagreb, Croatia
Bernard Diomede 2000-2001,
Guadeloupe, France
Richie Partridge 2000-2004,
*Dublin, Republic
Of Ireland*
Salif Diao 2002-2005,
Kedogou Tallie, Senegal
Bruno Cheyrou 2002-2004,
Suresnes, France
John Welsh 2002-2005,
Liverpool, England
Harry Kewell 2003-2008,
Smithfield, Australia
Anthony Le Tallec 2003-2005,
Hennebont, France

Forwards

**Robbie Fowler 1992-2001,
and 2006-2007,**
Liverpool, England
Michael Owen 1996-2004,
Chester, England
Karlheinz Riedle 1997-1999,
Simmerberg-Weiler, Germany
Sean Dundee 1998-1999,
Durban, South Africa
Jon Newby 1998-2000,
Warrington, England
Titi Camara 1999-2000,
Conakry, Guinea
Erik Meijer 1999-2000,
Meersen, Holland
Neil Mellor 1999-2005,
Sheffield, England
Emile Heskey 2000-2004,
Leicester, England
Jari Litmanen 2001-2002,
Lahti, Finland
Nicolas Anelka 2001-2002,
Versailles, France
Milan Baros 2001-2005,
Valassake, Czech Republic
El Hadji Diouf 2002-2004,
Dagar, Senegal
**Florent Sinama-Pongolle
2003-2006,**
Saint-Pierre, France

Players Used: 66
By position: Goalkeepers: 8
Defenders: 22, Midfielders: 22
Strikers: 14
By nationality: England: 19,
France: 10, Norway: 6, Germany:
4, Republic Of Ireland: 5, Czech
Republic: 3, Holland: 2, Wales: 2,
Scotland: 2, Senegal: 2, USA: 1,
Poland: 1, Cameroon: 1, Finland:
1, Switzerland: 1, Portugal: 1,
Croatia: 1, Australia: 1, South
Africa: 1, Guinea: 1, Croatia: 1
* Although born in different countries,
players marked with an asterisk either
went on to play international football for
another nation or were considered to
be of a different nationality.

FRENCH LESSONS

The arrival of Gerard Houllier to the Liverpool coaching hierarchy in 1998 brought a Gallic flavour to Anfield. The man from Lille quickly brought a French influence to the squad after being handed sole charge of the team in November of that year.

Initially recruited that summer as joint-manager with Roy Evans, Houllier brought in a whole team of Frenchmen before leaving the role in 2004. However, few of the Reds' French contingent were big successes. The first, Jean-Michel Ferri, was a case in point, making just two appearances after being signed for £1.5 million from Istanbulspor as midfield cover for captain Paul Ince.

The Istanbul link was significant, however as the biggest influence the Reds' French players have had on the family came in the Turkish capital following Houllier's departure. Houllier's 'French Gems' Florent Sinama-Pongolle and Anthony Le Tallec played their parts in helping Rafael Benitez's team to the UEFA Champions League final in 2005. Djimi Traore started the final against AC Milan, and produced his best display for Liverpool as they overcame a 3-0 deficit to end the night – or following morning – by parading the famous trophy in front of their jubilant supporters.

Djibril Cisse also figured in that final as a late substitute for Milan Baros in normal time. Cisse, signed by Houllier before he departed the club, had a mixed time at Anfield, in part due to injuries. But the former Auxerre striker kept his head to slot home one of the penalty kicks in the dramatic shoot-out which saw Liverpool crowned champions of Europe.

French influence: Jean-Michel Ferri (below) and Djimi Traore (below right, centre) enjoyed differing fortunes at Anfield

Cup hero: Djibril Cisse, on target during the 2006 FA Cup final, holds aloft the trophy

Cisse also played a key role on the big stage the following season in what turned out to be his final appearance for the club. His fine goal in the FA Cup final against West Ham at Cardiff brought Liverpool back into the game after they trailed 2-0 to the Hammers inside 28 minutes. It paved the way for yet another penalty shoot-out success following a dramatic 3-3 draw after extra time.

Other recruits such as Bruno Cheyrou and Bernard Diomede failed to provide the Kop with the French flair they had expected. But looking to the future, striker David Ngog has made a promising start to his Liverpool career after being brought in by Rafael Benitez in the summer of 2008. And following the takeover by Fenway Sports Group in the autumn of 2010, a Frenchman will have a big influence on new arrivals from 2011 with Damien Comolli being brought in to the club as director of football strategy.

Arles, France
Djibril Cisse

Arles has a huge Roman influence. Taken in 123BC, it became a key city through a canal link to the Mediterranean Sea.

Arles became the HQ for Roman Emperors during military campaigns and is home to a collection of Roman and Romanesque Monuments. The collection is listed as a UNESCO World Heritage Site.

Vincent van Gogh spent 15 months there from February 1888, producing over 300 paintings and drawings, including Starry Night Over the Rhone and Café Terrace at Night. It was in Arles on the night of December 23, 1888, that the Dutch artist cut off part of his ear with a razor blade while in a brothel.

Jeanne Louise Calment lived in Arles for her entire life before her death on August 4, 1997, at the age of 122 years and 164 days old – giving her the longest confirmed human life span in history.

OUT OF AFRICA

The impact made by Liverpool's South African players is covered in Journey Three of this book. However, the rest of the continent has also provided Liverpool with half-a-dozen players during the last decade or so.

Rigobert Song went on to become an iconic figure in the history of African football. The Indomitable Lion won an astonishing 137 caps for Cameroon, appearing in four World Cup and numerous African Cup of Nations tournaments, winning the competition twice in 2000 and 2002. He was brought to Liverpool by Gerard Houllier in the late 1990s, and figured in several defensive positions.

He was followed to Anfield by fellow African Titi Camara. The Guinea international became a cult figure at the club and was a firm fans' favourite during his short stay at Anfield before he moved on to West Ham United.

The next Africans to arrive at Anfield came in the summer of 2002 on the back of impressive performances at the World Cup finals. Houllier splashed the cash on Senagalese stars El-Hadji Diouf and Salif Diao. The Liverpool manager promised fans that Diouf would have fans on the edge of their seats but he failed to justify his price tag, while Diao struggled to press his claims to be a regular in the starting line-up.

More recently, midfielder Momo Sissoko blossomed after being signed by Rafael Benitez from his former club Valencia. The French-born Mali international quickly established himself as one of the most promising holding midfielders in the game, before a serious eye injury affected his confidence and form.

The last African to play for the Reds was another French-born player. Youngster Nabil El-Zhar arrived at Liverpool from St Etienne in 2006, but the forward has found his opportunities few and far between. A full Moroccan international, he spent the 2010/11 season on loan at Greek side PAOK.

Made their mark: Momo Sissoko impressed during his Reds' spell Opposite page: Fans' favourite Titi Camara pays tribute to his father, who had passed away only hours before, after scoring against West Ham in 1999

"Guinea international Titi Camara became a cult figure and was a firm fans' favourite during his short stay at Anfield"

RAFAEL BENITEZ TREE
– June 16, 2004 to June 3, 2010

Players

Goalkeepers

Jerzy Dudek 2001-2007,
Rybnik, Poland
Chris Kirkland 2001-2004,
Leicester, England
Scott Carson 2005-2006,
Whitehaven, England
Jose Reina 2005-Present,
Madrid, Spain
Daniele Padelli 2007-2007,
Lecco, Italy
Charles Itandje 2007-2008,
Bobigny, France
Diego Cavalieri 2008-2010,
Sao Paulo, Brazil

Defenders

Jamie Carragher 1996-Present,
Liverpool, England
Stephen Warnock 1998-2007,
Ormskirk, England
Sami Hyypia 1999-2009,
Porvoo, Finland
* Djimi Traore 1999-2006,
Laval, France
Stephane Henchoz 1999-2004,
Billenz, Switzerland
John Arne Riise 2001-2008,
Molde, Norway
Steve Finnan 2003-2008,
Limerick, Republic Of Ireland
Zak Whitbread 2003-2005,
Houston, USA
Josemi Rey 2004-2005,
Malaga, Spain
David Raven 2004-2005,
Wirral, England
Mauricio Pellegrino 2005-2005,
Leones, Argentina
Antonio Barragan 2005-2006,
Sevilla, Spain
Miki Roque 2005-2006,
Tremp, Spain
Jack Hobbs 2005-2007,
Portsmouth, England

Defenders

Jan Kromkamp 2006-2006,
Makkinga, Holland
Daniel Agger 2006-Present,
Hvidovre, Denmark
Fabio Aurelio 2006-2010;
2010-Present,
Sao Carlos, Brazil
Gabriel Paletta 2006-2007,
Buenos Aires, Argentina
James Smith 2006-2006,
Liverpool, England
Stephen Darby 2006-Present,
Liverpool, England
Alvaro Arbeloa 2007-2009,
Salamanca, Spain
Emiliano Insua 2007-Present,
Buenos Aires, Argentina
Martin Kelly 2007-Present,
Bolton, England
Daniel Ayala 2007-Present,
Sevilla, Spain
Martin Skrtel 2008-Present,
Handlova, Slovakia
Andrea Dossena 2008-2009,
Lodi, Italy
Philipp Degen 2008-Present,
Holstein, Switzerland
Glen Johnson 2009-Present,
London, England
Sotirios Kyrgiakos 2009-Present,
Trikala, Greece
Jack Robinson 2010-Present,
Warrington, England

Midfielders

Steven Gerrard 1997-Present,
Whiston, England
Dietmar Hamann 1999-2006,
Waldasson, Germany
Vladimir Smicer 1999-2005,
Vernerice, Czech Republic
* Darren Potter 1999-2007,
Liverpool, England
Igor Biscan 2000-2005,
Zagreb, Croatia

Midfielders

Richie Partridge 2000-2004,
Dublin, Republic Of Ireland
Salif Diao 2002-2005,
Kedogou Tallie, Senegal
John Welsh 2002-2005,
Liverpool, England
Harry Kewell 2003-2008,
Smithfield, Australia
Anthony Le Tallec 2003-2005,
Hennebont, France
Xabi Alonso 2004-2009,
Tolosa, Spain
Antonio Nunez 2004-2005,
Madrid, Spain
Mark Smyth 2002-2005,
Liverpool, England
* Mohamed Sissoko 2005-2007,
Mont Saint Agnain, France
Boudewijn Zenden 2005-2007,
Maastricht, Holland
* Mark Gonzalez 2005-2007,
Durban South Africa
Jermaine Pennant 2006-2008,
Nottingham, England
Danny Guthrie 2006-2007,
Shrewsbury, England
Lee Peltier 2006-2007,
Liverpool, England
* Nabil El Zhar 2006-Present,
Ales, France
Javier Mascherano 2007-2010,
San Lorenzo, Argentina
Yossi Benayoun 2007-2010,
Dimona, Israel
Lucas Leiva 2007-Present,
Dourados, Brazil
Sebastian Leto 2007-2007,
Alejandro Korn, Argentina
Damien Plessis 2007-2009,
Neuville-Aux-Bois, France
Albert Riera 2008-2010,
Mallorca, Spain
Jay Spearing 2008-Present,
Wirral, England
Alberto Aquilani 2009-Present,
Rome, Italy
Maxi Rodriguez 2010-Present,
Rosario, Argentina

Forwards

Robbie Fowler 1992-2001
and 2006-2007,
Liverpool, England
Neil Mellor 1999-2005,
Sheffield, England
Milan Baros 2001-2005,
Valassake, Czech Republic
Florent Sinama-Pongolle
2003-2006,
Saint-Pierre, France
Luis Garcia 2004-2007,
Badalona, Spain
Djibril Cisse 2004-2006,
Arles, France
Fernando Morientes 2005-2006,
Cilleros, Spain
Peter Crouch 2005-2008,
Macclesfield, England
Dirk Kuyt 2006-Present,
Katwijk, Holland
Craig Bellamy 2006-2007,
Cardiff, Wales
Ryan Babel 2007-2011,
Amsterdam, Holland
Fernando Torres 2007-2011,
Madrid, Spain
Andriy Voronin 2007-2009,
Odessa, Ukraine
Dani Pacheco 2007-Present,
Malaga, Spain
Robbie Keane 2008-2009,
Dublin, Republic Of Ireland
David Ngog 2008-Present,
Gennevilliers, France
Nathan Eccleston 2009-Present,
Manchester, England

RAFA ROOTS

Rafael Benitez's route to success with Liverpool can be traced back to his time serving Real Madrid. A midfielder, he appeared only in the lower categories of the club, where he remained for seven years. A serious injury dashed his hopes of establishing himself any higher, and he left to join AD Parta in 1981.

Below: Rafael Benitez smiles for the cameras at his official Anfield introduction, June 2004

Players Used: 83
By position: Goalkeepers: 7, Defenders: 30, Midfielders: 29, Strikers: 17
By nationality: England: 22, Spain: 13, France: 7, Argentina: 6, Holland: 4, Republic of Ireland: 4, Italy: 3, Brazil: 3, Switzerland: 2, Czech Republic: 2, Poland: 1, Norway: 1, Finland: 1, USA: 1, Denmark: 1, Slovakia: 1, Greece: 1, Germany: 1, Croatia: 1, Australia: 1, Senegal: 1, Chile: 1, Israel: 1, Wales: 1, Ukraine: 1, Mali: 1, Morocco: 1
* Although born in different countries, players marked with an asterisk either went on to play international football for another nation or were considered to be of a different nationality.

Benitez played for three-and-a-half seasons in the Spanish Second and Third Divisions before ending his career at Linares. While there he was dogged by a knee injury and after missing an entire season with the problem, he was forced to retire at the age of 26. Benitez did at least have something to fall back on, having completed a degree in Physical Education at the Polytechnic University of Madrid. From there it was time to begin his fledgling coaching career.

Benitez started with the Castilla B youth team, coaching the side to two league titles in three seasons. His final year, 1989, also saw him obtain the qualification of 'national football coach'. From there, he returned to Real Madrid, where he was appointed as coach of the youth team's B side on a part-time basis. At the same time he was putting his degree in PE to good use working as a fitness trainer and staff co-ordinator at the Abasota gymnasium in Madrid.

Having won another league title with the B side, Benitez took charge of the Madrid Under-19s side, winning the Spanish U19 Cup in 1991 and 1993 – the latter year also seeing the side clinch a league and cup double. The success earned promotion to work as assistant for Real Madrid B during the 1992/93 season, before he became head coach the following season. Benitez was already proving to be a single-minded young manager with a clear vision of how the game should be played.

By the end of this first season he had led them to seventh in the Spanish Second Division. Real Madrid boss Vincente del Bosque was impressed with Benitez's training methods and tactical awareness, and appointed him as his assistant for the last few months of the 1993/94 season. He returned to coach the B side for the following campaign, before deciding to emerge from del Bosque's shadow. Real Valladolid offered Benitez the chance to become manager in 1995, and he decided the time was right to quit the Bernabeu.

Up to this point management had come easily to Benitez, but it wasn't long before he discovered the harsh realities of La Liga. After just two wins in 23 games and with Valladolid firmly rooted to the bottom of the table, Benitez left the club.

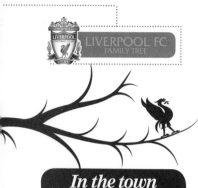

In the town where I was born

Aluche, Madrid

Rafa Benitez

Rafa Benitez spent his early years in the Aluche district of the Spanish capital. Aluche is a barrio of the city, situated in the south-west, in the Latina district. Aluche takes its name from the Luche creek that formerly flowed through the neighbourhood.

With 75,871 inhabitants, it is the largest of Madrid's barrios (according to the 2001 census). Many of its streets are named after towns and villages of the province of Toledo.

Benitez grew up on General Romero Basart Street before his family moved to Majadahonda, a district situated 16 kilometres north-west of Madrid. After a few years, the family settled in the popular suburb of Pozuelo de Alarcon.

He wasn't unemployed for long. Osasuna, then in the second tier, appointed Benitez as their manager in 1996 but after just one win in his first nine games he was out of work again. Despite now having a record of three wins in 32 games as a manager, he was still in demand and Extremadura appointed him as their boss. It was to be a solid marriage. With 23 wins in 42 games he steered them to promotion in his first season – although keeping them in La Liga would prove a lot harder. They finished 17th and lost a relegation play-off to Villarreal. Benitez quit and decided to study coaching methods in England and Italy, spending time at clubs including Arsenal and Manchester United.

Benitez returned to coaching in 2000, leading Tenerife back into the top flight. That prompted Valencia, who were losing Hector Cuper to Inter Milan, to offer him the manager's job at the Mestalla. Valencia fans weren't overwhelming in their appproval of the appointment but by the end of the 2001/02 season, Benitez had landed them their first Spanish title for 31 years. They finished fifth the following season and then in 2004 won La Liga again, as well as the UEFA Cup.

However, Benitez was unhappy with the direction his club was taking. He wanted to overhaul his playing staff and inject fresh life into the squad. Benitez claimed he asked sporting director Jesus Garcia Pitarch – in charge of all transfer activity at the club – for a sofa [a defender], but instead received a lamp [an attacking midfielder]. It was the beginning of the end for Benitez.

Summer 2004 saw changes at Anfield. Gerard Houllier's tenure at the club was at an end, and a new direction was sought. Benitez's impact at Valencia did not go unnoticed by the club hierarchy, and a second successive Anfield overseas appointment was confirmed.

Benitez immediately sought to instil a Spanish influence, with Xabi Alonso and Luis Garcia among the first influx of players brought in, mainly from La Liga. The new manager also instigated a change in backroom staff, bringing a fresh outlook from his homeland. However, inconsistency in the league proved a problem in his first season – the club finishing fifth – although he did reach the League Cup final.

There were, though, some impressive European performances, Benitez's astute tactical approach ensuring a growing challenge in the Champions League. Bayer Leverkusen, Juventus and Chelsea were defeated in the knockout phase as the Reds reached Istanbul, the club's first final in the competition for 20 years. Subsequent events against AC Milan are well documented – the comeback from 3-0 down to 3-3 in the

Best in Europe:
Skipper and manager
show off the
Champions League
trophy in 2005

space of six minutes, miraculous goalkeeping from Jerzy Dudek and penalty shoot-out glory creating a new chapter in club folklore. All achieved with the aid of the inspirational qualities – and tactical tweaking – of the manager.

Despite that success, long-term stability was sought. Pepe Reina was brought in to replace Dudek, while Daniel Agger, Momo Sissoko and Peter Crouch were amongst early Benitez purchases. Premier League form picked up, with the Reds finishing two places higher in third, achieving automatic Champions League qualification. Although the defence of the trophy fell at the last 16 phase, the European Super Cup had been won – while the Reds finished just short in the Club World Championship. However, the FA Cup was brought back to Anfield after a five-year absence. Another memorable showpiece – this time against West Ham – saw Liverpool hit back twice from 2-0 and 3-2 down to draw 3-3 thanks to skipper Steven Gerrard's last-minute stunner, before holding their nerve in the penalty shoot-out.

New owners arrived and though a league challenge never materialised in 2006/07, the club reached a Champions League final for the second time in three years, a run that included a memorable victory over Barcelona at the Nou Camp. Unfortunately, AC Milan gained revenge in the Athens final.

Benitez brought in Fernando Torres, breaking the club's transfer record and his goals were key in helping the Reds top the Premier League for the first time in his stint at the Liverpool helm. A stronger challenge would arise in 2008/09,

'Memorable wins – including a league double over Manchester United – saw the club finish as runners-up'

as memorable wins – including a league double over Manchester United – saw the club finish as runners-up, losing only two league matches in the process. A convincing 5-0 aggregate success also came against Real Madrid in the Champions League, although the challenge for European glory would end at the last-eight stage.

The 2009/10 season would be Benitez's last, poor early season form ruling out a title bid. A seventh-placed finish would be the lowest in his tenure, and also meant the club would be without Champions League football for the first time in seven seasons. A semi-final defeat to Atletico Madrid in the Europa League would prove Benitez's last tilt at success, and his departure was confirmed in June 2010 – bringing the curtain down on six eventful seasons.

Pointing the way: Rafa directed matters from the touchline while head coach of Valenica

SPANISH STARS

Up until the summer of 2004, Liverpool had no history of Spanish players on the club's books. That all changed with the appointment of Rafael Benitez as manager.

As well as bringing with him Spanish coaching staff, the former Valencia boss swooped to bring in a quartet of stars from his homeland. The arrivals enabled the new-look Liverpool team to have an exotic feel to it. First to arrive was defender Josemi and he was quickly followed by winger Antonio Nunez in the deal which saw Michael Owen leave for Real Madrid.

Ahead of the transfer window closing that August, Benitez completed deals for two major signings. Midfield playmaker Xabi Alonso was recruited from Real Sociedad in a £10.7 million deal, and quickly became a fans' favourite with an ability to create, as well as score spectacular goals (sometimes from within his own half).

Another popular player, 'five foot seven of football heaven' according to a popular Kop song, was attacking wide midfielder Luis Garcia, snapped up from Barcelona for £6 million. Then, when Benitez sought attacking reinforcements that January, he brought in Real Madrid favourite Fernando Morientes in a deal worth £6.3 million.

Three more Spaniards arrived the following summer. Young defenders Antonio Barragan and Miki Roque would make only one senior appearance each before moving on, but the third arrival was to play an important part for the remainder of the decade.

Pepe Reina was snapped up from Villarreal for £6 million and helped the club to a dramatic penalty shoot-out FA Cup win over West Ham at the end of his first season. He has gone on to become a big favourite with Kopites, setting clean sheet records and has been an ever present Premier League presence from 2007/08 up until this book was published (February 2011).

In January 2007, Alvaro Arbeloa bolstered the Reds' options in the full-back positions following his arrival from Deportivo La Coruna. In the summer of '07, Benitez splashed out a club record fee on Atletico Madrid striker Fernando Torres. The investment in the Spain international would prove worth every penny as he quickly set about becoming a Kop idol. He would eventually leave for Chelsea for a British record fee in January 2011.

While Torres took the headlines, the arrival of Spanish youngster

Setting the trend: Josemi (below) and Antonio Nunez (bottom), the first wave of Spanish players brought to the club by Rafa

Dani Pacheco almost slipped under the radar. The diminutive attacker arrived from Barcelona, with the Reds paying compensation to the Catalans.

In August 2008, the Reds added to their Spanish contingent with the signing of winger Albert Riera for £8 million. The final Spanish star to arrive to date was teenage Sevilla defender Daniel Ayala, who joined the club in September 2009.

Benitez parted company with Liverpool at the end of the 2009/10 season, by which time the Reds' squad had been sprinkled with a Spanish flavour. The Spanish theme also gave rise to several treasured anthems during Rafa's reign.

The tribute to Luis Garcia mentioned earlier was by no means the only refrain inspired by the Reds' Spanish stars. The most popular among them was sung to the tune of the 1987 UK number one hit single *La Bamba* by Los Lobos, and paid homage to the Reds' fleet of Spaniards.

In the 2004/05 season, the lyrics went:

'Ra Ra Ra Ra Rafa Benitez (x2), Xabi Alonso, Garcia and Nunez.'

As players came and went, the surnames Reina, Torres, Arbeloa and Riera were added to replace those of the departed (with Josemi also getting an occasional airing in the song's early days).

Below: Looking to the future: Dani Pacheco, hoping to establish himself in the Reds' first team. Below, right: Luis Garcia's winning goal in the 2005 Champions League semi-final against Chelsea. On the opposite page, a selection of Liverpudlian Spaniards (clockwise): Xabi Alonso, Alvaro Arbeloa, Fernando Torres, Pepe Reina, Fernando Morientes and Daniel Ayala

What's in a name?

Rodriguez

An Iberian name, its roots are in the Christian name Rodrigo.

It is thought to have been born out of the Germanic name Hrodric, meaning a compound of hrod 'renown' and ric 'power(ful)'.

In the town where I was born

Rosario, Argentina
Maxi Rodriguez

The largest city (1.1m) in the Santa Fe province, Rosario is a major shipping centre thanks to the Parana River.

Home to the Argentine Flag Memorial, it was inaugurated in 1957 to mark the anniversary of the death of Manuel Belgrano – the man who created the Argentine flag.

ARGENTINA

Following Argentina's World Cup triumph in 1978, three members of their squad came to ply their trade in England. Ossie Ardiles and Ricky Villa are fondly remembered at Spurs, but Alberto Tarantini's spell at Birmingham ended with him wading into the crowd to throw a punch at a heckler.

Liverpool's interest in Argentinian footballers came much later. The first to wear the famous red shirt was Mauricio Pellegrino in 2005. A key figure in Rafa Benitez's defence at Valencia, he joined his former coach at a Anfield. Although he played only 13 games, the Cordoba-born player later returned to the club to work as Benitez's first-team coach.

Another central defender, Gabriel Paletta, joined the Reds in July 2006. He came from the capital city of Buenos Aires as did the next Argentine to sign for the Reds, Emiliano Insua, the young left-back who established himself as a regular during the 2009/10 season.

Alejandro Korn-born winger Sebastian Leto joined the club in August 2007, but work permit problems restricted him to less than a handful of first-team games for the club.

Arguably the most successful Argentinians to represent Liverpool are the other pair to have played for the club. Javier Mascherano, from San Lorenzo, became a key member of the Liverpool line-up for three years prior to his switch to Barcelona in the summer of 2010. The tough-tackling midfielder also went on to captain his country under Diego Maradona during his spell at Anfield. He was joined at Anfield in January 2010 by international team-mate Maxi Rodriguez, an exciting winger who grew up in the Rosario region of the nation.

**In the town
where I was born**

**Dourados,
Brazil**
Lucas Leiva

BRAZIL

Brazil's footballers have dazzled the world with their flair and colour for many a year.

Throughout the 1980s and 1990s, Liverpool were linked with swoops for several of Brazil's best but it wasn't until the summer of 2006 that the Reds unveiled a Samba star of their own.

Left-back Fabio Aurelio was the man in question, joining from Rafa Benitez's former club Valencia. The man from Sao Carlos has seen his Liverpool career hampered by injuries.

He was joined in the dressing room by a fellow Brazilian as midfielder Lucas Leiva signed from Gremio in 2007. Lucas was brought up in Dourados, a city situated in the state of Mato Grosso do Sul, 140 miles south west of the state capital Campo Grande.

Completing Liverpool's links with Brazil is goalkeeper Diego Cavalieri, who joined from Palmeiras in 2008. Cavalieri, who hails from Sao Paulo, was unable to force his way into the first team on a regular basis due to the outstanding form of Pepe Reina. He made just 10 cup appearances for the club before joining Italian side Cesena in the summer of 2010.

The city has a population of around 200,000 people, situated in Mato Grosso do Sol, 140 miles south-west of the state's capital, Campo Grande. The economy relies on arable agriculture with sugar cane, soya and maize the most common items.

It is 75 miles from Paraguay and there is a strong ethnic and cultural union between the city and the country. Around 30% of the population have a family link.

Czech mates (clockwise from top: Patrik Berger and Vladimir Smicer celebrate FA Cup success in 2001; Smicer wheels away in celebration after netting in the 2005 Champions League final; Milan Baros holds aloft the trophy in Istanbul

CZECH REPUBLIC

Since 1996 the Reds have employed the services of three attack-minded players from the Czech Republic.

First to arrive on the back of performances at Euro 1996 was Patrik Berger, a man born in the capital Prague.

Berger became fondly thought of by the Kop and left the club with a record of 35 goals in 196 games in a spell just shy of seven years.

In May 1999, he was joined by Vladimir Smicer, who would go on to become one of the stars of Liverpool's 2005 UEFA Champions League triumph.

Smicer, from the northern town of Decin, scored one of the Reds' goals as they produced an incredible fightback against AC Milan. As well as firing a 20-yard drive past Dida, he then went on to score a crucial penalty in the shoot-out to win Liverpool the famous trophy for the fifth time.

The third member of the Reds' Czech contingent also figured in that success.

Milan Baros was born in Valasske in the Zlin region of the country. He joined Liverpool from Banik Ostrava in July 2001 and shot to prominence during Euro 2004 when he finished the competition as winner of the Golden Boot. But after 27 goals in 108 games for the Reds, he left for Aston Villa at the end of the 2004/05 season.

GERMANY

Towards the end of the 1990s and early part of the 21st century, Liverpool had something of a Germanic influence.

Of four players to wear the Liverbird upon their chests, two were undoubted successes – while the other two did not make such an impact.

First to arrive was striker Karlheinz Riedle, who was actually born in East Germany. After enjoying plenty of good times with Borussia Dortmund, he made the move to English football just months after scoring twice in the Champions League final against Juventus.

Despite his pedigree, Riedle was more miss than hit at Anfield, eventually finishing with a goalscoring ratio of not quite one every five games.

Dietmar Hamann made far more of an impression after signing from fellow Premier League side Newcastle United in July 1999. A pivotal part of the team for the next seven years, the midfielder went on to win the Champions League with the club.

Hamann's influence was such that he was shortlisted for the Liverpool Hall of Fame for the decade 2000-2010, reaching the final 10.

Another to make a good contribution to the Reds' cause was defender Markus Babbel.

The man from Munich was able to play at centre-back or right-back and played a significant role as the team won a cup treble in 2001.

Less than two months after Babbel's arrival, his Germany team-mate Christian Ziege joined from Middlesbrough.

The left-sided Berlin-born player came with a good pedigree but struggled to produce his best form for the club, moving on after just a single season.

What's in a name?

Riedle

There may not be 57 varieties – but there are several variations on Karlheinz's surname.

It is said to be a variant of the South German name Riedel, a pet form of the name Riede. Meanings come from the phrase 'mossy area' from the word Ried, and also the verb 'ridden', which translates as 'to ride'.

Hamann

Although predominantly a German name, Didi's surname is also found in parts of Denmark. It is a much reduced form of the Christian name Johannes (John) and Mann 'man', i.e. 'John's man (servant)'.

In the town where I was born

Katwijk-aan-Zee, Holland

Dirk Kuyt

A Dutch fishing village with a population of around 13,700, it is part of the larger municipality of Katwijk. It translates literally as Katwijk-on-Sea, and in Roman times was a place of strategic importance. As a result, Katwijk-aan-Zee would be the point that many travellers would either start from, or change at, to voyage to Great Britain.

While Liverpool has Scouse, Katwijk-aan-Zee also has its own regional dialect known as 'Katwijks'. It is one of the 'South Holland' dialects, considered to be one that is least effected by standard Dutch. Heavily influenced by language used in the 17th century, it is still spoken by many locals.

HOLLAND

The Dutch have always enjoyed a reputation for skill and creativity on the football field. The very mention of the name conjures up images of Johan Cruyff at his pomp and the 'brilliant orange' producing their breathtaking brand of 'total football.'

Gerard Houllier became the first Liverpool manager to turn to Holland in 1999, when he made a double Dutch swoop for goalkeeper Sander Westerveld and striker Erik Meijer.

Westerveld, who was born in Enschede, was one of two keepers Houllier famously signed on the same day, with Chris Kirkland also unveiled at the same time. He spent two seasons at the club after arriving from Vitesse Arnhem, a spell which culminated in him helping the club to their cup treble of 2001.

Meijer became a cult figure with Liverpool supporters, and was affectionately nicknamed 'mad Erik'. The man from Meersen scored just twice in 27 games for the Reds before moving on before Christmas 2000, but travelled to Dortmund for Liverpool's UEFA Cup final in 2001 and was seen partying with Liverpool supporters before the match.

Liverpool's third Dutchman arrived in the summer of 2005, Middlesbrough's Bolo Zenden joining on a Bosman transfer. A year later the Maastricht-born midfielder was joined at Anfield by compatriots Jan Kromkamp, a defender born in Makkinga and Dirk Kuyt, a striker from the seaside resort of Katwijk aan Zee.

To date, Kuyt is probably Liverpool's biggest Dutch success, passing 50 goals for the club during the 2009/10 season.

Amsterdam-born Ryan Babel took the Reds' Dutch contingent to six when he was snapped up from Ajax in 2007, his inconsistent spell ended when he left to join German Bundesliga side Hoffenheim in the January 2011 transfer window.

ISRAEL

Liverpool have been served by three Israelis down the years, although the first was technically an Egyptian!

Israeli international defender Avi Cohen signed for Liverpool from Maccabi Tel Aviv in 1979, but was actually born in Cairo. The most famous of his 24 games in a red shirt came at Anfield in May 1980 with Liverpool needing victory against Aston Villa to claim the league title.

Cohen put the ball in his own goal but quickly made amends with a screamer at the other end to help the Reds to a 4-1 victory. Cohen, whose son Tamir signed for Bolton in 2008, sadly passed away in December 2010, aged 54, from injuries suffered in a motorcycle crash.

Little was known about Haifa-born Ronny Rosenthal when he joined in March 1990. However, when he scored a hat-trick in his first start at Charlton, Reds fans certainly took notice. His goals helped secure the club's 18th title triumph. In all, Rosenthal was at Anfield for just short of four years but he is often remembered for his near gravity-defying miss at Villa Park in September 1992.

Most recently, Liverpool have enjoyed the services of Dimona-born Yossi Benayoun. Signed in 2007, he was a skilful addition to the Reds' squad and could lay claim to scoring hat-tricks for Liverpool in the Premier League, FA Cup and UEFA Champions League. He left for Chelsea in the summer of 2010.

Champion: Ronny Rosenthal – helped the Reds to title glory in 1990

Below: Alberto Aquilani in action during his first season at Anfield

ITALY

Italy may be home to some of football's finest footballers, but the nation has yet to make much of an impact at Anfield. To date only three Italians have represented the club in a senior fixture – and none of the trio has been a success.

Goalkeeper Daniele Padelli became the first Italian to play for the Reds when he appeared in the final league game of the 2006/07 season against Charlton Athletic. It proved to be his only outing.

Hopes were high that defender Andrea Dossena would make more of an impression after joining from Udinese for a reported £7 million at the start of the 2008/09 season. However, he was unable to live up to the fee – but did score in memorable wins against Real Madrid at Anfield and Manchester United at Old Trafford.

Finally, Alberto Aquilani was signed as a big-money replacement for Xabi Alonso during the summer of 2009. He failed to shine, however, and was shipped out on loan to Juventus for the 2010/11 season.

FROM BOSTON TO THE BUSINESS OF SUCCESS

NEW LIVERPOOL FC OWNERS WITH EYES ON THE MAIN PRIZES

The Fenway Sports Group, fronted by John W Henry and Tom Werner, have already made a big impact in implementing change at Anfield. Keen to restore LFC family values and traditions – while helping the club challenge for honours – they have already made their mark in their appointment of Kenny Dalglish, one of the finest players – and managers – in the club's history

A NEW ERA

The Liverpool family is always expanding and there have been plenty of changes and additions in recent times. Most notable of all is a returning favourite son: Kenny Dalglish.

King Kenny, as his nickname suggests, has long been Anfield royalty and in January 2011 he was sitting on the throne once more. The man who most Reds' fans consider to be Liverpool's greatest player brought three league championships and two FA Cups to the club during five full seasons as player-manager between 1985-90.

His presence alone lifted the mood and gave the man himself the opportunity to take care of what he termed "unfinished business", lingering from his abrupt departure in 1991. Even in the years away from the club, the ties that bind remained strong. In his recent book 'In My Liverpool Home', Dalglish explained:

"The people of Liverpool have always been in my heart. From the moment Billy Shankly invited me down from Scotland for a trial in 1966, the first stirrings of a love affair began. When Bob Paisley signed me from Celtic in 1977, giving me a chance to perform in front of the Kop, that passion deepened. Even when I moved away, finding employment at Blackburn Rovers, Newcastle United and briefly back up at Celtic, memories of special times drifted through my mind."

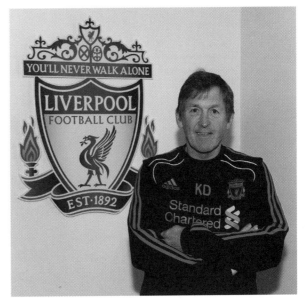

Back where he belongs: Kenny Dalglish, soon after his appointment as Reds boss once again

Dalglish was given the top job by Liverpool's new owner, the Fenway Sports Group (FSG), which is run by American businessmen John W Henry and Tom Werner. FSG, through parent company New England Sports Ventures (NESV), bought the club in October 2010 following the removal of previous owners Tom Hicks and George Gillett. Henry is the principal owner of FSG while Werner is the chairman of Liverpool Football Club. NESV already owned the Boston Red Sox baseball team so Liverpool have effectively acquired a 'sister' sporting organisation, one that has a similar devoted following amongst its supporters.

It has been a turbulent time for the club. Before the Hicks and Gillett ownership era concluded, Rafael Benitez's six-year

managerial reign came to an end following the 2009/10 season. Benitez was replaced by Roy Hodgson but his time in charge did not work out and he left by mutual consent after six months. Hodgson's departure paved the way for the second coming of Dalglish as manager during a tumultuous first month of 2011 – when Liverpool underwent significant upheaval.

Dalglish wasn't able to ease himself back into the job, having to deal with fixtures against Manchester United and Everton in his first week before an extraordinary transfer saga unfolded. Out went Fernando Torres for a British record fee and in came Andy Carroll – a club record purchase from Newcastle United – and Uruguay World Cup star Luis Suarez, recruited from Ajax.

A new era has begun in the rich history of Liverpool FC with new owners, a new manager and new players. They all have one thing in common: Membership of the Liverpool family.

Eyes on the prize: Fenway Sports Group heads John W Henry and Tom Werner view the European Cups amassed in the club museum at Anfield

AMERICAN DREAMING OF RED SUCCESS

John W Henry gave an exclusive interview to the club's official magazine soon after taking over ownership of Liverpool Football Club in October 2010. His encouraging words, noting the club's proud tradition and legacy of success, was music to the ears of the LFC family keen to see the club re-ignite their position as one of the biggest names in world football.

"We're incredibly pleased", the Fenway Sports Group head commented. "Talking to all the partners in the States, they're extremely happy. There were many days where I was wondering whether or not we'd be going home. There were days where I was confident but there were a lot of twists and turns here. It was a terrific team who did a tremendous job and I'm just happy it ended successfully."

After months of negotiation, speculation and uncertainty, the club could again look to move forward. Owner of one of the biggest names in baseball, the Boston Red Sox, Henry noted links between both teams.

"There are a lot of similarities and that was something we've been discussing. We found more and more similarities between Liverpool 2010 and the Red Sox of 2001. For instance the stadium was a big issue in Boston in 2001 and we went in there not knowing what we should do, whether we should build a new ball park or refurbish Fenway. We have the same issue here. We have to listen, learn, talk to the community, talk to the council, talk with the supporters, but the biggest issue of all is really what makes the most sense for Liverpool long term."

"We're going to have to work very hard. There's a lot of work to be done to get this club to where it needs to be in the grand scheme of things. We really, through all the work we've done over the last two months, saw the challenges and problems which exist and we've got to work to address those. There is a great nucleus here off the field and on the field and we think we can build from that, but it's not going to be easy. We've got real challenges."

Henry's overall message to the fans was a positive one, words that should help inspire fans who have witnessed uncertainty and instability on and off the pitch in recent years.

"All I can say at this point is we're going to work as hard for you as we possibly can and there's no doubt about it, you deserve it. You have supported this club through the worst of times now and we're going to do everything in our power to make the supporters proud of their club and of us. It's a big challenge but I think we're up for that challenge."

Above all, I would like to be remembered as a man who was selfless, who strove and worried so that others could share the glory, and who built up a family of people who could hold their heads up high and say...

We are Liverpool.

Billy. Shankly

BILL SHANKLY
Manager 1959-74

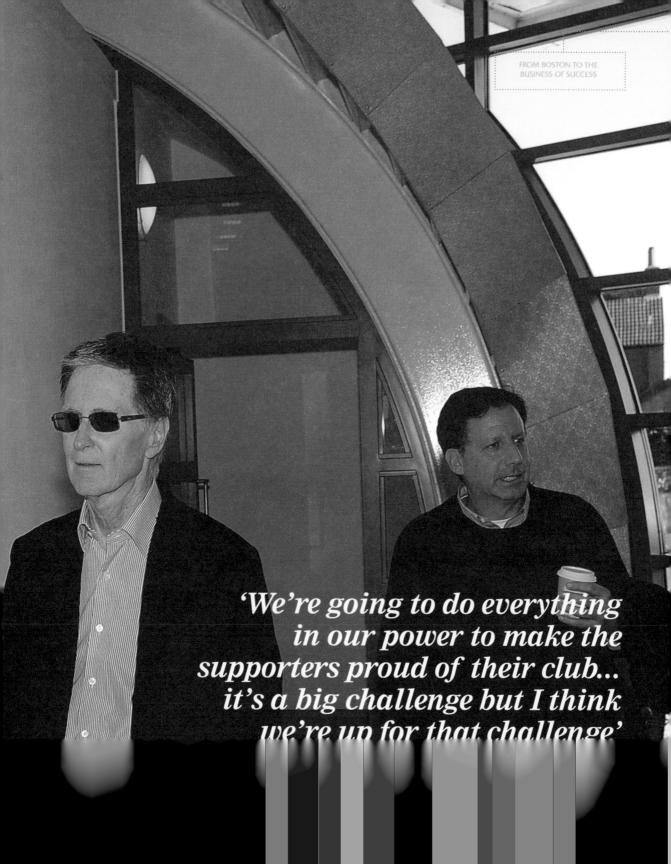

'We're going to do everything
in our power to make the
supporters proud of their club...
it's a big challenge but I think
we're up for that challenge'

FAMILY RECORDS

The following pages offer a complete record of Liverpool FC first-team achievements, the greatest players in the club's history, the players who have played in a first-team match and the full list of player nationalities

APPEARANCES

Most first-team appearances:	Ian Callaghan (857)
Most league appearances:	Ian Callaghan (640)
Most FA Cup appearances:	Ian Callaghan (79)
Most League Cup appearances:	Ian Rush (78)
Most European appearances:	Jamie Carragher (129)
Most European Cup final appearances:	Phil Neal (5)
Most goalkeeper appearances:	Ray Clemence (665)
Most consecutive appearances:	Phil Neal (417, (October 1976-September 1983)
Most seasons ever-present:	Phil Neal (9)
Longest serving player:	Elisha Scott (21 years, 52 days)
Oldest player:	Ted Doig (41 years, 166 days; v Newcastle United, 1908)
Youngest player:	Jack Robinson (16 years, 250 days; v Hull City, 2010)
Longest-serving manager by time:	Tom Watson (18 years, 263 days)
Longest-serving manager by matches:	Bill Shankly (783)

GOALS

Most first-team goals:	Ian Rush (346)
Most league goals:	Roger Hunt (245)
Most FA Cup goals:	Ian Rush (39)
Most League Cup goals:	Ian Rush (48)
Most European goals:	Steven Gerrard (38)
Highest-scoring substitute:	David Fairclough (18)
Most hat-tricks:	Gordon Hodgson (17)
Most hat-tricks in a season:	Roger Hunt (5 in 1961/62)
Fastest hat-trick:	Robbie Fowler (4 mins, 33 seconds v Arsenal, 1994)
Most league goals in a season:	Roger Hunt (41 in 1961/62)
Most goals in a season (all comps):	Ian Rush (47 in 1983/84)
Most penalties scored:	Jan Molby (42)
Most games without scoring:	Ephraim Longworth (371)
Youngest goalscorer:	Michael Owen (17 years, 144 days; v Wimbledon, 1997)
Oldest goalscorer:	Billy Liddell (38 years, 55 days v Stoke City, 1960)
Most goals in a game:	5 by Andy McGuigan (v Stoke, 1902) John Evans (v Bristol Rovers, 1954) Ian Rush (v Luton Town, 1983) Robbie Fowler (v Fulham, 1993)

Most league goals scored in season: 106 in 30 games (1895/96)
Fewest league goals scored in season: 42 in 34 games (1901/02) and 42 in 42 games (1970/71)
Most league goals conceded in season: 97 in 42 games (1953/54)
Fewest league goals conceded in season: 16 in 42 games (1978/79)

HONOURS

Most medals:	Phil Neal (20)
Most League Championship medals:	(8) – Phil Neal, Alan Hansen
Most FA Cup winners medals:	(3) – Bruce Grobbelaar, Steve Nicol and Ian Rush
Most League Cup winners medals:	(5) – Ian Rush
Most European Cup winners medals:	(4) – Phil Neal
European Footballer of the Year:	Michael Owen in 2001
European Golden Boot winner:	Ian Rush in 1983/84 (32 goals)
FWA Footballer of the Year:	(11) 1974 – Ian Callaghan; 1976 – Kevin Keegan; 1977 – Emlyn Hughes; 1979 – Kenny Dalglish; 1980 – Terry McDermott; 1983 – Kenny Dalglish; 1984 – Ian Rush; 1988 – John Barnes; 1989 – Steve Nicol; 1990 – John Barnes; 2009 – Steven Gerrard.
PFA Player of the Year:	(5) 1980 – Terry McDermott; 1983 – Kenny Dalglish; 1984 – Ian Rush; 1988 – John Barnes; 2006 – Steven Gerrard.
PFA Young Player of the Year:	(5) 1983 – Ian Rush; 1995 and 1996 – Robbie Fowler; 1998 – Michael Owen; 2001 – Steven Gerrard.
Manager of the Year:	(11) – Bill Shankly (1973); Bob Paisley – (1976, 1977, 1979, 1980, 1982, 1983; Joe Fagan – (1984); Kenny Dalglish – (1986, 1988, 1990)

Knighthood:	Sir John Smith
OBE:	Bill Shankly, Bob Paisley, Gerard Houllier (honorary) Roger Hunt, Emlyn Hughes, John Toshack
MBE:	Tommy Smith, John Barnes, Ian Callaghan Ray Clemence, Kenny Dalglish, Gary McAllister, Steven Gerrard
CBE:	Sir John Smith

MATCHES

Record victory: 11-0 v Strømsgodset (European Cup Winners' Cup first round, Sept 1974)

Record defeat: 1-9 v Birmingham City (Division Two, Dec 1954)

Record league win: 10-1 v Rotherham Town (Division Two, February 1896)

Record FA Cup win: 9-0 v Newton (second qualifier, October 1892)

Record FA Cup defeat: 0-5 v Bolton Wanderers (fourth round, first leg, January 1946)

Record League Cup win: 10-0 Fulham (second round, first leg, September 1986)

Record League Cup defeat: 3-6 v Arsenal (fifth round, January 2007)

Most league wins in a season: 30 from 42 games (1978/79)

Fewest league wins in a season: 7 from 30 games (1894/95)

Most league defeats in a season: 23 from 42 games (1953/54)

Fewest defeats in a season: Unbeaten in 28 games (1893/94)

Record run without conceding a goal: 11 games (Pepe Reina, October-December 2005)

Most games at Anfield without conceding: 10 games (October 2005-January 2006)

ATTENDANCES

Highest league home attendance: 58,757 v Chelsea (1949/50)

Highest FA Cup home attendance: 61,905 v Wolves (1951/52, fifth round)

Highest League Cup home attendance: 50,880 v Nottingham Forest (1979/80, semi-final, second leg)

Highest European home attendance: 55,104 v Barcelona (1975/76, UEFA Cup semi-final, second leg)

Lowest league home attendance: 1,000 v Loughborough Town (1895/96)

Lowest league home attendance (post-war): 11,976 v Scunthorpe United (1958/59)

Lowest FA Cup home attendance: 4,000 v Newton (1892/83, second qualifying round) v Barnsley St Peters (1894/95, first-round replay) v Burton Swifts (1896/97, first round)

Lowest FA Cup home attendance (post-war): 11,207 v Chester City (1945/46, third round, second leg)

Lowest League Cup home attendance: 9,902 v Brentford (1983/84, second round, second leg)

Lowest European attendance: 12,021 v Dundalk (1982/83, European Cup first round, first leg)

Record highest home attendance: 61,905 v Wolves (1951/52, FA Cup fifth round)

Record lowest attendance: 1,000 v Loughborough Town (1895/96)

Liverpool FC's Official Hall of Fame

1890s
HARRY BRADSHAW and MATT McQUEEN

1900s
ALEX RAISBECK and JACK COX

1910s
ARTHUR GODDARD and EPHRAIM LONGWORTH

1920s
ELISHA SCOTT and DON MACKINLAY

1930s
GORDON HODGSON and JIMMY McDOUGALL

1940s
ALBERT STUBBINS and JACK BALMER

1950s
BILLY LIDDELL and ALAN A'COURT

1960s
ROGER HUNT and RON YEATS

1970s
RAY CLEMENCE and IAN CALLAGHAN

1980s
ALAN HANSEN and KENNY DALGLISH

1990s
JOHN BARNES and IAN RUSH

2000s
STEVEN GERRARD and JAMIE CARRAGHER

COMPLETE LIST OF LIVERPOOL FC PLAYERS BY NATIONALITY
(Players must have played in a senior fixture for LFC 02/02/2011)

On the player information, the first date is the year the player signed for LFC and the second the date of his last senior appearance.
*Although born in different countries, players marked with an asterisk either went on to play international football for another nation or were considered to be of a different nationality.

ENGLAND (361)

Alan A'Court	1952-1964, Rainhill, England
Gary Ablett	1983-1992, Liverpool, England
Andrew Aitken	1930-1930, Newcastle, England
Messina Allman	1908-1909, Burslem, England
David Amoo	2007-present, Southwark, England
Eric Anderson	1951-1956, Manchester, England
Thomas Armstrong	1920-1920, Preston, England
Alan Arnell	1953-1961, Chichester, England
Steve Arnold	1970-1971, Wembley, England
Alf Arrowsmith	1960-1968, Manchester, England
Charlie Ashcroft	1943-1955, Chorley, England
Jack Balmer	1935-1952, West Derby, England
John Bamber	1915-23, Peasley Cross, England
Alan Banks	1958-1961, Liverpool, England
William Banks	1913-1915, Cramlington, England
Henry Barkas	1930-1931, Wardley Colliery, England
Nick Barmby	2000-2002, Hull, England
* John Barnes	1987-1997, Kingston, Jamaica
Fred Baron	1925-1927, Prudhoe, England
Kevin Baron	1945-1954, Preston, England
Harold Barton	1928-1934, Leigh, England
Wilf Bartrop	1914-1915. Worksop, England
Peter Beardsley	1987-1991, Newcastle, England
Frank Becton	1895-1898, Preston, England
Augustus Beeby	1908-1910, Ashbourne, England
Thomas Bennett	1916-1919, Walton, England
Arthur Berry	1908-1909; 1912-1912, Liverpool, England
Louis Bimpson	1953-1959, Rainford, England
Robert Blanthorne	1905-1907, Birkenhead, England
Ernie Blenkinsop	1934-1937, Cudworth, England
Phil Boersma	1968-1975, Kirkby, England
George Bowen	1901-1901, Walsall, England
Sam Bowyer	1907-1912, Northwich, England
James Bradley	1905-1910, Goldenhill, England
Thomas Bradshaw	1893-1898, Liverpool, England
Philip Bratley	1914-1915, Rawmarsh, England
Ken Brierley	1948-1953, Ashton-under-Lyne, England
Tom Bromilow	1919-1930, Liverpool, England
Joseph Brough	1910-1911, Burslem, England
Derek Brownbill	1972-1973, Liverpool, England
Les Bruton	1932-1933, Foleshill, England
Fred Buck	1903-04, Newcastle-under-Lyme, England
Ben Bull	1895-1896, Leicester, England
Keith Burkinshaw	1953-1955, Highan, England
David Burrows	1988-1993, Dudley, England
Tom Bush	1933-1947, Hodnet, England
Gerry Byrne	1953-1969, Liverpool, England
Ian Callaghan	1960-1978, Liverpool, England

Bobby Campbell	1954-1961, Liverpool, England
Don Campbell	1950-1958, Bootle, England
John Carlin	1902-1907, Liverpool, England
Willie Carlin	1958-1959, Liverpool, England
Len Carney	1939-1947, Liverpool, England
Jamie Carragher	1996-present, Liverpool, England
Scott Carson	2005-2006, Whitehaven, England
Jimmy Carter	1991-1991, Hammersmith, England
Jimmy Case	1973-1981, Liverpool, England
John Chadburn	1903-1903, Mansfield, England
Edgar Chadwick	1902-1904, Blackburn, England
Harry Chambers	1915-1928, Willington Quay, England
John Charlton	1929-1931, Leadgate, England
Phil Charnock	1992-1992, Ormskirk, England
Francis Checkland	1918-1921, Seaforth, England
Bert Childs	1953-1953, Liverpool, England
Phil Chisnall	1964-1966, Manchester, England
Tom Chorlton	1904-1910, Heaton Mersey, England
James Clark	1928-1931, Newcastle-upon-Tyne, England
Ray Clemence	1967-1981, Skegness, England
Nigel Clough	1993-1995, Sunderland, England
William Cockburn	1924-1926, Willington Quay, England
Joe Cole	2010-present, Islington, England
James Collins	1936-1937, London, England
Stan Collymore	1995-1997, Stone, England
Tom Cooper	1934-1939, Fenton, England
Charles Cotton	1903-1904, Plymouth, England
Jack Cox	1897-1909, Liverpool, England
Edmund Crawford	1932-1933, Filey, England
Russell Crossley	1947-1954, Hebden Bridge, England
Peter Crouch	2005-2008, Macclesfield, England
Daniel Cunliffe	1897-1898, Bolton, England
William Cunningham	1920-1922, Radcliffe, England
Benjamin Dabbs	1932-1937, Oakengates, England
Stephen Darby	2008-present, Liverpool, England
John Davies	1900-1902, Liverpool, England
Gerald Dewhurst	1894-1894, London, England
Julian Dicks	1993-1994, Bristol, England
Joe Dickson	1952-1956, Liverpool, England
Joseph Dines	1912-1912, King's Lynn, England
Cyril Done	1938-1952, Liverpool, England
Robert Done	1926-1934, Runcorn, England
John Durnin	1986-1988, Liverpool, England
Harry Eastham	1936-1947, Blackpool, England
Nathan Eccleston	2008-present, Manchester, England
Dick Edmed	1926-1930, Gillingham, England
Alun Evans	1968-1972, Bewdley, England
John Evans	1953-1957, Tilbury, England
Roy Evans	1965-1973, Liverpool, England

Chris Fagan	1970-1971, Manchester, England	David Hodgson	1982-1984, Gateshead, England
David Fairclough	1974-1983, Liverpool, England	Ralph Holden	1911-1913, Blundellsands, England
Philip Ferns	1958-1965, Liverpool, England	James Holmes	1895-1898, Preston, England
Patrick Finnerhan	1897-1898, Northwich, England	Mike Hooper	1985-1993, Bristol, England
Fred Finney	1945-1946, Prescot, England	Fred Hopkin	1921-1931, Dewsbury, England
Matthew Fitzsimmons	1936-1938, Liverpool, England	Fred Howe	1935-1938, Bredbury, England
Dick Forshaw	1919-1927, Preston, England	Raby Howell	1898-1901, Sheffield, England
Robbie Fowler	1992-2001 and 2006-2007, Liverpool, England	Emlyn Hughes	1967-1979, Barrow-in-Furness, England
Abraham Foxall	1899-1899, Sheffield, England	James Hughes	1904-1909, Bootle, England
Jim Furnell	1962-1963, Clitheroe, England	Laurie Hughes	1943-1957, Liverpool, England
Tom Gardner	1929-1930, Huyton, England	Roger Hunt	1958-1969, Golborne, England
James Garner	1922-1925, Manchester, England	Thomas John Hunter	1899-1902, Unknown, England
James Garside	1904-1906, Manchester, England	William Hunter	1908-1909, Sunderland, England
Howard Gayle	1977-1981, Toxteth, England	Paul Ince	1997-1999, Ilford, England
Fred Geary	1895-1898, Hyson Green, England	Thomas Ince	2008-present, Stockport, England
Steven Gerrard	1997-present, Whiston, England	Colin Irwin	1974-1981, Liverpool, England
Cyril Gilhepsy	1921-1925, Fencehouses, England	Brian Jackson	1951-1958, Walton-on-Thames, England
Rob Glassey	1933-1936, Chester-le-Street, England	James Jackson	1925-1933, Newcastle-upon-Tyne, England
John Glover	1900-1903, West Bromwich, England	David James	1992-1999, Welwyn Garden City, England
Arthur Goddard	1902-1914, Heaton Norris, England	Norman James	1929-1932, Liverpool, England
Bertram Goode	1908-1909, Chester, England	William Jenkinson	1919-1920, Golborne, England
James Gorman	1906-1908, Middlesbrough, England	David Johnson	1976-1982, Liverpool, England
Frank Grayer	1912-1914, Southampton, England	Dick Johnson	1920-1925, Gateshead, England
Thomas Green	1901-1903, Rock Ferry, England	Glen Johnson	2009-present, London, England
Michael Griffin	1907-1909, Middlesbrough, England	Tosh Johnson	1934-1936, Dalton-in-Furness, England
Harry Griffiths	1905-08, Middlesbrough, England	Barry Jones	1989-1991, Prescot, England
Gordon Gunson	1930-1933, Chester, England	Bill Jones	1938-1954, Whaley Bridge, England
Danny Guthrie	2006-2007, Shrewsbury, England	Harold Jones	1952-1953, Liverpool, England
Jack Haigh	1949-1952, Rotherham, England	* Rob Jones	1991-1998, Wrexham, Wales
Charles Hakefost	1914-1914, Sunderland, England	Charlie Jowitt	1896-1897, Liverpool, England
Edmund Hancock	1931-1933, Rotherham, England	Stanley Kane	1935-1936, Workington, England
Alf Hanson	1931-1938, Bootle, England	George Kaye	1941-1947, Liverpool, England
Sam Hardy	1905-1912, Chesterfield, England	William Keech	1895-1895, Irthlingborough, England
Steve Harkness	1989-1999, Carlisle, England	Kevin Keegan	1971-1977, Armthorpe, England
Chris Harrington	1920-1921, Edge Hill, England	Joe Keetley	1923-1924, Derby, England
James Harrop	1907-1912, Sheffield, England	Martin Kelly	2008-present, Bolton, England
Ted Harston	1937-1937, Barnsley, England	Phillip Kelly	1892-1893, Liverpool, England
Billy Hartill	1936-1936, Wolverhampton, England	James Kelso	1892-1892, Unknown, England
Tony Hateley	1967-1968, Derby, England	Arthur Kelvin	1892-1892, Unknown, England
Emile Heskey	2000-2004, Leicester, England	Alan Kennedy	1978-1985, Sunderland, England
Charles Hewitt	1907-1908, Greatham, England	Ray Kennedy	1974-1981, Seaton Delaval, England
Joe Hewitt	1904-1909, Chester, England	Brian Kettle	1973-1977, Prescot, England
Jack Heydon	1949-1953, Birkenhead, England	Kevin Kewley	1972-1978, Liverpool, England
Dave Hickson	1959-1961, Salford, England	Peter Kippax	1948-1949, Burnley, England
Alan Hignett	1963-1965, Liverpool, England	Chris Kirkland	2001-2004, Leicester, England
Samuel Hignett	1906-1907, Liverpool, England	Paul Konchesky	2010-present, Barking, England
Joseph Hoare	1903-1904, Southampton, England	Frank Lane	1971-1972, Wallasey, England
Jack Hobbs	2005-2007, Portsmouth, England	Chris Lawler	1960-1975, Liverpool, England
Alf Hobson	1936-1938; 1945-46, County Durham, England	Herbert Leavey	1910-1911, Guildford, England

COMPLETE LIST OF LIVERPOOL FC PLAYERS BY NATIONALITY
(Players must have played in a senior fixture for LFC to 02/02/2011)

Sammy Lee	1976-1986, Liverpool, England	Stan Palk	1940-1948, Liverpool, England
Hugh Lester	1911-1912, Liverpool, England	Jack Parkinson	1902-1914, Bootle, England
Harry Lewis	1916-22, Birkenhead, England	John Parkinson	1899-1899, Blackpool, England
Kevin Lewis	1960-1963, Ellesmere Port, England	Steve Parr	1948-1953, Preston, England
Alec Lindsay	1969-1977, Bury, England	Jimmy Payne	1944-1956, Liverpool, England
John Lipsham	1906-1907, Chester, England	Albert Pearson	1919-1921, Tynemouth, England
Doug Livermore	1965-1970, Liverpool, England	Joe Pearson	1892-1892, Liverpool, England
Larry Lloyd	1969-1974, Bristol, England	Lee Peltier	2006-2007, Liverpool, England
Frank Lock	1953-1955, London, England	Jermaine Pennant	2006-2008, Nottingham, England
Ephraim Longworth	1910-1928, Halliwell, England	Steve Peplow	1966-1969, Liverpool, England
Harry Lowe	1911-1919, Whitwell, England	Bill Perkins	1899-1903, Wellingborough, England
Thomas Lowry	1963-1965, Liverpool, England	Fred Perry	1954-1955, Cheltenham, England
Tommy Lucas	1916-1932, St Helens, England	Keith Peters	1936-1939, Port Sunlight, England
Joe Lumsden	1897-1898, Derby, England	George Pither	1926-1928, Kew, England
Terry McDermott	1974-1982, Kirkby, England	Peter Platt	1902-1904, Oldham, England
John McKenna	1906-1907, Near Liverpool, England	Darren Potter	1999-2005, Liverpool, England
Peter McKinney	1920-1921, Consett, England	Henry Race	1927-1930, Evenwood, England
John McLaughlin	1969-1974, Liverpool, England	Bernard Ramsden	1935-1947, Sheffield, England
Steve McMahon	1985-1991, Liverpool, England	David Raven	1999-2005, Wirral, England
Steve McManaman	1990-1999, Liverpool, England	Archie Rawlings	1924-1926, Leicester, England
Tony McNamara	1957-1958, Liverpool, England	Sam Raybould	1900-1907, Steveley, England
Tom McNulty	1954-1957, Salford, England	Jamie Redknapp	1991-2001, Barton-on-Sea, England
Billy McOwen	1892-1894, Blackburn, England	Wally Richardson	1892-1893, Liverpool, England
Joe Maloney	1951-1953, Liverpool, England	John Roberts	1933-1933, Blundellsands, England
Mike Marsh	1987-1993, Kirkby, England	Syd Roberts	1929-1936, Bootle, England
William Henry Marshall	1901-1902, Unknown, England	Jack Robinson	2010-present, Warrington, England
Jimmy Melia	1954-1964, Liverpool, England	Michael Robinson	1983-1984, Leicester, England
Neil Mellor	1999-2005, Sheffield, England	Robbie Robinson	1904-1912, Sunderland, England
Arthur Metcalf	1912-1915, Sunderland, England	Fred Rogers	1933-1939, Frodsham, England
Gordon Milne	1960-1967, Preston, England	Tom Rogers	1907-1911, Prescot, England
Ray Minshull	1946-1950, Bolton, England	Arthur Rowley	1951-1953, Fazakerley, England
John Molyneux	1955-1962, Warrington, England	Neil Ruddock	1993-1997, Wandsworth, England
William Molyneux	1963-1965, Liverpool, England	Colin Russell	1978-1981, Liverpool, England
Richard Money	1980-1981, Lowestoft, England	Dave Rylands	1970-1974, Liverpool, England
Ronnie Moran	1952-1965, Crosby, England	Jack Sambrook	1922-1923, Wednesfield, England
Fred Morris	1958-1959, Pant, England	Charles Satterthwaite	1899-1901, Cockermouth, England
John Morrissey	1957-1961, Liverpool, England	Percy Saul	1906-1909, Rotherham, England
Bobby Murdoch	1957-1959, Garston, England	Roy Saunders	1948-1958, Salford, England
Danny Murphy	1997-2004, Chester, England	Ted Savage	1931-1937, Louth, England
Phil Neal	1974-1985, Irchester, England	John Scales	1994-1996, Harrogate, England
Jon Newby	1998-2001, Warrington, England	Alan Scott	1929-1931, Birkenhead, England
John Nicholson	1957-1959, Liverpool, England	Tom Scott	1925-1927, Newcastle-upon-Tyne, England
Harold Wheeler Nickson	1945-1945, Liverpool, England	Mark Seagraves	1983-1986, Liverpool, England
Steve Ogrizovic	1977-1980, Mansfield, England	John Sealey	1962-1965, Wallasey, England
Jon Otsemobor	2002-2003, Liverpool, England	John Shafto	1936-1939, Humshaugh, England
Michael Owen	1996-2004, Chester, England	Les Shannon	1944-1948, Liverpool, England
Cyril Oxley	1925-1926, Worksop, England	Albert Shears	1924-1928, Newcastle-upon-Tyne, England
Fred Pagnam	1914-1919, Poulton-Le-Fylde, England	Jackie Sheldon	1913-1921, Clay Cross, England
Bob Paisley	1939-1954, Hetton-le-Hole, England	Jonjo Shelvey	2010-present, Romford, England

Bill Shepherd	1945-1951, Liverpool, England
John Shield	1935-1936, South Shields, England
Danny Shone	1921-1925, Wirral, England
Jack Smith	1951-1953, Birkenhead, England
James Smith	2006-2006, Liverpool, England
Sydney Smith	1903-1903, Liverpool, England
Tommy Smith	1962-1978, Liverpool, England
Mark Smyth	2002-2004, Liverpool, England
Alex South	1954-1955, Brighton, England
Nigel Spackman	1987-1988, Romsey, England
James Speakman	1908-1913, Huyton, England
Sam Speakman	1912-1919, Huyton, England
Jay Spearing	2008-present, Wirral, England
Eddie Spicer	1939-1953, Liverpool, England
Fred Staniforth	1913-1913, Kilnhurst, England
General Stevenson	1898-1899, Burnley, England
Paul Stewart	1992-1993, Manchester, England
Harry Storer	1895-1899, Butterley, England
Trevor Storton	1972-1974, Keighley, England
James Stott	1893-1894, Middlesbrough, England
Geoff Strong	1964-1970, Kirkheaton, England
William Stuart	1911-1912, Unknown, England
Albert Stubbins	1946-1953, Wallsend, England
Nick Tanner	1988-1992, Bristol, England
Harold Taylor	1932-1937, Hanley, England
Phil Taylor	1936-1954, Bristol, England
Jack Tennant	1933-1935, Newcastle-upon-Tyne, England
Michael Thomas	1991-1998, Lambeth, England
Charlie Thompson	1929-1931, Forest Hall, England
David Thompson	1996-2000, Birkenhead, England
Max Thompson	1974-1975, Liverpool, England
Peter Thompson	1963-1972, Carlisle, England
Phil Thompson	1971-1983, Kirkby, England
Fred Tomley	1953-1955, Liverpool, England
John Tosswill	1912-1913, Eastbourne, England
Geoff Twentyman	1953-1959, Carlisle, England
Dave Underwood	1953-1956, London, England
Harold Uren	1906-1912, Bristol, England
Barry Venison	1986-1992, Consett, England
Alan Waddle	1973-1977, Wallsend, England
Harold Wadsworth	1919-1924, Bootle, England
Walter Wadsworth	1912-1926, Bootle, England
Peter Wall	1966-1970, Westbury, England
Jimmy Walsh	1922-1928, Stockport, England
Paul Walsh	1984-1987, Plumstead, England
Mark Walters	1991-1995, Birmingham, England
Stephen Warnock	1998-2007, Ormskirk, England
William Watkinson	1946-1950, Prescot, England
Alex Watson	1985-1989, Liverpool, England

Henry Welfare	1912-1913, Liverpool, England
John Welsh	2002-2005, Liverpool, England
Alf West	1903-1909; 1910-1911, Nottingham, England
Johnny Wheeler	1956-1961, Crosby, England
Dick White	1955-1962, Scunthorpe, England
John Whitehead	1894-1895, Liverpool, England
Albert Whitehurst	1928-1929, Fenton, England
Jack Whitham	1970-1972, Burnley, England
George Whitworth	1950-1952, Eckington, England
Barry Wilkinson	1954-1959, Bishop Auckland, England
Bryan Williams	1945-1953, Liverpool, England
Charlie Wilson	1897-1905, Stockport, England
David Wilson	1967-1967, Nelson, England
David A. Wilson	1899-1899, Unknown, England
Don Woan	1950-1951, Liverpool, England
Arthur Worgan	1894-1894, Aigburth Vale, England
Mark Wright	1991-1997, Dorchester, England
Stephen Wright	1996-2002, Liverpool, England
Vic Wright	1934-1937, Walsall, England

SCOTLAND (150)

George Allan	1895-1897; 1898-1899, Linlithgow Bridge, Scotland
Bernard Battles	1896-1897; 1898-1898, Springburn, Scotland
John Bovill	1911-1913, Rutherglen, Scotland
Tom Bradshaw	1930-1937, Bishopton, Scotland
John Browning	1934-1939, Alexandria, Scotland
Matt Busby	1936-1939, Orbiston, Scotland
Joe Cadden	1948-1952, Glasgow, Scotland
James Cameron	1894-1894, Glasgow, Scotland
John Cameron	1892-1893, Unknown, England
Ken Campbell	1911-1920, Cambuslang, Scotland
William Chalmers	1923-1925, Aberdeen, Scotland
Frank Christie	1949-1950, Perthshire, Scotland
Thomas Cleghorn	1896-1899, Leith, Scotland
James Cleland	1895-1895, Lanarkshire, Scotland
Robert Colvin	1897-1898, Kirkconnel, Scotland
Peter Cormack	1972-1975, Edinburgh, Scotland
Herbert Craik	1903-1903, Greenock, Scotland
Robert Crawford	1909-14, Blythswood, Scotland
John Curran	1894-1895, Belshill, Scotland
Kenny Dalglish	1977-1990, Glasgow, Scotland
David Davidson	1928-1930, Aberdeen, Scotland
James Dawson	1912-1914, Edinburgh, Scotland
William Devlin	1927-1927, Bellshill, Scotland
Douglas Dick	1893-1894, Greenock, Scotland
Ned Doig	1904-1908, Letham, Scotland
John Drummond	1894-1895, Edinburgh, Scotland
Billy Dunlop	1895-1909, Kilmarnock, Scotland
John Easdale	1937-1947, Dumbarton, Scotland

COMPLETE LIST OF LIVERPOOL FC PLAYERS BY NATIONALITY
(Players must have played in a senior fixture for LFC to 02/02/2011)

Willie Fagan	1937-1951, Musselburgh, Scotland
Thomas Fairfoul	1913-1915, West Calder, Scotland
Robert Ferguson	1912-1915, Cleland, Scotland
Harold Fitzpatrick	1907-1907, Ayr, Scotland
George Fleming	1901-1905, Bannockburn, Scotland
Gary Gillespie	1983-1991, Stirling, Scotland
Samual Gilligan	1910-1912, Dundee, Scotland
John Givens	1894-1894, Glasgow, Scotland
Archie Goldie	1895-1900, Hurlford, Scotland
William Goldie	1897-1903, Hurlford, Scotland
Patrick Gordon	1893-1894, Glasgow, Scotland
Tom Gracie	1912-1914, Glasgow, Scotland
Bobby Graham	1961-1972, Motherwell, Scotland
Brian Hall	1968-1976, Glasgow, Scotland
Andrew Hannah	1892-1895 Renton, Scotland
Alan Hansen	1977-1990, Sauchuie, Scotland
Jim Harley	1934-1948, Methil, Scotland
James Harrower	1958-1961, Alva, Scotland
Abraham Hartley	1897-1898, Dumbarton, Scotland
Alastair Henderson	1931-1932, Shettleston, Scotland
David Henderson	1893-1894, Stirling, Scotland
Hugh Henderson	1894-1894, Unknown, Scotland
James Henderson	1893-1893, Scotland
Ray Houghton	1987-1992, Glasgow, Scotland
John Hunter	1899-1902, Johnstone, Scotland
* Don Hutchison	1990-1994, Gateshead, England
Robert Ireland	1929-1930, Darvel, Scotland
Alan Irvine	1986-1987, Broxburn, Scotland
Neil Kerr	1894-1895, Bowling, Scotland
Bill Kinghorn	1938-1939, Strathblane, Scotland
Peter Kyle	1899-1900, Cadder, Scotland
Tommy Lawrence	1957-1971, Dailly, Scotland
Hector Lawson	1924-1924, Shettleston, Scotland
Tommy Leishman	1959-1962, Stenhousemuir, Scotland
Billy Liddell	1939-1960, Townhill, Scotland
John Lindsay	1928-1929, Cardenden, Scotland
George Livingstone	1902-1903, Dumbarton, Scotland
Norman Low	1933-1936, Aberdeen, Scotland
Kevin MacDonald	1984-1988, Inverness, Scotland
Donald MacKinlay	1910-28, Newton Mearns, Scotland
Gary McAllister	2000-2002, Motherwell, Scotland
Doug McAvoy	1947-1948, Kilmarnock, Scotland
Neil McBain	1928-1928, Campbelltown, Scotland
James McBride	1892-1894, Renton, Scotland
Donald McCallum	1901-1903, Unknown, Scotland
William McCann	1894-1895, Renfrewshire, Scotland
John McCartney	1892-1898 Newmilns, Scotland
John McConnell	1909-1912, Cambusnethan, Scotland
Andrew McCowie	1896-1899, Cambuslang, Scotland

John McDonald	1909-1912, Kircaldy, Scotland
Jimmy McDougall	1928-1938, Port Glasgow, Scotland
Robert McDougall	1913-1914, Glasgow, Scotland
John McFarlane	1928-1929, Shettleston, Scotland
Andy McGuigan	1900-1902, Newton Stewart, Scotland
Jimmy McInnes	1938-1939, Ayr, Scotland
Duncan McLean	1892-1895 Dumbarton, Scotland
James McLean	1903-1903, Edinburgh, Scotland
John McLean	1894-1895, Port Glasgow, Scotland
Tommy McLeod	1945-1948, Musselburgh, Scotland
Jock McNab	1919-1928, Cleland, Scotland
Harry McNaughton	1920-1920, Edinburgh, Scotland
Archie McPherson	1929-1934, Alva, Scotland
Bill McPherson	1906-1908, Beith, Scotland
Joe McQue	1892-1898, Glasgow, Scotland
Hugh McQueen	1892-1895, Harthill, Scotland
Matt McQueen	1892-1899, Harthill, Scotland
Danny McRorie	1930-1932, Glasgow, Scotland
Malcolm McVean	1892-1897 Jamestown, Scotland
Bobby Marshall	1897-1898, Edinburgh, Scotland
Dominic Matteo	1992-2000, Dumfries, Scotland
Bill Michael	1896-1897 Wilshaw, Scotland
John Miller	1892-1893 Dumbarton, Scotland
John Miller	1918-1920, Motherwell, Scotland
Tom Miller	1912-1920, Motherwell, Scotland
Frank Mitchell	1919-1921, Elgin, Scotland (100)
Hugh Morgan	1898-1900, Longriggend, Scotland
Tom Morrison	1927-1934, Coylton, Scotland
Alex Muir	1947-1948, Inverkeithing, Scotland
Bill Murray	1927-1929, Alexandria, Scotland
David Murray	1904-1905, Glasgow, Scotland
Robert Neill	1896-1897, Govan, Scotland
Jimmy Nicholl	1914-1915, Port Glasgow, Scotland
Steve Nicol	1981-1994, Ayrshire, Scotland
John Ogston	1965-1967, Aberdeen, Scotland
Ronald Orr	1908-1911, Bartonholm, Scotland
George Paterson	1937-1939, Aberdeen, Scotland
James Penman	1919-1920, Kelty, Scotland
David Pratt	1923-1927, Lochore, Scotland
Bob Pursell	1911-1919, Campbelltown, Scotland
Alex Raisbeck	1898-1909, Polmont, Scotland
Tom Reid	1926-1929, Motherwell, Scotland
John Robertson	1900-1902, Newton Mearns, Scotland
Tom Robertson	1898-1902, Renton, Scotland
Ian Ross	1965-1972, Glasgow, Scotland
Jimmy Ross	1894-1897, Edinburgh, Scotland
Sydney Ross	1892-1893 Edinburgh, Scotland
Bill Salisbury	1928-1929, Glasgow, Scotland
James Scott	1910-1912, Stevenston, Scotland

Sam Shields	1949-1949, Denny, Scotland
Bert Slater	1959-1962, Musselburgh, Scotland
Don Sloan	1908-1909, Rankinston, Scotland
Alexander Smith	1937-1937, Buckie, Scotland
Jimmy Smith	1929-1931, Old Kilpatrick, Scotland
John Smith	1892-1893, Ayrshie, Scotland
Graeme Souness	1978-1984, Edinburgh, Scotland
David Speedie	1991-1991, Glenrothes, Scotland
Ian St John	1961-1971, Motherwell, Scotland
Willie Steel	1931-1934, Blantyre, Scotland
Willie Stevenson	1962-1967, Edinburgh, Scotland
James Stewart	1909-1913, Dumbarton, Scotland
Bobby Thomson	1962-1964, Menstrie, Scotland
John Walker	1898-1902, Coatbridge, Scotland
William Walker	1897-1898, Unknown, Scotland
Gordon Wallace	1961-1965, Lanark, Scotland
John Wark	1984-1987, Glasgow, Scotland
William White	1901-1902, Edinburgh, Scotland
Tom Wilkie	1895-1898, Edinburgh, Scotland
Danny Wilson	2010-present, Livingston, Scotland
Dave Wright	1930-1934, Kirkcaldy, Scotland
Tom Wyllie	1892-1893 Maybole, Scotland
Ron Yeats	1961-1971, Aberdeen, Scotland
Tommy Younger	1956-1959, Edinburgh, Scotland

NORTHERN IRELAND (9)

Willie Donnelly	1896-1897, Magherafelt, N Ireland
Sam English	1933-1935, Coleraine, Northern Ireland
David Hannah	1894-1897, Raffrey, Northern Ireland
William Hood	1937-1937, Belfast, Northern Ireland
Billy McDevitt	1923-1924, Belfast, Northern Ireland
David McMullan	1925-1928, Belfast, Northern Ireland
Billy Millar	1928-1928, Ballymena, Northern Ireland
Elisha Scott	1912-1934, Belfast, Northern Ireland
Sammy Smyth	1952-1954, Belfast, Northern Ireland

REPUBLIC OF IRELAND (15)

* John Aldridge	1987-1989, Liverpool, England
* Phil Babb	1994-1999, London, England
Jim Beglin	1983-1987, Waterford, Republic of Ireland
Steve Finnan	2003-2008, Limerick, Republic of Ireland
Steve Heighway	1970-1981, Dublin, Republic of Ireland
Robbie Keane	2008-2009, Dublin, Republic of Ireland
Mark Kennedy	1995-1998, Dublin, Republic of Ireland
Bill Lacey	1912-1924, Wexford, Republic of Ireland
* Mark Lawrenson	1981-1988, Preston, England
* Jason McAteer	1995-1999, Birkenhead, England
Brian Mooney	1983-1986, Dublin, Republic of Ireland
Richie Partridge	2000-2004, Dublin, Republic of Ireland
* Kevin Sheedy	1978-1982, Builth Wells, Wales

Steve Staunton	1986-1991 and 1998-2000, Drogheda, Republic of Ireland
Ronnie Whelan	1979-1994, Dublin, Republic of Ireland

WALES (26)

Harry Beadles	1921-1923, Llanllwchaiarn, Wales
Craig Bellamy	2006-2007, Cardiff, Wales
Reginald Blore	1959-1959, Wrexham, Wales
John Hughes	1903-1904, Flint, Wales
William Hughes	1893-1894, Caernarfon, Wales
Alan Jones	1957-1963, Flint, Wales
Joey Jones	1975-1978, Llandudno, Wales
John Jones	1924-1925, Holyhead, Wales
Lee Jones	1992-1996, Wrexham, Wales
Mervyn Jones	1951-1953, Bangor, Wales
Paul Jones	2004-2004, Chirk, Wales
Ron Jones	1938-1939, Mold, Wales (Killed in action)
Ray Lambert	1939-1955, Bagillt, Wales
George Latham	1903-1908, Newtown, Wales
Billy Matthews	1916-1921, Plas Bennion, Wales
Layton Maxwell	1999-1999, St Asaph, Wales
Richard Morris	1902-1905, Newtown, Wales
Edward Parry	1921-1925, Colwyn Bay, Wales
Maurice Parry	1900-1909, Trefonen, Wales
Ernest Peake	1908-1914, Aberystwyth, Wales
John Price	1954-1955, Aberystwyth, Wales
Tony Rowley	1953-1958, Porthcawl, Wales
Ian Rush	1980-1987; 1988-1996, St Asaph, Wales
Dean Saunders	1991-1992, Swansea, Wales
Cyril Sidlow	1946-1950, Colwyn Bay, Wales
John Toshack	1970-1977, Cardiff, Wales

ARGENTINA (6)

Emiliano Insua	2007-present, Buenos Aires, Argentina
Sebastian Leto	2007-2007, Alejandro Korn, Argentina
Javier Mascherano	2007-2010, San Lorenzo, Argentina
Gabriel Paletta	2006-2007, Buenos Aires, Argentina
Mauricio Pellegrino	2005-2005, Leones, Argentina
Maxi Rodriguez	2010-present, Rosario, Argentina

AUSTRALIA (3)

* Craig Johnston	1981-1988, Johannesburg, South Africa
Brad Jones	2010-present, Armadale, Australia
Harry Kewell	2003-2008, Smithfield, Australia

BRAZIL (3)

Fabio Aurelio	2006-2010, 2010-present Sao Carlos, Brazil
Diego Cavalieri	2008-2010, Sao Paulo, Brazil
Lucas Leiva	2007-present, Dourados, Brazil

COMPLETE LIST OF LIVERPOOL FC PLAYERS BY NATIONALITY
(Players must have played in a senior fixture for LFC to 02/02/2011)

CAMEROON (1)
Rigobert Song   1999-2000, Nkenlicock, Cameroon

CROATIA (1)
Igor Biscan   2000-2005, Zagreb, Croatia

CZECH REPUBLIC (3)
Milan Baros   2001-2005, Valassake Mezirici, Czech Republic
Patrik Berger   1996-2003, Prague, Czech Republic
Vladimir Smicer   1999-2005, Vernerice, Czech Republic

DENMARK (4)
Daniel Agger   2006-present, Hvidovre, Denmark
Jan Molby   1984-1995, Kolding, Denmark
Torben Piechnik   1992-1993, Copenhagen, Denmark
Christian Poulsen   2010-present, Asnaes, Denmark

FRANCE (14)
Nicolas Anelka   2001-2002, Versailles, France
Pegguy Arphexad   2000-2002, Guadeloupe, France
Bruno Cheyrou   2002-2004, Suresnes, France
Djibril Cisse   2004-2006, Arles, France
Bernard Diomede   2000-2001, Guadeloupe, France
Jean-Michel Ferri   1998-1999, Lyon, France
Charles Itandje   2007-2008, Bobigny, France
Anthony Le Tallec   2003-2005, Hennebont , France
Patrice Luzi   2002-2004, Ajaccio, France
David Ngog   2008-present, Gennevilliers, France
Damien Plessis   2007-2009, Neuville-aux-Bois, France
Florent Sinama-Pongolle   2003-2006, Saint-Pierre, France
Djimi Traore   1999-2006, Laval, France
Gregory Vignal   2000-2003, Montpellier, France

FINLAND (3)
Lauri Dalle Valle   2007-2010, Kontiolahti, Finland
Sami Hyypia   1999-2009, Porvoo, Finland
Jari Litmanen   2001-2002, Lahti, Finland

GERMANY (4)
Markus Babbel   2000-2002, Munich, Germany
Dietmar Hamann   1999-2006, Waldasson, Germany
Karlheinz Riedle   1997-1999, Simmerberg-Weiler, Germany
Christian Ziege   2000-2001, Berlin, Germany

GREECE (1)
Sotirios Kyrgiakos   2009-present, Trikala, Greece

GUINEA (1)
Titi Camara   1999-2000, Donka, Guinea

HOLLAND (6)
Ryan Babel   2007-2011, Amsterdam, Holland
Jan Kromkamp   2006-2006, Makkinga, Holland
Dirk Kuyt   2006-present, Katwijk, Holland
Erik Meijer   1999-2000, Meersen, Holland
Sander Westerveld   1999-2001, Enschede, Holland
Boudewijn Zenden   2005-2007, Maastricht, Holland

HUNGARY (1)
Istvan Kozma   1992-1992, Paszto, Hungary

ISRAEL (3)
Yossi Benayoun   2007-2010, Dimona, Israel
* Avi Cohen   1979-1981, Cairo, Egypt
Ronny Rosenthal   1990-1993, Haifa, Israel

ITALY (3)
Alberto Aquilani   2009-present, Rome, Italy
Andrea Dossena   2008-2009, Lodi, Italy
Daniele Padelli   2007-2007, Lecco, Italy

MALI (1)
* Mohamed Sissoko   2005-2007, Mont Saint Agnain, France

MOROCCO (1)
* Nabil El Zhar   2006-present, Ales, France

NORWAY (6)
Stig Inge Bjornebye   1992-1999, Elverum, Norway
Vegard Heggem   1998-2000, Trondheim, Norway
Frode Kippe   1999-2001, Oslo, Norway
Bjorn Tore Kvarme   1997-1999, Trondheim, Norway
Oyvind Leonhardsen   1997-1999, Kristiansund, Norway
John Arne Riise   2001-2008, Molde, Norway

POLAND (1)
Jerzy Dudek   2001-2007, Rybnik, Poland

PORTUGAL (2)
Raul Meireles   2010-present, Porto, Portugal
* Abel Xavier   2002-2002, Nampula, Mozambique

SENEGAL (2)
Salif Diao   2002-2005, Kedogou Tallie, Senegal
El Hadji Diouf   2002-2004, Daqar, Senegal

SERBIA (1)
Milan Jovanovic   2010-present, Bajina Basta, Serbia

SLOVAKIA (1)

Martin Skrtel   2008-present, Handlova, Slovakia

SOUTH AFRICA (13)

Lance Carr	1933-1936, Johannesburg, South Africa
Sean Dundee	1998-1999, Durban, South Africa
Hugh Gerhardi	1952-1953, Johannesburg, South Africa
* Mark Gonzalez	2005-2007, Durban South Africa
* Jimmy Gray	1926-1928, Glasgow, Scotland
* Bruce Grobbelaar	1981-1994, Durban, South Africa
Gordon Hodgson	1925-1935, Johannesburg, South Africa
Dirk Kemp	1936-1939, Cape Town, South Africa
Berry Nieuwenhuys	1933-1947, Kroonstad, South Africa
Robert Priday	1945-1949, Cape Town, South Africa
Arthur Riley	1925-1939, Boksburg, South Africa
Doug Rudham	1954-1959, Johannesburg, South Africa
Harman Van Den Berg	1937-1939, Cape Town, South Africa

Slovakian Red: Martin Skrtel

SPAIN (13)

Xabi Alonso	2004-2009, Tolosa, Spain
Alvaro Arbeloa	2007-2009, Salamanca, Spain
Daniel Ayala	2007-present, Sevilla, Spain
Antonio Barragan	2005-2005, Sevilla, Spain
Luis Garcia	2004-2007, Badalona, Spain
Fernando Morientes	2005-2006, Cilleros, Spain
Antonio Nunez	2004-2005, Madrid, Spain
Dani Pacheco	2007-present, Malaga, Spain
Jose Reina	2005-present, Madrid, Spain
Josemi Rey	2004-2005, Malaga, Spain
Albert Riera	2008-2010, Mallorca, Spain
Miki Roque	2005-2006, Tremp, Spain
Fernando Torres	2007-2011, Madrid, Spain

SWEDEN (1)

Glenn Hysen   1989-1992, Gothenburg, Sweden

SWITZERLAND (2)

Philipp Degen	2008-present, Holstein, Switzerland
Stephane Henchoz	1999-2004, Billenz, Switzerland

UKRAINE (1)

Andriy Voronin   2007-2009, Odessa, Ukraine

URUGUAY (1)

Luis Suarez   2011-present, Salto, Uruguay

USA (2)

Brad Friedel	1997-1999, Ohio, USA
Zak Whitbread	2004-2005, Houston, USA

FAMILY PARTIES
FAMILY REUNIONS
A SCRAPBOOK OF HAPPY MEMORIES

MERSEYSIDE'S
WINNING TEAM

¡HALA
ROJOS, A
GLORIA!

YOU'LL NEVER WALK A

FROM ALL THE PLAYERS - THANK YOU!   WE WILL NEVER WALK ALONE

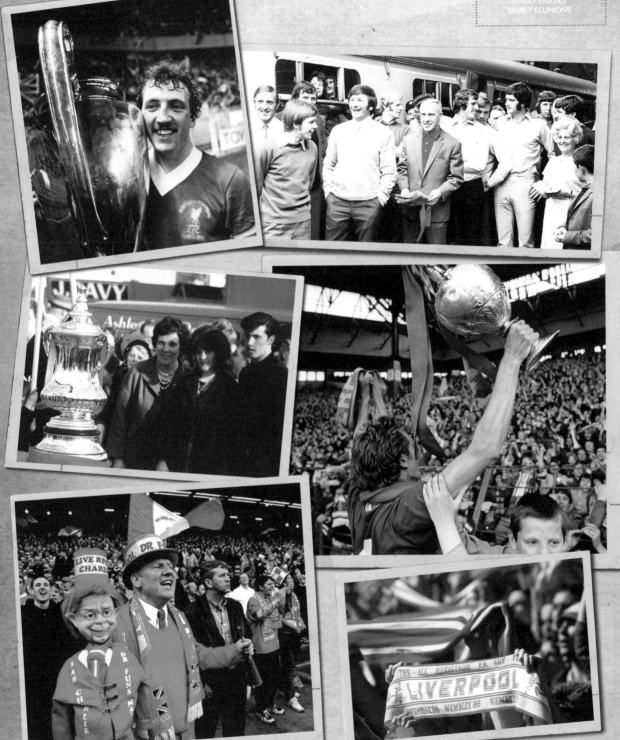

Compiled from loyal fans who subscribed to the official Liverpool FC Family Tree. They take their place alongside legends from the official Liverpool FC Hall of Fame.

LIVERPOOL FC FAMILY TREE FANS' SCROLL

ALAN A'COURT
Pam Aindow
Wayne Stafford Ainscough
Stafford Ernest Ainscough
Walid Aldoori
Rashid Al-Dossary
Fajer Al-Dossary
Angelica Alimpuangon
Alyssa Lois Alimpuangon
Cyril Alimpuangon
Ethel Alimpuangon
Annie E Allan
Josh Allott
Tahani Al Tahani
Siti Amelya
Nathan Anderson
Nattapol Apikeeratikul
Mike Arands
Tony J Archer
Mark A Archer
Eric J Archer
Dorothy R Archer
Craig Archer
Chris Armitt
Kurtis Armitt
Sasiwimon Arphathananuwat
Natasha Astill
Kevin Atter
Francis Ayombil
Frederick Ayombil
Kirsty Elizabeth Ayre
Courtney Ayre
Elizabeth Ayre
Nor Abu Bakar

David Norm Baker
Denise Magg Baker
David Ed Baker
Alexandra K Bakis
Alfred Stanley Ball
William Edward Ball
Rachel Alicia Ballentyne
David John Ballentyne
Joseph Charles Ballentyne
JACK BALMER
Davide Balzarotti
Brian Banks
Mark Banks
Elliot Banks
Eduardo Filipe Baptista
Ricardo Joao Baptista
Nicolau Filipe Baptista
Ariana Baptista
Laura Acacio Baptista
S. Santhanaraj Baratharaj
Frank Barker
John Barker
Joseph Barker
Thomas Barker
Andy Barlow
Freya Barnard
Anthony Barnes
JOHN BARNES
Peter Baron
Harold J Barr
Ann-Marie Barton
Dania Nur Batrisyia
Katie Batt
Sarah M Beasley
Matthew P Beasley

Garry Beattie
Russell Bedford
Amelie Nevaeh Bedford
Kevin Begley
Helen Begley
Anna Begley
Rachel Begley
Justin Belcher
Kyle Belcher
Jamie Belcher
Naveen S A Benazir
Marni J Beninger
Sara M Bennett
Janet Bennett
Bill Bennett
Jim Bermingham
Catherine Bermingham
Sophie Bermingham
Thomas Berry
William Best
Anthony M Bigeni
Mohd Nadiz Bin Zaidi
Magaras G Bingi
Wally Bird
Lawrie Bolton
Ian Booth
Elliott Booth
Harry Booth
Shawn J G Borrows
Adam Benjamin Borrows
Kev Bourne
Rachel Bourne
James Box
HARRY BRADSHAW
Kenny Bradshaw
Catherine Brady
Thessaloniki Branch

Albie Bray
Mal D Breeze
Lorraine L E Breeze
David Anthony Brennan
Stephen Daniel Brennan
Stephen Anthony Brennan
Stephen Charles Brennan
Patrick Brickley
Paddy Brickley
Gretta Brickley
Mark Bridges
Beanie Bridson
Annie C Britton
Sean E Britton
Katarina Brkljacic
Gary Broadbent
Mckenzie Michael Broadbent
Jamie Broadbent
Ellie Leigh Broadbent
Ian Brooks
Maureen Brooks
Keira Brooks
Nicole Brooks
John A Brooks
Alison E Brooks
Kayleigh E Brooks
Tara E Brooks
Christopher Broughton
Eric Brown
David Brown
Liz Brown
Tony C Brown
Amy Ngo Brown

Claire Brown
Jennifer Brown
Nigel Browne
Caroline Browne
Steven Browne
Sally Bruce
Faye Bruce
Dougie Bruce
Michelle Buchanan
Jeff Buchanan
Tayler Buchanan
Mehboob Ali Bukhari
Mohsin Ali Bukhari
Omar Ali Bukhari
Reina Yasmeene Bukhari
Evgeny Burminsky
Richard Burnett
Chris Burns
Damian Burton
Colin Burton
Anthony A Butler
Sheila Butler
Chloe J Butler
Sophie E Butler
Rose Buttery
Peter Byrne
Gary Byrne
Paul Byrne
Gary Byrne
Jason R Byrne
Fraser G E Byrne
Ophelia G Byrne
Aaron Cadby
Bob Caddick
Maureen Caddick
Brian Cadman
Karen Cadman
IAN CALLAGHAN

Brenton Cannizzaro
Robyn Cannizzaro
Eric Cannizzaro
Caesar Cannizzaro
JAMIE CARRAGHER
Freddie Carroll
Eleanor Carter
Alan Carter
John William Carter
David Mark Carter
Raymond Cassidy
Lawrence Cauchi
Nicolas Cauchi
Maria Concetta Cauchi
Kara Cauchi
Deepak Chakravarty
Jennifer Chakravarty
Dimitrios Chalkidis
Darren Chantler
Morten Dyhr Christensen
Annaling Chua
Robin Clague
Janet Clague
Jamie Clague
Louise Clague
Stan Clarke
Graham Clarke
Megan Clarke
Martin Clarke
Terry Clarke
Ian John Clarke
RAY CLEMENCE
Keith K Coker
Joseph Collins
Ernie Collins
Dilys M Collison
Philip Connell
Stephen Connell

David Connell
Simon Connell
Luke Conroy
Gemma Conway
Alex Cooper
Keith Cooper
Alison Cooper
Daniel Cooper-Kamodsky
Thomas Corcoran
Craig L Cotham
Melville Cove
Gerald Cove
Elizabeth Cove
Owen Cove
JACK COX
Rich Cree
Alan Critchlow
Thomas Crowe
Janet Crowe
Bernie Cullen
Ian Curtis
Kelly Cyr
KENNY DALGLISH
Alon Dambovski
Jumpol Dangsagul
Worawat Dangsagul
Mark Darvill
Angela Darvill
Colin Datson
Anthony Dass David
Maria David
Zoltán Deák
Joshua Dearden
Lee W Delaney
Aileen Dempsey
Tony Dempsey
James Dempsey
Aaron Dempsey
Ray Denning
Harry Denning
Ellen Denning
Michael Denning
Esther Dent
Victor Deynego
Faisal A Dialdin
Maria Dickenson
Ashley Dignam
Katie Ditch
Dawn Ditch
Peter J Ditchburn
Leon J Doherty
Carole Doherty
Kane Doherty
James Doherty Snr
Eric Doig
Scott Donegan
Jack Donegan-Jones
Mark Douglas
Carl Douglas
Sarah Downes
Donna Doyle
Ian Doyle

Martin Doyle
Gary Dredge
Margaret Dredge
Amy Dredge
Ben Dredge
Emma Driscoll
Miles Driscoll
Ernest David Duffy
Christopher Dullaghan
Robbie S Duncan
Lora H R Duncan
Lisa Dunn
Caitlin Dunn
Maniam Durai
Ian Dutton
Eric Earle
Samantha Eaton
Paul Eccleston
Lorna Eccleston
Chloe Eccleston
Georgia Eccleston
Fred Eccleston
Paul Eccleston
Chloe Eccleston
Georgia Eccleston
Carol Edwards
Ian John Edwards
John Edwards
Nick Edwards
Joan Elliott
Victoria Ellis
Lynn Ellis
Brian Ellis Jnr
Brian Ellis Snr
Veronica Ellis-Robinson
Sue Embley
Brian Embley
Anthony Emery
Agnes Eng Shieh Pei
Stacey Concetta Esham
Alun Edward Evans
Gareth James Evans
Lynn Pamela Evans
James Raymond Evans
Jean H Evans
Geoff M Evans
Sam J Evans
David Fairhurst
Kevin Fairhurst
Frank Falzon
Karl Falzon
Catherine Falzon
Iddon Family
Naima Fares
Aniq Farhan
Afif Farhan
Hugh Farrelly
Michael Farrelly
Neil Faulkner
Darwish Hafiy Fayyadh

Becca Fenney
Neil Ferris
Pete Ffoulkes Jnr
Pete Ffoulkes Snr
Tommy Fielder
Kylan Fitzsimons
Nicky Fitzsimons
Shane Fitzsimons
Dave Fitzsimons
Steven Flaherty
Nicola Fletcher
Michael Fotiadis
Rita Foumia
Jeremy Fowler
Gordon France
Oliver France
Samuel France
Charlie France
Marge France
Carla France
Daniel Frøystadvåg
Daniel Galvan Duque
Noel Galvin
Hugh Gamble
Ian Gamble
Jenna Gamble
Karen Lynn Gamble
Charlie Gant
Dave Gant
Jack A W Gant
Charlotte E Gant
Gorka Lopez Garcia
David Garde
Robbie Scott Garde
Chantelle Garde
Margie Garde
Sharon Gardiner
Michael Gardner
Jean Gardner
David Gardner
Kevin Gardner
Derek Gardner
Cliff R Garwood
Pam R Garwood
Nerys M Garwood
Mario Gatt
Leanne M Gatt
Alexandra M Gatt
Catherine H Gavin
Catherine H Gavin
STEVEN GERRARD
Anthony Giblin
Cameron Gibson
Becky Gibson
Francesca Gibson
Karen Gibson
Susan Giles
Dave Gill
Carly Gill
Mani Gill
David A Gillan
Brian Gillingham
Robin Gilmour

Katie Gilmour
Ron Glass
Shakeel Deepaksing Goburdhun
Surekha Atmani Goburdhun
Yovna Goburdhun
Rachna Goburdhun
ARTHUR GODDARD
Alex Goodall
Isabel Goodall
Becci Goode
Tommy Goode
Darren M Goodley
Andy B Gordon
Harry A D Gordon
Dave Gould
Theresa Gould
Gareth Gould
Nathan Gould
Harold Gouthwaite
Geoffrey Gouthwaite
Paul Gouthwaite
Cayden-Paul Gouthwaite
Stacey Evelynn Gouthwaite
Aaron Gouthwaite
Nanggai Govindan
Karen Gowing
Wally Gowing
Francis J Graham
Peter Graham
Jennifer M Graham
James A Graham
Richard Grant
Gemma Grant
Jack Grant
Anna Gredler
Shane Green
Althea Green
Mark Green
Damon Greenhalgh
Paul Gresham
Daniel Gresham
Nick Gresham
Daren Greville
Gayle Greville
Scully Greville
Antony Griffin
Jason Griffin
James Griffiths
Luke Griffiths
Erin Griffiths
David Keith Griffiths
Eddie Griffiths
Israel Grinblatt
Yogev Grinblatt
Snir Grinblatt
Yavanna Gubay
Shafiq Luqman Guee
Luqman Guee
Tony Gustafson
Lynn Gustafson

Steve A Hadley
Phil Hall
Macey Hall
Anthony Hall
Gillian Hallowell
David Hallowell
Mary Halstead
Harvey D Hamer-Jager
Cherith Hancock
ALAN HANSEN
Jesper Hansen
Anders Christian Hanssen
Norman Hardy
Yvonne Harris
Al Harris
Jen Harris
Nicola Harris
Lee Harris
Karen Harvey
Iain G Harvey
Elizabeth Harvey
Paul Hawksbee
Margaret Esme Hayward
Arthur Hayward
Michael John Hayward
Stacey Heaney
Lily Heaney
Victoria Heaney
Laurence Heaney
Lynsey Hehir
Philip P Hendy
Christopher C Hendy
David W C Heyneke
Colin Hignett
Graham Hignett
Maisie Hignett
Dave Hill
Andrew Hilton
William Hilton
Thomas Jack Hodgers (TJ)
GORDON HODGSON
Paul W Holmes
Matthew W Holmes
Jackie Holmes
Edward John Holmes
Lesley Honan-Loucks
Carl Hooper
Fergal Horan
Sophie Horan
Jessica Horan
Alan Howard
Michael Howard
Thomas Howard
John Howarth
Phillip Howarth
Myra Howarth
Kok Sen Huang
Jason M J Hudd
Colette Hughes

Michael Hughes
John Hughes
Kimberley M Hughes
Chloe E Hughes
Logan Huigsloot
Vince Huigsloot
ROGER HUNT
Catherine Hunt
Karen Hunt
Amanda Hunt
Philip Hunter
Jacqueline Hunter
Steven Hurrell
Stan Hutchings
Shahida Ibrahim
Albert Irvine
Jonny Isaksen
Beverley Jackson
Feras R Jad
Emily B James
David C James
Andrea M James
Ian M James
Emily James
Sophie L James
Kacy M James
Ilu Järvinen
Andrew J Jeffery
Jack L R Jeffery
Thomas O Jeffery
John Jenns
Ann Jenns
Colin Jenns
Joeffrin Joeffrin
James Johnson
Shannon Johnson
Ryan Johnson
Gareth Jones
Shannon Jones
Roby Jones
Darryl E Jones
Graham Jones
Brian Jones
Jasmine Jones
Poppy Jones
Heath Jones
Sara Jones
Mark Jones
Dave Jones
Anat Jungjit
Jutharat Junsakul
Hasuni Kahwaji
Nadine Kahwaji
Gazwan J R Kahwaji
Zeyn Kahwaji
Shiva Pushani Kalaiselvan
Shiva Shobitha Kalaiselvan
Mohammed Kamal
Adrian Kang Soon Lai
Solomon Kantanka
Osei Kantanka

Alfred Kantanka
Denzel Kantanka
Antonia Kaputkin
Natasha Keane
John Keating
John Francis Keating
Kevin Kellaghan
Gillian Kellaghan
Jamie Kellaghan
Niall Kelly
Christopher Kelly
Alan Kelly
Maggie Kelly
Phillip Kelly
Graeme Kelly
Rachel Kelly
Joshua Kelly
Lexie Kelly
Andrew J Kennedy
Michael A Kennedy
Jane M Kennedy
Alan P Kennedy
Cian Kennefick
Boon Tat Ker
Alfred Kershaw
Patrick Kershaw
Michael Kershaw
Liam Kershaw
Jordan Keyes
James Keyes
Carl T Keyes Jnr
Carl Keyes Snr
Aisha Al Khalifa
Alan P Kilby
Maureen G Kilby
Jason Kilvo
Kilvington
Andy J King
Owen Kinnin
Olivia Kinnin
Thomas Kirby
Irene Kirby
Joanne R Kirwin
Terry Kissock
June Kissock
Howard Klarfeld
James Kneale
Irene Kneale
Kevin Kneale
Joshua Kneale
Robert A Knowles
Andrew R Knowles
Thomas H Knowles
Denis Knowles
Torben Måge Kofoed
Patrik Kolshus
Sofie G Kolshus
Marius Kolshus
Emma Kolshus
Sergey Korziuk
Anthony Kourellias
Michael Kourellias
James Kourellias

Hasse Kuhn
Einar Kvande
Sindre Hyldbakk
Kvande
Marit Hyldbakk
Kvande
Even Hyldbakk
Kvande
Tony Laird
Andrew Anthony
Laird
Kevin Laird
Anuj Lama
Ashish Lama
Michael Vincent
Lappin
Rhys Lappin
Erik Baggerud Larsen
Frederick Lawson
Mark Lawson
Chris Laycock
Andrew Laycock
Matt Laycock
Tim Layland
Holly Le Marinel
Alistair Leather
Sydney Gary
Leatherbarrow
Sid Leatherbarrow
Alice Leatherbarrow
Michael J Lee
Peter Lee
Helen Leeming
Waraporn Leesakul
Wareeporn Leesakul
Sean C Legassie
Nathan L Legassie
David George Lewis
Paul Lewis
Kyle Lewis
BILLY LIDDELL
Kevin J Loftus
Denise Loftus
Cian M Loftus
Nia Haf Loftus
James Long
EPHRAIM
LONGWORTH
Edwin Gerald
Lourdes
Gloria Lourdes
Daniel Lovett
Shaun J Lucking
John E Lucking
John M Lucking
Ruth M Lucking
Arska Lukkarinen
Joy D Lush
Maria Lye
Terence Lynch
Veronica Lynch
Phelim Lynch
Gillian Lynch
Stephen Lyon

Noel Lythgoe
Mike Lythgoe
Alexander Lythgoe
James Lythgoe
Mohamed Maail
Fergus Mackinnon
Rhona Mackinnon
Angus Mackinnon
Uddle Maher
Abbie Malton
Anthony Mamo
Grace Mamo
Owen Gerrard Mamo
David Mandel
Jasse Marin
Lila Marin
Jaana Marin
David Mars
Alex Marsh
Chris Marshall
Alan Marshall
Carol Marshall
Bob D Marshall
Caroline W Marshall
Helen F Marshall
Richard Marston
Niamh Marston
Gavin D Martin
Darren Martin
Jensen Martin
John Martin
Natalie Martin
Rodney S
Masarirambi
Michael Mason
Paul Mason
Richard Matthews
Luke Matthews
Jordan Matthews
Ellis Matthews
Darja Mauser
JIMMY McDOUGALL
Theresa T McArthur
James J McArthur
Julie J McArthur
Gary Leslie McGowan
Leslie Keith McGowan
Elizabeth Anne
McGowan
Malcolm J McArthur
Callum McArthur
Lucinda H J McArthur
Eleanor L McArthur
Ian McCabe
Terry McCabe
Scott McCardle
Fraser McCardle
Euan McCardle
Edward McCarthy
Edward McCarthy
Claire P McCarthy
Ian McClenahan
Callum J McCormick

Stephen McCormick
Anne McCormick
Emma L McDermott
William McGinnigle
Jessica McGinnigle
Joel McGinnigle
Carl J McGuiness
Mark McGurgan
Martina McGurgan
Steven McGurgan
Caroline McKenna
DON MACKINLAY
Brian G McLoughlin
Hilda McLoughlin
MATT McQUEEN
Tony McShane
Josh McShane
Harry McShane
Nathan McShane
Payam Mehdipour
Tom R Mehlum
Sebastian Mehlum
Tonje Cecilie Mehlum
Henrik Mejer
Gite Mejer
Jens Mejer
Sarah Mejer
Andrew J Mellor
Timothy C Mellor
Frederick N Mellor
Aubrey J Mellor
Guee Luck Meng
Mandy Mercer
Claire S Metcalf
Ian Mills
Charlie Mills
Olivia Mills
Franz Mittendorfer
Maria Mittendorfer
Michaela Mittendorfer
Noah Mittendorfer
David Moen
John T Moffett
Dennis Mogg
Mike Mogg
Liam Monk
Amileigh Monk
Jacob Monks
Gerard Montgomery
Kay Montgomery
Sean M Montgomery
Florence Moody
Ivor J Moody
Ivor J W Moody
Ben S Moody
Valerie J Moore
Jonathan Morcom
Samuel Morcom
Sam Morcom
Samuel William
Morcom
Mike Morgan
Barry Morgan

Gareth Morgan
Gary Morgan
Phil Morgan
Eileen Morgan
John Morgan
Joyce Morgan
Hannah Morgan
Leon Morgan
Irene Morgan
Elizabeth Morgan
Isobel Morrison
Billy Moss
Peter Mouat
Anna Moyes
Stefan Mueller
Martin Mueller
Tom Murphy
John Murphy
Elizebeth Murphy
John Murphy
Aileen Murphy
Joe Murphy
Chris M Murphy
Claire M Murphy
Oliver J Murphy
Charlie J Murphy
Loraine Murphy
Gregory Murphy
Christopher Murphy
Alex Murphy
Lynsey Murray
Bill Murray
Patricia Murray
Frank Murray
Catherine E Murray
Stephen Murray
Tony Musker
Margaret Musker
Paul Robert Myers
Stig Myklebust
Elisabeth Myklebust
Morten Hundvin
Myklebust
Kasper Myklebust
Easentheren Naidoo
Eganthren Naidoo
Jake Needham
Sally Needham
Clare Neely
Jason M J Nelson
Miron Netschaew
David Newby
Jon Newby
Jim Newby
Thomas Møller
Nielsen
Erik Nielsen
Elizabeth Nikolaisen
Norarina Norarina
Tommy Noton
Philip Noton
Upasana Nunkumar
Darren O' Brien

Eoin O' Brien
Fiona O'Brien
Gavin O'Brien
Rosin O'Brien
Karl O'Brien
Shane O'Brien
Terry O'Keefe
Claudia Oakley
Samantha Oakley
Alexandra Oakley
David Oates
Philip J Ohare
Mark O Ohare
Liam O'Leary
Tyrone O'Neill
Flinn Patrick O'Neill
Lucinda Rose O'Neill
Lisa Maree O'Neill
KP Onn
Ryan O'Quigley
John O'Quigley
NasserA Oraik
Terry Osborn
Lizzy Osbourne
Joey O'Toole
Patrick O'Toole Jnr
Patrick O'Toole Snr
James Owen
Harry Page
George Pakiufakis
Yiorgos Pakiufakis
Claire Palmer
Solomon Papaloizou
Gary Parker
Thomas Parkinson
Peter Parkinson
Cameron Parkinson
Wendy Parkinson
Isobel Mary Parry
Anthony Parsons
Sue Parsons
Don Passey
Jack Patterson
Leo J Patterson
Amber Z Patterson
Nina Patterson
Rob W Paul
Nofal Paulus
Lisa Paulus
Jaran Pedersen
Russell A Pemberton
Marion Pepeunig
Caitlin Perkins
Johnathon Perkins
Liam Perkins
Tukka Pete
Gábor Peterdi
Zalán Peterdi
Ádám Peterdi
Ronald Phillips
Norman Phillips
Stephen Phillips
Jeffrey Phillips

Ernie Pinch
Tony Pinch
Jimmy Poland
Geraldine Poland
Gerard Poland
Amy Poland
David J Pollock
Jaya Pushani Ponnudurai
Ian Porter
Garry Porter
Sue Porter
Alfie G Potter
Lewis A Potter
Dan Powell
F... Powell
... ...ll

Fer... ...sey
Ryan R...
Damon Ramsey
Anne B Randall
Ethan Randells
Chloe Randells
Phillip Randells
Martin E Randle
Andrew M J Randle
Jaime J P Randle
Jonathan D Randle
Lee Ratcliffe
Jamie D Rees-Winter
Victoria A Rees-Winter
Bryony Z Rees-Winter
Louise J Reid
Dave Ginger Rhyl
Gemma Richards
Alan Richards
Joseph Richards
Geoff Richards
Alan Richards
Gordon A Richardson
Christine Riddell
David Riley
Philip Riley
Julie-Ann Riley
Lorna Riley
Paul John Ritchie
Sarah Rivers
David Robb

Marco Robb
Dewi W Roberts
Michala J Roberts
Kathryn Roberts
Jacqueline Roberts
Kevin Roberts
Shaun Roberts
Mark Robertshaw
David Robinson
Thomas Robinson
Joe Roche
Thomas J Rogers
Toby Rogers
Colin Rogers
Michael K Rogers
Natalie E Rogers
Caleb M Rogers
Calvin D K Rogers
Joan Rogers
Chutipong Romsonthi
Sirirat Romsonthi
...ilo Ronzani
... ...nzani
... Rose
...ca Rose
...ert Ross
...ean Ross
Kaitlin Ross
James Ross
Mick Rowan
Nina Anastazia Ruchko
Shelia Ruse
Sammy Ruse
IAN RUSH
Michael J Russo
Oleg Ryzhkov
Serge Saint-Jean
Nicola Salters
Pamela J Sansom
Stephen Santhanaraj
Stephen S Santhanaraj
Jenni R Sanzotera
Matthew E Schmidt
Marcia A Schmidt
ELISHA SCOTT
Stan Scotland
Jason Scrymgeour
Maddie Scrymgeour
Mirron Scrymgeour
Gillian Scrymgeour
Latifah Rohaniah Selamat
Markus Seppälä
Gavin T Shelley
Paul A Sherborne
Tórfinn S Simonsen
John A Simpson
May Simpson
Shabnam R Singh
Rehan R Singh
Ranjit Singh

Athear Sipi
Mark Sixsmith
Christopher Sixsmith
Steven Sixsmith
Harry Sixsmith
Edward Sixsmith
Sandra Sixsmith
Ian Sixsmith
Paula Sixsmith
Jon Sjåtil
Krishan Sjåtil
Andrew Skelding
Elzbieta Skiba
Matthew Skinner
Tracey Skipper
Lorraine Skipper
Daniel Skipper
Jack Skipper
Michael Slater
Joanne Slater
David Slinn
Kevin Slinn
Daniel Slinn
Matthew Slinn
Billy Sloan
William J Sloan
Deborah Sloan
Curtis W Sloan
Gerry Smith
Robin Smith
Sonny Smith
Søren Mundt Sørensen
Michael J Spear
Bethanie A Spear
Alisha M Spear
Robert Speed
Gavin Speed
Benjamin Speed
Oliver Speed
Karina Spiegel
Heike Sprote
Poppet Sprote
Steven Thomas Stanley
Joanna Marie Stanley
Keith Stanton
Katie Stanton
Ian Stapleton
Valerie Stapleton
Michael J.F Steer
Peggy M Steer
Malcolm J Steer
Santhanaraj Stephen
Shelley A Stephens
Peter Stevens
Reece Stevens
John Stevenson
Ian M Stevenson
Michael J E Stevenson
Nell Stewart
Stuart Stirling
Graeme Stirling
Lewis Stirling
Douglas Stirling

Lee Stockdale
Thomas William Stockton
Mark J Stokes
Graham Stonadge
Karen Stonadge
Robbie Stonadge
Chris Stonadge
Trond Straume
Bastian Straume Grebstad
Nikolai Straume Grebstad
Steve Strickland
Melvin Stubbs
ALBERT STUBBINS
Phil Sumner
Lars Busk Svendsen
Helen Swift
Thomas Swift
Christopher Swift
Lewis W Talbot
Justin Tan
Lin Vin Tan
Ignatius Tan Yik Kai
Duncan Tanner
Ju Tanner
Micky Taylor
E Team
Anastasios Thanoglou
Evangelos Michael Theodoulou
Alexandros Marios Theodoulou
Christakis Theodoulou
Linda Christine Theodoulou
Clive Thomas
Shan Thomas
Cerys Thomas
Bethan Thomas
Huw Thomas
Sasha Thompson
Maximilian Thompson
Daniel Nicolas Thømt
Paul Timmins
Peter Timson
David Todd
Kelly-Anne Todd
Malcolm E Todd
Brenda J Todd
Eric J Todd
Michael Todd
Dominic P Toller
Owen J Toller
Honey-Louise D Toller
John Toner
John-Paul Tooley
Maibritt T M Tórfinnsdóttir
Sigurð E

Tórfinnsson
Jonn Rói Tórfinnsson
Martin Travis
Edward Travis
Niamh Travis
Edward Treble
Edward Treble
Ian Treble
David Treble
Margaret Trevena
Christine Trevena
Terry Tribue
Rob Tubb
Pauline Tubb
Joel Tubb
Sophie Tubb
Gillian Tubb
Graham Tubb
Carol Turner
Frederick D Turner
Ian F Turner
Joanne H Turner
Paul William Tyrer
Gareth V Underwood
Carys S Underwood
James R Underwood
Chang Su Qin
Valerie Sebastian
Ralph Van Pletzen
Cor van Zanten
Corina van Zanten
Shane van Zanten
Michael Ventre
Anthony Ventre
Chang Xin Ying Vernice
Chang Kah Chun Vincent
Dejan Vlaski
Mladen Vlaski
Irina Vlaski
Ana Vlaski
Laura Vranos
Alan Waddington
Graeme Waddington
Tracy Waddington
Brian Wainwright
Paul J Waltho
Daniel P Waltho
Callum T Waltho
Lauren E Waltho
Cleasie Ward
Alan Warden
Jade Wardle
Paisley Ware
R Wareham
Craig Warman
Thomas Francis Waters
Tommy Waters
Gary Watson
Debbie Watson
Angela Watson

Roy Watson
Janet Weedall
Craig Weedall
Matthew Wells
Barrie Wells
Stephen White
Adam John White
Heidi White
Diane White
Craig Whiteley
Lisa Whiteley
Deanna Whiteley
Jim Whiteley
Bill Whorton
Pauline Whorton
Stefanie Wilken
Tracey Anne Willacy
Lauren Elizabeth Willacy
Fredrik Wille
Karen Wille
Ludvig Wille
Paul Willey
Jamie Williams
Daniel Williams
Tyler C Williams
Timmy J Williams
Sinead Williams
Sylvia-Rose Williams
Phil The Rev Williams
Paul Willis
Vicky Willis
Edward James Winrow
James Winrow
Diane Winrow
Craig Winstanley
Mark Winstanley
Michael A Winter
Linda A Winter
David Woerner
Siew Kan Wong
Chee Chiew Wong
Raymond Wong
Paweena Wongwiwattanawut
Craig M Woodhouse
Gavin C Woodrow
Diane L Woodrow
Suzanne Woodward
Susan Worrall
Francis Worsley
Samuel Worsley
Alice Worsley
Bridgetta Worsley
RON YEATS
Yien Hoe Yeo
Alison Young
Karen Po-Man Yu
Paulina Po-Lan Yu
BoBo Po-Sau Yu
Paul Yuen
Maxim Zhukov

Other great official titles for the LFC family bookshelf – prices from £3.99

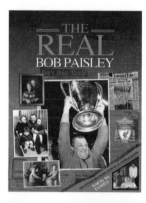

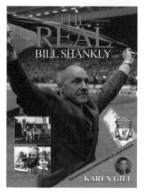

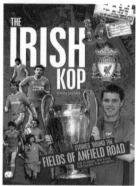

All of these titles, and more, are available to order by calling 0845 143 0001,
or you can buy online at www.liverpoolfc.tv/match/magazine

EXPERIENCE THE NEW

ANFIELD STADIUM TOUR

THE HOME OF LIVERPOOL FOOTBALL CLUB

BOOK TODAY
VISIT WWW.LIVERPOOLFC.TV/TOURS
OR CALL 0151 260 6677

THE
OFFICIAL
LIVERPOOL FC
FaMiLY Tree